# T

## MYTH

## OF TOMORROW

# THE

# MYTH

## OF TOMORROW

### SEVEN ESSENTIAL KEYS FOR LIVING THE LIFE YOU WANT TODAY

## Gary Buffone, Ph.D.

McGraw-Hill

New York    Chicago    San Francisco
Lisbon    London    Madrid    Mexico City    Milan
New Delhi    San Juan    Seoul    Singapore
Sydney    Toronto

The **McGraw·Hill** Companies

1 2 3 4 5 6 7 8 9 0   DOC/DOC   0 9 8 7 6 5 4 3 2

ISBN 0-07-138917-2

This publication is designed to provide accurate and authoritative information in regard to the subject matter covered. It is sold with the understanding that the publisher is not engaged in rendering legal, accounting, or other professional service. If legal advice or other expert assistance is required, the services of a competent professional person should be sought.

> —*From a declaration of principles jointly adopted by a committee of the American Bar Association and a committee of publishers.*

 This book is printed on recycled, acid-free paper containing a minimum of 50% recycled de-inked fiber.

McGraw-Hill books are available at special quantity discounts to use as premiums and sales promotions, or for use in corporate training programs. For more information, please write to the Director of Special Sales, Professional Publishing, McGraw-Hill, Two Penn Plaza, New York, NY 10121-2298. Or contact your local bookstore.

*To my wife, Norma,
whose love has filled
my heart and lifted
my spirit*

# CONTENTS

# ACKNOWLEDGMENTS

This book is a synergistic creation of many hearts and minds. First and foremost, I want to acknowledge my dear parents for their constant demonstrations of love over these many years. I thank my devoted wife, Norma, for her unwavering support and confidence throughout our relationship, and my daughters, Jennifer and Jill, who have taught me lessons only children can teach. In this vein, I want to thank my community of friends who have offered both interest and encouragement over the long haul—Doug McNamera, Charlie and Chris Booras, Steve and Chris Carpenter, Connie Lyons, Pat Boger, Jim Penrod, and Pat and Wayne Hogan, to name the most important.

I wish to extend a special thank you to my mentors who guided me in the writing aspects of this project. Frank Green offered valuable insights in the early work and encouraged me as a writer. Most importantly, Debi Moss inspired me by sharing her own writing experiences and by reviewing and discussing my work. Debbie's incisive comments and enthusiastic support buoyed my spirits and kept me focused at those critical times when I questioned the value of continuing. She was my muse, becoming a dear friend in the process.

I am grateful for the wise guidance of my literary agent, Ken Atchity, who believed in the value of this book's message. His knowledge of the publishing world and the consistent presence and help of Felippe Marques helped make this journey both exciting and bearable. I would also like to express my gratitude to my McGraw-Hill editor, Nancy Hancock, for her sensitivity and professional competence in the refinement of this manuscript.

I would lastly thank the many wonderful and loving clients who were and are my guides. They have demonstrated to me the importance of seeking growth after tragedy to feel whole. Whether they survived rape, abuse, serious accidents, combat, loss of loved ones, violence, or the ravages of disease, they have patiently taught me about courage, hope, life, and ultimately, death. Their energy, courage, humor, and determination, even in the face of insurmountable odds and at times indescribable horror, continue to inspire me every day. It is to them, and to all the exceptional survivors, that this book is dedicated.

# THE
# MYTH
## OF TOMORROW

# PART ONE

# THE
# BLESSINGS
## of
# TODAY

# CHAPTER ONE

# Astray in a Dark Wood

*A new philosophy, a new way of life,*
*is not given for nothing. It has to be*
*paid dearly for and only acquired with*
*much patience and great effort.*
*—Fyodor Dostoyevsky*

It's so easy to waste the little time we have.

In the world today there's still considerable confusion and uneasiness about how to live. Like the great Italian poet Dante we find ourselves wandering "astray in a dark wood," searching for a new path that leads to greater satisfaction, fullness, and meaning. Having achieved our set dreams, material or otherwise, we're still dissatisfied, yearning for greater passion and fulfillment. Bogged down in the everyday, we know something doesn't feel right, even if we have trouble articulating it.

Yet to discover a life bristling with greater passion and purpose we must first confront some of life's most difficult, yet meaningful questions.

How do we wish to live?
Do we feel secure and loved within ourselves and with others?
How much joy can we feel?

Can we freely share our happiness with those we love?
Does our life have meaning?

As a psychologist, what I see clearly are people awash in these concerns. Every day I talk with executives feeling depressed in their high-paying yet meaningless work; wives suffering from the intense loneliness of their marriage; highly successful professionals riddled with self-doubt; cancer patients who bravely battled their illness yet are unsure how to make their lives more satisfying; accident survivors seeking new meaning in their second chance at life.

How can we reclaim what is most important in our lives? What can scrape away the usual distractions of our everyday world, focusing us on a deeper experience of ourselves, relationships, and of life itself?

This shift isn't accomplished by listening to simple platitudes or through quiet armchair contemplation. Information and insight doesn't change anyone; inspiration does.

Think of all the many people who know exactly what and how to change their lives yet sit idle, doing nothing to make their lives better. We need a stiff shot of inspiration to transform our lives, and the most potent boost comes from facing the ultimate truth that our time is running out, that the cosmic clock is always ticking.

We all want to make our lives better. We may be waiting for the right time to change our careers, slow down and spend time with our family, fulfill a secret dream, take a fantasy trip, pursue a cherished hobby, downsize or upgrade our life, have children, get married, or concentrate on what really matters. Yet we postpone doing anything, we put it off, or make plans forever filed away.

It's so easy to put the important things in our lives on the back burner, to jot down our resolutions and dreams on a perpetual "to do" list, thinking that we'll get to them tomorrow. But our best laid plans and dreams somehow slip away, leaving our lives filled only by the empty confusion and busyness that stands in the way of the life we truly want. The clock keeps ticking as our deepest, heartfelt desires and wishes fade before our very eyes, with our postponement creating the very foundation for our later regrets.

What will it take to get you to make the decision to have the life you really want? What will spark you to turn your dreams into a living reality?

I'm confronted daily by the changes people want to make in their lives, their hopes, their dreams, their innermost desires. Some of these changes are small, like going after an important promotion, and others life shattering, like escaping an abusive marriage. Yet as important as these needs are, these individuals hold off and do nothing, somehow hoping these changes will occur magically without intention or effort.

Now don't get me wrong, true change is hard work. Big shifts, transformational changes, don't come easily or for no reason. You don't just wake up one morning and decide to turn your life upside down. Something or someone first has to grab you by the shoulders, get your attention, and shove you in a new direction.

Take Tom, a 53-year-old commercial real estate developer who came to see me at his cardiologist's urging after suffering from stress-related chest pain, angina. A tall, heavily built fellow bristling with impatience, Tom clearly had "better things to do." He fidgeted at the edge of his chair as he quickly blurted out how his being there was for his wife and doctor, not for him. "I don't really know why I'm here. One, I don't believe anything's wrong. Two, I've got a thousand things to do today more important than talking to a shrink about stress. Everybody's stressed, big deal."

It became evident in our first meeting that Tom had no intention of addressing his problem. He was on a mission to "succeed," and nothing, including his heart, could stand in his way. "OK, OK, I know I need to slow down, but the pills the doctor gave me seem to relieve the pain so I can work. Sure, I run myself hard, so what? Everybody I know works 90-hour weeks. I'll take time off to relax after I retire, but not now," he hissed, with obvious irritation in his voice.

He glared at me for the next 20 minutes as we spoke of his condition and the options open to him. No one was surprised when after our initial session Tom dropped out of treatment.

I hadn't seen Tom for a few years when I noticed him on my schedule one Thursday morning. He had called with a message telling me something important had happened and that he wanted to talk. We met in my office the next week.

"I remembered what we talked about a couple of years ago and things have changed. You know I'd talked about taking time off to be with my kids for years, but kept putting it off. I always had the best of intentions but figured my family could wait until later. Well, I had a wake-up call. After the first heart attack…oh, you don't know about that. It happened a few months after we met together. Anyway, my doctors told me then that I needed to cut back. I didn't listen to them and a few months ago my second heart attack almost killed me.

"It took almost losing everything, not knowing whether I'd live or die, to finally get me thinking maybe this is it. I'd never seen myself as mortal, but that second heart attack put my life in bold relief. It was like somebody had turned up the volume on my life. Most people don't understand me when I talk about my lucky heart attack. But it was the only thing that could've saved me, to get me to look at my life differently."

Tom had neglected his family for years, despite their pleas to spend time with them. "I've pissed most of my life away on nonsense. For that one moment, lying there on the kitchen floor with this intense pain in my chest, looking up into my daughter's terrified face, time stopped and my life shifted. I was lucky I even made it to the hospital."

His near-death encounter had shaken him to the core, opening his eyes to the beauty, kindness, and love that had been there for him all along. "Now I get up every morning thanking God that I have one more day. Every day, I do my best to enjoy it. I smile more, play with my kids, and take trips with my wife. Things that seemed so important before, work, the size of my bank account, new cars, things that I used to let consume me don't occupy me as much. Now when I look back, I see it took almost dying to get my attention."

Tom is certainly not alone in his experience, for nothing challenges us to live life more than the thought of losing it. When we awaken to see our time as limited, we refuse to retreat back to our "old" lives but rather start living from our true selves. On a practical level, this may mean we ditch a dead-end career, move to our dream destination, heal or end relationships, or bring new meaning into our lives. I've met many people who were "stuck" on hold until a major crisis turned their lives upside down—and just as often, right side up.

I've spent the last several years searching for the active ingredient in these dramatic life reversals. I've hunted for the therapeutic "holy grail," a potent catalyst that could accelerate profound, positive human growth, growth usually accomplished only through years of therapy. I've searched to discover the inspirational formula that would help people not just awaken to their lives, but also live their lives more fully and completely. What could possibly provide such a motivational boost, this ultimate psychic "kick in the pants"?

What I've discovered is something I knew all along; that deep reflection and transformational change are best potentiated by certain urgent life crises, such as serious accidents or illness, divorce, and death. But of these, none concentrates the heart and mind more, convincing us to stop postponing what is truly important, than confronting the single thought of our own end.

## BEYOND SURVIVAL

Like Tom, many of my patients have experienced traumatic life crises and, from this, rediscovered life's fragility and the importance of paying attention to the time they have on this earth. Whether they've been shaken by the loss a family member, a heart attack or cancer diagnosis, violence, or a serious car accident, their tragedies forced these exceptional people to take a hard look at how they were living their lives while gifting them the wisdom to make more of the time they had left. They had not only survived their trauma but had also used it to make their lives better. But how could a life-threatening tragedy make our lives fuller?

Psychiatrist Irving Yalom reminds us that "although our physical death destroys us, the idea of death can save us."[1] Yet how can the idea of our end redeem us? Existentialist Martin Heidegger concluded in his work *Being and Time* that the awareness of our end spurs us to shift from one mode of existence to a higher one.[2]

I've witnessed this shift in many clients who were suddenly shaken by their recognition of the delicate fragility of life into a new state of mindfulness, causing change at a very deep level. Although these exceptional people had experienced horrible tragedies that were nearly fatal, they refused to be victims, but rather took charge of their lives in ways they had never done before. You may ask, how does this happen?

Heidegger believed we either live in a "state of forgetfulness of being or in a state of mindfulness of being." When we live in a state of forgetfulness of being, we live in the world of things, immersing ourselves in the diversions of life. We become mired in the mud of habit, in dull and repetitive routines, in the "should" of living. We seek distractions—food, people, work, alcohol—to avoid facing whatever frightens us. By surrendering ourselves to the forces of the ordinary world, we lose touch with what matters most in our lives.

It's easy to get stuck in the everyday without even realizing what has occurred. We become unconscious, surrendering control of our lives to forces within or outside of ourselves, allowing our lives to career slowly out of control.

I recall first meeting Jackie, a frail, weary-eyed woman who seemed much older than her 48 years. "I'm exhausted. I work all day, spend time with my family at night, take care of my elderly mother on the weekends, and feel as if I'm constantly 'on call.' I just can't seem to find any time for myself. I think I'm doing everything I should do, but I feel lousy most of the time."

Jackie, a consummate high school English teacher, struggled with recurring depression. Successful in her profession and family, she was barely surviving, constantly depleted by her attempts to be all things to all people. Always drained by her frenetic pace, she never took time to reflect on her own feelings and desires. "My life seems like one long workday. I'm so consumed with getting the work done, pleasing my parents, and keeping the principal happy that I never stop long enough to see what I'm doing with my life.

"I know I'm unhappy, in fact, even I figured out I was depressed before my husband told me. I don't know what's wrong. I'm an excellent teacher. I've got a loving husband and four great kids and two grandchildren. There's no reason I should feel this way." And yet she did.

And then there's Roger, wrapped up in his own confusion. A tall, lanky, impeccably dressed gentleman, he quickly abandoned any formality as he dove into his confession at the threshold to my office. "I don't know what's come over me. I'm financially secure, have a great wife and kids, a good job, and yet I seem to be doing things that I know are self-destructive. The last couple of years as I've hit my forties, I've been drinking more and am obsessed with sex. I've had two affairs and I can't get women off my mind."

A pillar of the community and successful architect, Roger had no idea what was causing this dramatic change in his behavior. Devoutly religious, he was racked by guilt and knew he was risking everything. As we talked more over the next weeks, Roger began to realize that the specific women involved were not really all that important to him.

"I can see that these women, even though they're attractive, are almost like interchangeable parts in a machine. I don't really know them, nor do I want to get involved emotionally or anything. I'd rather not know anything about them. I'm not so much attracted to the person, but more the feeling I get when I'm with them.

Tom, Jackie, and Roger lived their lives in a state of forgetfulness. Though conscious of their unhappiness and dissatisfaction, they still wandered astray in their own dark woods, unsure of how to change or grow. Their work, busyness, sex, and drinking only distracted them from the life they yearned for. Their suffering teaches us that surrendering our conscious choices, that living in a state of forgetfulness, only takes us further away from the life we want to live. The way we deal with these decisions forever determines both the quality and the quantity of our life.

Tom believed he'd live forever. Distracted by his need to succeed at any cost, he sacrificed his family and nearly his life. "I thought I was invincible." Tom, like many of us, used his feeling of invincibility to shield himself from the fact that his time was limited and that change was needed. Even though Tom knew he was neglecting his health and family, he expected to take care of them later.

A "yes-woman," Jackie had lived a life of self-denial. "I never have time to stop and even think about what I'm doing. Years ago, I lost control of my life. I know I want to change, but I just can't say no to people."

Feeling trapped by her routines and responsibilities, she became machinelike, reflexively doing whatever was asked of her. Jackie sought refuge in her activity, assuming one day her life would somehow magically be better. Like Jackie, we hide in the illusion that we can always change our life *tomorrow*, and in this belief we postpone living for one more day.

This persistent compulsion to put off to tomorrow what we can choose today is what I refer to as the "mañana syndrome." When we buy the illusion that we have unlimited tomorrows, then we operate on a deferred living plan, believing we'll begin our "better" life later. But this notion of having "all the time in the world" is a seductive lie. For when we take our life for granted, it loses its fullness and zest.

So what's the alternative to this life of quiet desperation? In the higher state of mindfulness of being, we marvel at the simplest wonders of life, continually aware of our living, mindful of the fragility of our existence, aware tomorrow may never come.

With no tomorrows, each day becomes important, each moment special. Every conversation, every action, every decision becomes pregnant with meaning and value. Nothing is taken for granted, nothing wasted. This heightened consciousness injects passion and purpose into each precious second.

Take a few moments and reflect on your own life. How do you spend your time? Are you conscious of your choices, mindful of life's infinite possibilities? Do you wake up and find yourself appreciating each new day, looking for opportunities to express your excitement and passion? Are you living the life you want?

Or are you trapped in the state of forgetfulness, numbed down in the habits, routines, distractions, and "shoulds" of life? How often do you feel that you are living life to the fullest?

It's easy enough to go astray, to lapse into forgetfulness. At one time or another we all get wrapped up in the little things, hav-

ing enough money, fixing the lawn mower, making the mort-
gage, buying a new car—all the small acts we do just to keep our
lives going.

But we must see this as a choice. Some people, like small birds
perched on the open door of their gilded cage, prefer the boredom
of their routines and habits to the anxiety of choice.

Why would anyone live this way, you may ask. Jackie offers
some insight into the power of the familiar: "I know how unhappy
and tired I am, but I'm afraid to do anything different. I'm scared
of having to make my own choices about what to do with my life.
In some ways it's just easier to keep doing the same thing." Like
Jackie, who recognizes the safety in her busyness and exhaustion,
we too can surrender our freedom out of fear of the full horizon
of experience.

Fortunately, although we may wander aimlessly at times, we
can always choose to take a new path, to live our lives more mindfully and fully. We can awaken and recognize the endless opportunities for happiness and fulfillment. For when we're willing to
enter the state of mindfulness of being, we exist authentically, directing our lives from our most basic values and feelings.

I often tell my patients who want to spark their lives to begin
making their choices based on what they would feel if they knew
they were only going to live another day, week, or year. That's one
way of giving people an immediate awareness of what they need
or feel, even if they've never paid attention to feelings. We can't
afford the luxury of forever when we need to change immediately,
and the best way to change is to ask yourself what you'd do if your
days were numbered.

In this more mindful state, we become fully self-aware, embracing the possibilities and adventure that is life. Shedding distractions, we confront our fears, and with our awareness of freedom
comes the anxiety and energy to realize our full potential.

Heidegger realized that we don't move from a state of forget-fulness to a more enlightened mindfulness by simply wishing it to be so. There's a world of difference between knowing what to do and actually doing it. Many of us know how to improve our lives yet do not act, instead putting off indefinitely the life we want. How do we shake these distractions to awaken to life's pos-sibilities? What can shove us from passive understanding to thoughtful action, from unconsciousness to mindful living?

This shift only comes through certain "urgent experiences" that kick, jolt, and tug us from the everyday state of forgetfulness to the state of mindfulness. These urgent crises—divorce, illness, fi-nancial downturns, death—have the power to turn our world up-side down. These same calamities disrupt our lives and become catalytic agents, working as a psychological boot in the pants.

Urgent life crises, often involving the threat of our extinction, are unparalleled in their power to move us to living life in a more authentic fashion, goading us into appreciating to the utmost what we have or can do today. The awareness of our own end is, as Tom described after his second heart attack, "like a Zen two-by-four upside my head."

Tom was jolted awake by his near-death encounter, shaken to his very core. "Even though my first heart attack jostled me, I never truly believed I would die until I was lying on that kitchen floor. Then it finally hit me that I may not live to take another breath. That fear, that my life was over, shook me to my bones. In a funny way, that second heart attack, facing the 'big sleep,' saved my life."

This idea that near-death crisis makes a positive contribution to life is not easily or widely accepted. Generally, we view our end as such a terrible event that we must dismiss it as the most negative aspect of living. But in this dismissal, we lose the powerful message that our time on this earth is finite, that these are the only mo-ments we have.

Jackie never considered that one day her life would end. When I asked her to contemplate this fact, she became flustered. "Don't say that. Why in the world would I want to think about dying? I'm upset enough without getting depressed about things like that."

"Why do you think it would be so depressing to consider?" I asked.

"Well, it just would. I don't like to think about it unless I have to, and right now I don't have to." She said this with increasing frustration, clearly disturbed by the notion. Jackie, like so many others, couldn't allow herself to see the advantages of facing her inevitable demise.

If you can, suspend judgment for a moment and imagine life without end. To many this would seem an ideal condition. Yet life shrinks when its end is denied. Homer illustrates this idea in the *Odyssey* in a passage where Ulysses meets Calypso, a sea princess and a child of the gods.[3] Calypso, a divine being, is immortal and will never die. Having never met a mortal before, Calypso becomes fascinated with Ulysses. As we read we begin to realize that Calypso envies Ulysses because he will not live forever. His life becomes more full of meaning, his every choice and action more significant, precisely because his time is so limited.

The very fact that our time is finite makes living precious. When we exclude the recognition of our end, when we lose sight of the real stakes involved, life becomes impoverished. It becomes easier to develop "mañana syndrome" and constantly postpone authentic living. People who presume that there is always tomorrow waste away in unproductive and meaningless jobs, joyless relationships, pointless worries, and vague plans for some distant future.

For just as hunger sharpens our appetite for food, the thought of mortality awakens our appetite for living. It gives us "permission" to do things that we would otherwise avoid doing. It pushes us to take time off to reflect, meditate, and chart a new course, making it easier to refuse unwelcome demands and obligations and to do things we had always put off. It enables us to ask for and give love, to speak our feelings, to be honest. It spurs us to change our lives in ways we would never dare to before.

The integration of acknowledging death in our life saves us, acting as a powerful catalyst to plunge us into more authentic life modes, enhancing each day with the full experiencing of life.

Our attitude toward our end greatly influences the quality of our life and the way we grow or falter. So when we say that thoughts of our end powerfully focuses our mind, the point, of course, is not so much our passing but rather the light that this knowledge sheds on our life. For if we accept that our time is limited, we will follow what we love, we will live deeply and attentively in every prized moment, we will live with reverence for all things and in gratitude for the gift of a single day upon this earth. By living fully in a day with no tomorrows, we become freed from procrastination and its inevitable cousin, regret.

But until we explode this myth of tomorrow, we can never move ourselves to this higher, more authentic mode of existence.

# CHAPTER TWO

# Exploding the Myth
# of Tomorrow

*Death tells us that we must live life now,*
*in the moment—that tomorrow is illusion…*
                    *—Leo Buscaglia*

To find a new beginning we must first embrace our end. "Before my heart attacks, no one could have ever convinced me that I needed to change my life. Now it amazes me to see how people are firmly convinced that they will live forever," said Tom after having almost died from his heart attack. We are nearsighted, blinded by our belief in tomorrow. What prevents us from recognizing our finiteness and accepting life's simple truth—that one day we will not exist?

## DEATH ANXIETY:
## WHISTLING PAST THE GRAVEYARD

We southerners have an expression, "whistling past the graveyard," to describe someone who uses some means, like whistling, to avoid facing an unpleasant reality. We all "whistle," in one form or another, as a way of coping with the fact that our time on this earth is passing.

Tom coped by losing himself in his work. In discussing this one afternoon in my office, Tom offered, "I used work to feel successful, powerful, vital. When I'd close a big deal and make a wad of cash, I was on top, invincible. It was a high, an addiction. Now I know it was what helped me escape my fear of ending up like my father—dead."

Jackie "whistled" with her maniacal activities, hoping her busyness would help her avoid facing the inevitable changes in her life. With her mother ill and dying, her children leaving home, her husband retiring, she was overwhelmed by the endings in her life. "I can't slow down, even though I know I need to rest. When I stop and sit still, I'm flooded with an unexplainable anxiety. As long as I'm busy, I don't have to think about it."

Roger drowned himself in alcohol and women to avoid dealing with his fear of mortality. "I never dealt with endings. I'd just go on with my life and pretend like nothing happened. It was only when I couldn't pretend anymore, when my father died and death got too close, that I lost it."

Transcending this fear of finitude is a major theme in human experience as is seen in our filling time, addiction to diversions, or the drive to get ahead. We must find some way to do away with our fear. But this is impossible. Only by confronting our anxiety directly, by accepting that our time is limited, can we flood our lives with new urgency and focus. But first we must explode the myth of tomorrow.

Tom, Jackie, and Roger certainly weren't alone in their discomfort. Anxiety about death is universal and has existed since the first humans huddled together around a fire out of a fear of what lurked in the darkness. What exactly are we so scared of?

When we more closely examine our death anxiety, we see this discomfort is a composite of a number of smaller, more discrete fears. When a large group of diverse people were asked to rank

their most common fears about death, they listed them in order
of descending frequency:

- My death would cause grief to my relatives and friends
- All my plans and projects would come to an end.
- The process of dying might be painful.
- I could no longer have any experiences.
- I would no longer be able to care for my dependents.
- I am afraid of what might happen to me if there is a life
  after death.
- I am afraid of what might happen to my body after death.[1]

Take a moment to reflect on your own apprehension. When
you think about your end, what do you feel anxious about? Although we may worry about pain, about our loved ones' reactions, or about an afterlife, these are not our central concern. Of
all of these anxieties, the fear of personal extinction, the fear of
"ceasing to be," the pain of missed opportunities, is at the vortex
of our dread.

Tom recalls his own visit to death's door. "I remember lying
in the hospital emergency room after that second heart attack. I'd
never been that scared. There I was, weak, sweating, this unbearable
chest pain, looking at the nurse's face to see how bad I was. I could
tell by her eyes she thought I wasn't going to make it. At that time,
my greatest fear was never seeing Marge and my kids again—that
all my hard work meant nothing with me gone. I'll never forget
those moments before they put me under."

What makes our physical end so poignant is its absoluteness.
There are no more relationships, enjoyable sensory experiences—
you give up everything you have known. Another client expressed
it poignantly: "Everybody's scared of death. Some moments I
know my life will end. I can see the light closing off, me disap-

pearing. I can't move I'm so scared." How do we cope with this fear that, left unchecked, becomes disabling?

## SHEDDING THE CLOAK OF DENIAL

As in Tom's case, the most common psychological defense or protection from death awareness is denial, the bedrock underlying the myth of tomorrow.

We all use psychological safety devices to deal with the world. Denial is a defense mechanism in which anxiety-provoking thoughts are kept out of or "isolated" from conscious awareness. Denial can be a marvelous coping device, getting us through times of acute crisis until we're psychologically ready to manage the situation more constructively.

Our denial of loss takes various forms. Most people simply believe death is something that will happen to the next guy or gal, certainly not to us, that somehow we alone are immune from extinction. We will live to a ripe old age or, better yet, forever. Even if we let ourselves believe the end will happen, it will not occur any time soon.

For many, it's the immediacy of our end we fervently deny. We promote the myth of tomorrow, wishing to believe that we'll always get another chance at living. We defer the life we really want, and in our postponement, day by day, squander away the only life we ever have.

This caution is offered by the Yaqui sorcerer Don Juan who says to Carlos Castaneda in *Journey to Ixtlan*:

> We don't have time, my friend, that is the misfortune of human beings. Focus your attention on the link between you and your death without remorse or sadness or worrying. Focus your attention on the fact that you don't have

time and let your acts flow accordingly. Let each of your
acts be your last battle on earth. Only under those conditions will your acts have their rightful power. Otherwise
they will be, for as long as you live, the acts of a timid man.[2]

Denial, like other self-protective mechanisms, certainly has its
place. Used adaptively, it enables us to better manage overwhelming emotional events, much like a surge protector keeps your
computer from being destroyed by a sudden electrical charge. But
when overused, denial blocks us from living life fully.

I've worked with numbers of patients over the years who have
experienced cancer, heart attacks, major surgeries, serious accidents, and other life-threatening circumstances. The majority of
these patients quite naturally use denial to cope with the trauma of
intrusive medical procedures, loss of work or sexual functioning,
and most significantly, the near-loss of their life. Where do they
cross the line from healthy to unhealthy denial?

Patients use denial most adaptively in the earliest stage, when
first coming to terms emotionally with their trauma. This defense
allows them to gradually recognize and deal with the sudden
changes and meaning associated with the event. Able to balance
the need to protect themselves psychologically with the need to
recognize the seriousness of their situation, they allow themselves
still to focus on taking steps to ensure their speedy recovery. This
form of denial is adaptive and promotes growth.

Other patients use denial to keep themselves from even recognizing that they are ill. Although it's common for cardiac suf-
ferers, particularly men, to deny or downplay their symptoms early
in their illness, people in serious denial will not recognize they
have symptoms and will delay or refuse life-saving medical care.

Even when these individuals seek or are forced into treatment,
they're unable to admit their illness, allow necessary medical pro-

cedures, or follow postintervention recommendations necessary to save their lives. This form of denial is not only unhealthy, it can be fatal.

Tom, after his first heart attack, disregarded his doctor's recommendations and threw himself back into his full work schedule, refusing to take time out for exercise, change his diet, or stop smoking. His response happens to be more often the rule than the exception.

Unless this unhealthy form of denial is broken, these patients usually don't recover well. If they aren't sick, why would they want to quit smoking, exercise, take medication, change their diet, or reduce their stress levels? Quite expectedly, these patients refuse to follow their physician's recommendations. Persistent denial, even in the face of substantial evidence to the contrary, can cost them their lives.

When an individual suddenly learns he or she has some life-threatening illness, the first reaction is some form of denial. It takes time and much psychological work to restructure one's lifelong assumptive world to incorporate this new information. Once someone's defense is truly undermined and that person realizes "My God, I could die," vulnerable and naked like everyone else, he or she feels confused, lost, and betrayed.

In life-threatening illnesses such as heart disease and cancer, patients initially cannot hear or grasp the serious nature of their diagnosis or cannot talk about their treatment or prognosis. Quite naturally, they find themselves flooded with existential anxiety, flailing their psychic arms just to keep their head above water. Much internal processing, usually interspersed with external feedback, information, and support, must occur to allow the knowledge to settle in and take hold.

For some, the awareness of mortality is so overwhelming and the anxiety so great that the recognition becomes temporarily debilitating. It's difficult to accept that our life is finite and that the world will continue without us. Despite our narcissism, we are still only one of many and the universe does not recognize our specialness; we are subject to the same laws of nature as everyone else.

The drive to succeed, to gain power, fame, fortune, status, to make ourselves special, is not unique to today's society. Human beings have always been driven to enlarge themselves by expanding their sphere of influence and control. We've somehow been led to believe that the more powerful and wealthy we become, the less chance we will be forced to take a glimpse at our own human frailty.

Sean, a client of mine, became a multimillionaire before he was 30. He had consulted me initially to help him to develop his executive team for his growing business. Wildly ambitious and hard driving, Sean grew his company from nothing, which only bolstered his feeling of invulnerability, believing there was no obstacle he couldn't overcome.

He conquered people the same way he had his businesses, with a vengeance. Those around him feared his tenacity and "take no prisoners" attitude. For many reasons, Sean felt he had the world by the tail.

He provided well for his family materially, yet gave little of himself. He seemed to have it all—the best toys, the right memberships, a cadre of golf buddies, what to Sean seemed like the "perfect life."

At the age of 39, he was diagnosed with inoperable brain cancer. Quite naturally, Sean sought out the best medical care money could buy, only to discover that his diagnosis was still terminal. When I met him again, he still couldn't grasp that all his money and power offered him no protection from death. He clung desperately to his "specialness," believing it to be the only thing shielding him from his mortality.

Only months before his demise, Sean began to change. He finally came to reconcile his vulnerability and accept his humanness, and with this, his end. In his remaining time, he shifted his focus to what was most important, his family and a long-lost spirituality. I remember one of our last conversations in which he talked about his two young sons.

"I want my boys to learn from my mistakes. I keep telling them not to be trapped by false values and the 'things' in life, to be more open and to care about people. I made them promise not to follow in my footsteps and make the same mistakes I have. If I leave them nothing else, I want them to pay attention to what's real in life, their heart and soul." He spent his last days in the bosom of his family and faith. Only then did Sean achieve some peace in his life.

As with Sean, every defense has its limitation. Although a repetitive exhilaration briefly accompanies each new achievement, possession, or "upward" movement, there comes a point where we must all face the fact that our time is limited. Reality always creeps in and presses on our self-deception, our psychic walls eventually crumbling under its weight.

We are all the same in our helplessness and mortality, for fate doesn't discriminate. As an Italian proverb shows, "At the end of the game, the king and pawn go back into the same box." Death is truly the great equalizer.

Denial is a powerful but not perfect protection. We each differ in the tenacity with which we cling to denial. Eventually, all denial crumbles in the face of overwhelming reality. Psychiatrist Elisabeth Kübler-Ross, in watching thousands of people die during her long career, reported she had seen only a handful maintain denial to the moment of their passing. Kübler-Ross wisely informs us, "It is the denial of death that is partially responsible for people living empty, purposeless lives; for when you live as if you'll live forever, it becomes too easy to postpone the things you know you must do."

## FROM FEAR TO GROWTH

We can all understand how our anxiety about dying kills our passion, dampening our zest for living. The opposite is just as true. As people live more fully, expand their horizons, and embrace those things most dear to them, their fears of passing subside. In other words, the more content and satisfied we are with our life, the less we fear losing it.

Studies of cancer patients' reactions during their terminal illness tell us that when their lives appeared satisfying, dying became less troublesome.[3] Their degree of satisfaction in their lives directly correlated with the levels of depression, anger, anxiety, and focus on the illness and death. I've witnessed this phenomenon in my clients who have faced their end. Those individuals who are best supported by satisfying relationships and work find dying less terrifying. In contrast, unhappy people are most panicked at the prospect of their time running out.

At first these results may seem confusing. We might think that the dissatisfied and disillusioned would welcome the relief that the end would bring. But the opposite seems truer: A sense of satisfaction and a feeling that life has been well lived mitigates the terror of death. In other words, living well is the best antidote to end-point anxiety.

Existential philosopher Friedrich Nietzsche eloquently explains: "What has become perfect, all that is ripe—wants to die. All that is unripe wants to live. All that suffers wants to live, that it may become ripe and joyous and longing—longing for what is further, higher, brighter."[4]

So our own end becomes a problem only because our daily life is a problem. People who are consumed with guilt, withdrawn from others, too dependent or independent, too ashamed or proud, overly ambitious or controlling—these are the most fearful. The ancient philosopher Seneca said, "Life, if lived well, is long enough."

Remember Jackie's despair over having sacrificed her life to please others? She was terrified by the very thought of dying. As we explored her anxiety, we discovered she feared dying because her life was so unfulfilling. "Even though I appreciate my work and kids, I can see more now how much I've missed in life. There's so much I haven't taken the time to do."

I asked Jackie what she would like to change about her life to make it more satisfying.

She replied, "That's a big part of the problem. I don't have a clue what I really want."

As she explored what she wanted, she became increasingly distressed. "I have these recurring nightmares about being killed by my mother while I'm sleeping. I'm lying there asleep and my mother walks in the room and holds a pillow over my face and I die. I wake up crying every time. I don't know what it means."

Over time, Jackie began to see the meaning in her dream. Having been raised in a strict Catholic home, she learned early how important it was to follow the rules. Her mother, an anxious, devout woman, often criticized Jackie, pointing out her many failings.

"I learned very young that if I didn't do just right, my mom would get angry and beat me. I can remember even when I was three or four, just after my little brother was born, being very careful not to do anything to make her mad. Dad was never around. I think he worked so much just to avoid her sharp tongue. She was vicious."

Jackie knew as a young child that her mother's love was highly conditional, that her feeling safe and loved depended entirely on her ability to please her mother, to be the "perfect" daughter. "I've always worked hard to make sure my mom was happy. It didn't matter how I felt or what I needed; it was always making her, and later anybody else, happy first. I've never stopped to ask myself

what I wanted or needed. The dream tells me my mother's perfectionistic demands were the pillow she used to snuff out my
life as a child, my knowing who I really was inside. It's no wonder I'm unhappy."

Jackie fought to revive the child within her. "I'm scared of
dying before I find myself—I want to live a life that's all my own.
Ironically, I'll know I've arrived when I can look death in the face
and not be so frightened. My life has been paralyzed by that fear."

Excessive attachment to life and fear of death leads to a constricted life—a life dedicated more to security, survival, safety, and
relief from pain than to growth and fulfillment. Individuals who
choose fear and contraction over joy and growth find themselves
strangled by the safety of their ho-hum existence. Only when
we're willing to push through our fears, can we open ourselves up
to the full range of human experience. Philosopher Joseph Campbell tells us, "The conquest of the fear of death is the recovery of
life's joy."

The only way to grow and live fully is by confronting what
we fear. This process of desensitization, or diminishing fears
through gradual or prolonged exposure to the feared object or situation, is a well-established mode of psychological treatment. With
repeated exposure, we can get used to anything. Many of us, without knowing, employ this exact procedure with everyday problems and fears.

I remember my first day as a prison psychologist. I clearly recall
my discomfort walking through the large iron gates and being
buzzed through the numerous security checkpoints, then finally to
be surrounded by hundreds of convicted criminals. Over several
weeks, however, it became just another day at work. The more we
face our fears, the smaller they become. People can conquer any
form of dread by repeatedly exposing themselves to what they fear
in small, graduated doses.

Wayne, a young man, consulted me for sleep problems. He was having recurring nightmares about death after the recent loss of his parents in an airplane accident. He tried everything to keep from having these dreams, including sleeping pills, alcohol, and staying up all night for days on end.

No matter what he tried, night after night, he would find himself dreaming that he was alone in a room with a dark and mysterious shadowy spirit. When the apparition would start to chase him, he would run away screaming. He could feel the spirit's intense presence as he ran and he would wake up sweating in heart-pounding terror.

As we explored his dream over the next weeks, I suggested we personalize death by giving it a name and asking it questions. As he became more comfortable in our discussions, Wayne developed a curiosity about the topic of death and dying. One night as the same dream unfolded, he stopped running and turned around and faced his pursuer. He said his interest in death at that moment was stronger than his fear. As he turned and faced death in his dream, it vanished and he never had the recurring nightmare again.

Another method of overcoming fear involves breaking it down to better understand it. We do this by examining the exact causes of our anxiety and then taking actions that give us a sense of greater control. By examining fears separately and rationally, we can devise strategies to allay some of the anxiety.

If, for example, we fear cancer, we may consult a doctor for pain medication, talk to a clergyman for spiritual guidance, call on supportive others to combat loneliness, and learn more about our illness and medical procedures. Having the courage to face our fears, to push through our anxieties, to overcome that which binds opens us up to whole new horizons of experience. For it is only the courageous who are able to break free of the bonds of fear and shift to the higher state of existence.

## MOVING TO THE NEXT LEVEL
## OF LIVING

As Heidegger has proposed, it requires an "urgent" experience to awaken us from a state of forgetfulness to a state of mindfulness. Without these experiences, we leave ourselves slumbering in our daily, routine existence, unaware of our deeper concerns and the potential their recognition brings to our lives.

Physiologically, we sleep at least one-third of our lives away, yet this fact does not reveal the complete picture. We are "leveled down" or psychologically asleep many more of our waking hours than we want to admit. We live much of our lives in this "everyday slumber," oblivious to what is most important in our lives. How many hours a week do you spend working, watching television, or lost in mindless acquisition of things that doesn't in any way enhance the quality of your life experience?

What of the best of life, the rush of joy, the tingle of excitement, the thrill of anticipation, the heat of intimacy, or the warm glow of contentment that makes life so worthwhile? Where is the quest for quality in our lives?

We can awaken ourselves if we recognize there is something to awaken for—a life more satisfying and meaningful than the one we now live. We can transform end-point anxiety into greater growth and fullness once we open ourselves to experience it. As psychiatrist Fritz Perls wrote in *Gestalt Therapy Verbatim*, "to suffer one's death and to be reborn is not easy."[5] And it is not easy precisely because so much of one has to change.

Perls described the process of shedding our thick edifice constructed of four layers. The first two are the everyday layers Perls refers to as the inauthentic levels of existence. These layers involve the tactics children learn to get along in society by the facile use of words to win approval and placate their adult superiors. These are the glib, empty talk, "cliche" and role-playing layers composing

our social mask. Many people live their lives never getting under-
neath them.

The third layer, harder to penetrate, is the impasse covering our
feelings of emptiness and loss, which is simply a part of the human
condition. These are the very feelings of disillusionment we try
to banish behind our own internal walls and defenses.

The final or fear of death layer is the layer of our true primitive
animal anxiety, the terror we hide even from ourselves. It is only
after we explode the fourth layer, says Perls, that we get to what we
call our authentic self, what we are without disguise, sham, and fear.

Many avoid this difficult process. Victor Frankl reminds us,
"What is to give light must endure burning." To move to the next
level, we must be willing to experience our greatest fears and
move beyond them.

We can learn from those who have gone before us on this path;
those who have squarely faced their end and lived to share their
lessons and insights. I will refer to those people who have encountered death, through their own direct experience or by the
loss of another, as *death survivors*. These individuals may have battled cancer or heart disease, lived through serious accidents, survived violence, or been near to someone who has died.

All warn us not to be seduced by the myth of tomorrow, that
life is not an audition. They caution not to put off what we want
or dream, but rather to live each day as if there were no tomorrows. These brave survivors have much to teach us. With this new
energy and knowledge, we can either choose to fall back asleep
and hold on to the familiar forgetfulness of being or transform our
lives in ways both new and significant.

If we let them, these wise and compassionate souls will guide
us, step by step, to the next level of living. Let us take the next
step together.

# CHAPTER THREE

# Embracing the King of Fears

*As you go the way of life, you
will see a great chasm. Jump.
It is not as wide as you think.*
— *Native American initiation rite*

"A change came over me which I believe is irreversible," Senator Richard Neuberger said months before he died of cancer. "Questions of prestige, of political success, of financial status, became all at once unimportant. In those first hours when I realized I had cancer, I never thought of my seat in the Senate, of my bank account, or of the destiny of the free world.... My wife and I have not had a quarrel since my illness was diagnosed. I used to scold her about squeezing the toothpaste tube from the top instead of the bottom, about not catering sufficiently to my fussy appetite, about making up guest lists without consulting me, about spending too much on clothes."

He continues, "I am either unaware of such matters, or they seem irrelevant. In their stead has come a new appreciation of things I once took for granted—eating lunch with a friend, scratching Muffet's ears and listening for his purrs, the company of my wife, reading a book or magazine in the quiet cone of my bed lamp at night, raiding the refrigerator for a glass of orange juice or slice of coffee cake. For the first time I think I actually am savoring life. I realize, finally, that I am not immortal.[1]

The side effects of mortality are not all bad. Near-death experiences offer the power for people to dramatically change their attitudes, beliefs, and behavior. By harnessing the death-rebirth experience, we provide a potent force for healing and change that can be applied at any moment in time.

How do we go about converting this anxiety into powerful living? How are we able to confront our fear of our own end in ways that open the door to higher levels of awareness and living? What can we learn from those who have faced urgent life crises that we may apply in our daily living?

## FROM END TO BEGINNING: DEATH CATALYZES CHANGE

Some of our greatest literary works have artfully portrayed the positive and profound effects of a close personal encounter with death. We see these changes are very similar to those occurring with people who have survived near-death experiences (NDE). Literary, research, and clinical reports consistently tell us that many death and trauma survivors effect dramatic life reversals.

In the vast majority of cases, NDEs occur in people diagnosed with life-threatening illnesses or who have clinically died and been resuscitated. Recall Tom's close encounter through his sudden heart attacks as one example.

In some instances, however, NDEs may involve perfectly healthy individuals who have been exposed to an intensely frightening or highly traumatic event perceived to be life threatening. These latter situations usually occur in people who have experienced a near-fatal accident or crime. In both instances, these individuals have a renewed sense of life.

Facing mortality leaves a profound, indelible impact. Those who have stared death in the face report afterward that their lives were altered in significant and drastic ways.

## RESARCH/CLINICAL EXPERIENCES

Clinicians encounter this death survivorship phenomenon with some frequency. We see this phenomenon in interviews with those who attempted suicide. Rosen tells us of several survivors who reported, "My will to live has taken over....There is a benevolent God in heaven who permeates all things in the universe." Another: "I have a strong life drive now.... My whole life is reborn.... I have broken out of old pathways.... I can now sense other people's existence." Another: "I feel I love God now and wish to do something for others." Another: "I was refilled with a new hope and purpose in being alive. It's beyond most people's comprehension. I appreciate the miracle of life—like watching a bird fly. Everything is more meaningful when you come close to losing it. I experienced a feeling of unity with all things and a oneness with all people. Since my psychic rebirth I also feel for everyone's pain. Everything is clear and bright."[2]

Russel Noyes studied more than 200 individuals with experiences involving auto accidents, mountain climbing falls, and drownings.[3] One-fourth described, even years later, that as a result of their experiences they were possessed by a "strong sense of the shortness of life and the preciousness of it...a greater sense of zest in life, a heightening of perception and emotional responsivity to immediate surroundings...an ability to live in the moment and to savor each moment as it passes... awareness of life and living things and the urge to enjoy it now before it is too late." These individuals described a "reassessment of priorities," of becoming more compassionate and more people-oriented than they were before their accidents.

Psychiatrist Irving Yalom interviewed a group of terminally ill cancer patients. With the exception of some hospitalized patients in great pain, many of the individuals interviewed by Yalom reported startling shifts and profound changes that can be characterized as therapeutic or "personal growth." These include:

- A rearrangement of life's priorities
- A sense of liberation and freedom: being able to choose not to do those things that they do not want to do
- An enhanced sense of living in the immediate present, rather than focusing on the past or postponing life until retirement or some other point in the future
- A more vivid appreciation of the elemental facts of life: the changing seasons, the ocean, falling leaves, the specialness of holidays, the wind, and so forth
- Deeper and more frequent communication with loved ones than before the crisis
- Fewer interpersonal fears, less concern about rejection, and a greater willingness to take risks in relating to others[4]

A survey of several hundred individuals in different life stages and ethnic groups asked the question, What would you want to do if you knew you had only six months to live? Young adults seemed to want to "grab all the gusto" they could by having experiences that would otherwise be missed and by spending time with loved ones. Young adults who are dying often feel angry that their life goals will not be realized and important relationships must be left behind.

Middle-aged adults were primarily concerned about the quality of their relationships and the welfare of loved ones. More senior adults, having realized many of their goals and raised their children, wanted to contemplate the meaning of their lives.

These findings are consistent with the theories of many developmental psychologists who see identity and intimacy concerns in early adulthood, caring for the younger generation as a concern in middle adulthood, and a quest for a sense of personal integrity in older years. These concerns are largely similar to those who have actually experienced near-death encounters.

I've witnessed a number of people transformed through similar experiences. Donna was a 39-year-old executive who had spent her life climbing the corporate ladder. A highly valued corporate bank executive, she traveled frequently and enjoyed the power and prestige accorded her position. She passed on marriage and children to pursue her career, making little time for even casual friendships. People in Donna's life were important only in so far as they could help her reach the "top."

In the shower one day, she noticed a lump in her breast but was able to convince herself it was "nothing." Several months passed before she saw her doctor, who ordered further tests. A biopsy revealed metastatic cancer and, with some hesitation, Donna underwent the recommended medical treatments. This was the first obstacle she was not able to overcome by simple determination and sheer will. Determined to beat the cancer, she put everything into getting better.

Unfortunately, as Donna pursued her treatment, she had difficulty keeping up with the heavy demands of her fast-paced travel and work, ultimately being placed on medical leave. Unable to work, she fell into a deep depression.

Within a few short months, Donna had been diagnosed with a terminal illness, lost her job, and realized she had nothing else in her life. She had long ago given up any significant relationships that could provide her with the support she so desperately needed. Like many people, she had embraced material things to satisfy a deep inner craving for love. Work had been a poor substitute.

When I first met Donna, she was in a terribly weakened state, both emotionally and physically. She came to quickly understand how she had severely constricted her life in her single-minded pursuit of success. She began to recognize the value of relaxing and enjoying the moment, stopping for the first time to become fully aware of all she encountered.

She began to take time to contact many of the friends that she had neglected over the years and made an effort to open herself to new people she met. She joined a cancer support group and spent time with others who were battling or who had survived their own struggle with the disease.

Donna also focused her energies on developing a relationship with her brother, from whom she had been estranged for years. For the first time, she was living her life fully. Her mood and outlook improved and became more positive. She had confronted her own death and now was consciously making decisions in her life, taking control of the full scope of her life for the first time.

In her own magical way, she had avoided the loneliness and death waiting always in the wings of her life's stage. By confronting her own demise, Donna transformed her life in a way few people can. She is just one example of how a personal confrontation with death can trigger profound life changes.

Interestingly, the changes reported by people experiencing NDEs are very similar to those changes usually accomplished only after years of therapy. The changes include reduced anxiety and specifically a reduced fear of death, increased concern for others, increased belief in an afterlife, improved mood, a lessened focus on material possessions and gain, and improved self-esteem.

However, in contrast to lengthy therapeutic efforts, NDE-related changes seem to be initiated by "urgent" experiences lasting as little as a few minutes. The simple *idea* of death plays a crucial role in the life experience of each of us. To face our own finitude transports us from a life characterized by mindless diversions and petty worries to a more authentic mode of existence.

What we need are ways to allow those of us who are not near death to experience the therapeutic potential of this transformation in ways that can dramatically alter our lives and existence. These dramatic awakenings do not have to be reserved for only those facing a terminal illness or narrowly escaping death, though squarely facing death is an essential first step. How can we become more aware of our mortality to facilitate greater personal growth and satisfaction? We need only to listen.

## SOUNDS IN THE NIGHT: IF ONLY THE LIVING WOULD LISTEN

We've all had the experience of being suddenly awakened by a sound in the middle of the night. If the sound is soft or recognizable, we quickly fall back asleep. Louder, strange sounds startle us and we are disturbed and fitful until we decide sleep is an acceptable response. If we remain anxious, then we must investigate the source of the sound and reassure ourselves we are safe, that the sound is only noise and not a threat. We clearly respond differently to our cat knocking over a picture and the breaking of a window.

Normal events in our life can act as sounds in the night of our existence. They vary in intensity and awaken us from our "everyday slumber" at times, leaving us to either immediately fall back asleep or to anxiously investigate the source of the noise.

Whether we like it or not, we're all exposed to an increased sense of our mortality by inevitable changes in our lives. These "sounds in the night" are sometimes soft, and at other times louder, disturbing reminders of the end. Occasionally, this psychic jostling occurs naturally or we may consciously seek it out.

Small deaths occur every day, in ways both subtle and obvious—a lost opportunity, a broken relationship, falling asleep. Let us look at some of the more likely ways in which we encounter this awareness of death while making no effort to do so. I have listed these natural brushes against death by order of their intensity, from the least to the most unsettling.

## Dreams and Fantasies: Whispers in the Night

We have all experienced fantasies, random thoughts, dreams, and nightmares with themes of death. This may involve a particularly terrifying nightmare occurring after a horror movie, a passing thought after learning about the demise of a casual friend, or pondering the question of what others may say about us at our funeral.

It only takes us being willing to monitor our dreams and fantasies to recognize such material. Discussions of unsettling movies, television shows, and books can certainly lead to this awareness.

I had this experience just the other day. As I was working on this manuscript, I noticed that the more writing I did, the more I became aware of thoughts about my own death. What would it mean to those around me, what would I leave behind as my legacy, would my loved ones be able to take care of themselves adequately? My increased exposure to the idea of death and its impact clearly triggered these random thoughts.

I found it interesting that I could translate this increased awareness in ways to make different choices in—and add quality to—my daily life. I became much more attentive and playful with my wife, rescued earthworms from the pavement on my morning runs, called an old friend whom I had put off contacting, and made a point of spending time doing things I enjoy.

*Anniversaries and Birthdays: A Cat's Meow*

Anniversaries and birthdays can be particularly potent reminders of our end. This becomes increasingly dramatic with increasing age and is further heightened by the "big" decade markers when we celebrate, as an example, a 50th birthday or anniversary. How many of us were slightly uncomfortable with the black banners celebrating a recent birthday?

We can become just as disturbed as we celebrate our children's aging. On our daughter's 29th birthday, my wife half-jokingly asked her to stop having birthdays. The pain elicited by these undeniable signs of the passage of time run deep and offer another, usually unwelcome, opportunity to recognize our own expiration date.

*Physical Changes: A Dog's Barking*

Sometimes simple, seemingly mundane reminders of aging offer us an opportunity for increased existential awareness. A daily glimpse in the mirror at times reveals a new wrinkle, more gray hairs, some extra weight, sun spots, fading vision, or balding. Sometimes these physical reminders alone can be enough to break through our denial.

We also notice these changes by glancing at old photographs or having someone point out how much we resemble our parents, at an age when they were considered old. This recognition occurs at the same time that we realize we do not have the same level of physical stamina, breath, speed, agility, or other attributes that we experienced in our youth.

An equally painful reminder can be our increasing reliance on over-the-counter pain medications and other aids to help us get by in ways we previously took for granted. It seems at times we are gradually "falling apart."

*Developmental Milestones: The Phone's Ringing*

A nearly universal marker we all share are the events associated with the different stages of our development, with certain transitions, such as midlife, proving particularly difficult.

Psychoanalyst Elliot Jaques stresses that people in midlife are particularly haunted by the idea that they have "stopped growing up and have begun to grow old."[5] Having reached what Carl Jung calls the "noon of life" and the achievement of independent adulthood, we become acutely aware that death cannot be far beyond.[6] Midlifers feel as if they have reached the crest in the hill and are now caught on a slippery slope downward into oblivion.

Of these developmental passages, reaching and dealing with midlife is the most significant. It is at this point that we face a most complex intersection of changes, including career questions, children leaving home, signs of aging, parents growing old and dying, and the increasing awareness of our own mortality. This can prompt a crisis resulting in the individual either becoming stuck or breaking through to a higher level of development. Recall Jackie's and Roger's experiences as they were challenged at midlife.

Along the same lines, we face further changes in career—and its ultimate junction, retirement. Confronting an ever-increasing awareness of death, many people experience a crisis when forced to give up the work that has defined their value and life. In fact, any major event, such as marital separation, divorce, or our children maturing and leaving home, is likely to prick at our well-established defense against death awareness.

*Severe Illness: Pounding on the Door*

One of the most obvious shocks to our defensive system of denial is the onset of a severe medical problem or illness. In the compelling study cited earlier, Russel Noyes interviewed 200 patients

who had experienced near-death through sudden illness or accidents and discovered a large number, over 25 percent, had developed a new and potent sense of death's inevitability. One study
participant described such death awareness in this statement: "I
have seen death in life's pattern and affirmed it consciously. I am
not afraid to live because I feel that death has a part in the process
of my being."

Though some of the study participants reported an increased
fear of death and vulnerability, the great majority reported that
their heightened death awareness proved to be a positive experience resulting in a greater sense of life's preciousness and a constructive realignment of life's priorities.

### Near-Fatal Accidents: Shattering Glass

A number of people every year have brushes with death in near-
fatal accidents. Serious automobile accidents, which occur daily,
are the most common. Other examples include victims of natural
or manmade disasters, crime, dangerous falls, near drownings, boating mishaps, and other situations where one narrowly escapes
being killed. Such sobering experiences often temporarily awaken
us from our daily routines and psychic numbness.

### Death of a Loved One: Footsteps on the Stairs

Certainly the most intense and disquieting life event that can
pierce the strongest defense is the death of a loved one. At
the least-intrusive level, this could involve the loss of a close
friend or colleague; at the most, the death of a parent, spouse,
or child.

Consider Carolyn, a close colleague and friend of mine, who
developed colon cancer at the age of 44 and died a short two years
later. We had worked closely together in the same office for several
years and over this time came to know each other well.

.

Given Carolyn's high energy and seemingly robust health, we were shocked upon learning of her diagnosis. After the initial surprise subsided, Carolyn seemed to take her condition in stride; she followed appropriate medical treatments and continued with her life. Her plucky spirit left her very open about her illness, and she talked about it honestly when asked by friends and patients.

Raised in a poor, alcoholic family, Carolyn had always fought for her life. She battled valiantly until finally succumbing to the cancer, surrounded by loving friends and family. She died as she had lived her life, courageously and with caring for those around her. Carolyn's death cracked my heart open and began my rebirth. As difficult as her loss was, she had taught us all something about how to live and die.

Even more significant is the loss of a parent, spouse, or child. Most of us have or will experience the loss of one or both of our parents. This usually occurs in midlife and adds to our growing awareness of our own mortality, common at this life stage.

This loss is moderated to some extent by several factors. We are usually in middle age and are less emotionally dependent on our parents and more involved in our own family. Moreover, we expect our parents will die someday and have had time to prepare ourselves. Nevertheless, their loss can be unsettling as we begin to realize that if this can happen to our parents, then it is only a matter of time until we succumb.

The literature on stress and life events lists death of a spouse as the most stressful event any of us can experience in our life. We are all familiar with the reports of one spouse dying soon after the death of the first.

Research shows surviving spouses progress through overlapping phases of yearning, disorganization, numbness, and reorganization. The widower experiences increased risks for emotional problems, illness, and particularly in the elderly, even death.

Arnold Toynbee in *Man's Concern for Death* reflects:

> I guess that if, one day, I am told by my doctor that I am
> going to die before my wife, I shall receive the news not
> only with equanimity but with relief. This relief, if I do feel
> it, will be involuntary. I shall be ashamed of myself for feel-
> ing it, and my relief will, no doubt, be tempered by concern
> and sorrow for my wife's future after I have been taken
> from her.[7]

Of all life events, perhaps none is more disturbing than the
death of a child. This bitterest of losses reminds all involved of their
helplessness. We believe parents are supposed to protect their children from harm and children aren't supposed to die before their
parents. Forced to recognize the limits of our own power to protect the child, we ourselves have no protection.

We are all vulnerable to an untimely demise. The loss of a
child, in addition to triggering powerful feelings of anger, grief,
guilt, and helplessness, has other significant implications. It signals
the failure of the parents' own immortality strivings, and most significantly, the parents' dreams once tied to the fate of their children
die as well.

### Near-Death Experiences: Someone's in the Room

Another potent reminder is the actual experience of death itself.
This occurs more frequently than we might imagine. A Gallup
poll estimated that 8 million Americans have undergone a near-
death experience.

While these naturally occurring reminders of death's presence
are numerous, only the most potent break through our ever-vigi-
lant system of denial. We need more conscious and intentional reminders to bring us to face the fact of death.

## CONSCIOUS ENCOUNTERS:
## THE WAKE-UP CALL

We are faced with intentional reminders of death every day. Montaigne, in his essay "That to Philosophize Is to Learn How to Die," cites a number of examples:

> ...we plant our cemeteries next to churches, and in the most frequented parts of town, in order.... to accustom the common people, women and children, not to grow panicky at the sight of a dead man, and so that the constant sight of bones, tombs, and funeral possessions should remind us of our condition...So I have formed the habit of having death continually present, not merely in my imagination, but in my mouth.

> And there is nothing that I investigate so eagerly as the death of men: what words, what look, what bearing they maintained at that time; nor is there a place in the histories that I note so attentively. This shows in the abundance of my illustrative examples; I have indeed a particular fondness for this subject. If I were a maker of books, I would make a register, with comments, of various deaths. He who would teach men to die would teach them to live.[8]

Aside from these natural or established reminders, some clinicians have offered therapeutic means to confront death anxiety. Various exercises include death imagery, which can be a powerful way to better focus on issues or tasks needing attention in our immediate lives. Often the client will be energized and focused to pursue some change in his or her life, resolve an issue with a friend or relative, spend more time with spouse or children, or simply make time to enjoy life more.

Despite the fact that these exercises can be interesting as well as powerful, they are nonetheless pretend. Though one can be involved in such an exercise for a certain time, denial quickly moves in to remind us that we still exist. No exercise is as powerful as spending time with those facing their own death.

This is illustrated by the best-selling book *Tuesdays with Morrie*, by Mitch Albom, who writes of his experience spending Tuesdays with his terminally ill college professor and the lessons he learned about life and death.[9] That this simple story became widely popular speaks to our fascination with death and our wish to learn from the process.

The novelist John Fowles writes, "Death's rather like a certain kind of lecturer, you don't really hear what is being said until you're in the front row." If we are to be altered by death, we must give it our full attention.

These types of exercises are one way to sit in the front row. Although they may not have the same potency as an actual near-death experience, they still have strong effects on the participants. In the words of sociologist William Thomas, "If men define situations as real, they are real in their consequences. Such experiences...tend to exert a powerful effect on a person's motivations, values, and conduct.... However one chooses to interpret near-death phenomena, they are unquestionably real in their effects."

Dr. Samuel Johnson said that the prospect of death wonderfully concentrates the mind. By becoming more aware of our own mortality, we can clarify what is most important in our lives while also discovering the motivation to enhance our future existence. What can we learn from others who have faced death to help us in our own discovery?

## THE SEVEN KEYS

What important life lessons can we learn from ordinary people placed in the extraordinary situation of being confronted by death? Can we benefit from their wisdom without our having to develop a terminal illness, sit on death row, face a firing squad, or have a near-fatal accident? In speaking with people who have grown personally from these situations, I have heard many lament, "Why did I have to go through this experience before I learned what is so important about life?"

There is remarkable agreement as to the key lessons learned by those who have faced their own death: a "death bed" wisdom that powerfully informs our daily life, offering each of us a way to assess the fullness of our own existence. These keys crystallize in seven life lessons.

## LIFE LESSON ONE

# DECIDE WHAT'S TRULY IMPORTANT IN LIFE

Confrontations with death compel us to stop and reevaluate our values and life. Seeing our time as limited forces us to rearrange our priorities while asking the question, "What is really important?"

Lance Armstrong spoke of this sudden shift in his book *It's Not About the Bike*:

> I thought I knew what fear was, until I heard the words, You have cancer. Real fear came with an unmistakable sensation; it was as though all my blood started flowing in the wrong direction. My previous fears, fear of not being liked, fear of being laughed at, fear of losing my money, suddenly seemed like small cowardices. Everything now stacked up differently: the anxieties of life—a flat tire, losing my career,

a traffic jam—were reprioritized into need versus want, real problems as opposed to minor scares. A bumpy plane ride was just a bumpy plane ride, it wasn't cancer.[10]

People who have brushed against mortality undergo a substantial values disruption and transformation. Psychologist Kenneth Ring has interviewed thousands of people who have narrowly escaped death and has written extensively of their experiences. In his *Lessons from the Light*, he notes, "Experiencer's resume life by living it more fully, loving more openly, and fearing death less, if at all.... Their life seems more grounded in a sense of purpose and is more consciously shaped by the spiritual values of love, compassion, and acceptance."[11]

People who have experienced near-death encounters change what they see as important in their lives. The more typical social "drivers" such as power, recognition, fame, money, work, and status suddenly lose their stranglehold. Since all such gains are finite, acquiring them fails to provide lasting satisfaction. Many of the common social-comparison games are no longer relevant and fall away.

Recall Tom after his second heart attack. "Most of my life was focused on getting ahead, making money, winning at any cost. Everybody saw me as supercompetitive. After my heart attacks, I finally realized that it didn't matter. Sure, I still enjoy the deal and the excitement when something comes together, but it's not my reason for living. Now my free time, being with my family, doing simple things, enjoying life, are what gets me up every morning."

Competitiveness becomes petty and cooperation paramount. People who have encountered death refocus their energies and time in developing more meaning in their life through giving to the community and others, deepening their personal relationships, and learning to know and accept themselves. A tremendous thirst for knowledge and understanding consumes their attention.

Life review is a common experience reported by people who come close to death. Many describe this as the most important element of the NDE. The popular conception of this experience is where "your life flashes before your eyes."

Researchers have seen this memory playback phenomenon with near-drowning victims and others who nearly perish. These individuals report the number, rapidity, and clarity of these images to be profound in their impact. They believe they have re-experienced their entire life, all at once and chronologically as well. The experience is educative, offering the most critical lessons needed to change their life for the better.

An example from one person in Kenneth Ring's book *Heading toward Omega* illustrates this process:

> I had a total, complete, clear knowledge of everything that had ever happened in my life . . . just everything, which gave me a better understanding of everything at that moment. Everything was so clear . . . I realized that there are things that every person is sent to earth to realize and to learn. For instance, to share more love, to be more loving toward one another. To discover that the most important thing is human relationships and love and not materialistic things.[12]

Participants report life review as a nonjudgmental process, a kind of "educational video" whereby they are able to relive every aspect of their life, their feelings, thoughts, actions, and the effect they had on others. The result is a startling recognition that everything we have done is revisited upon us; that we receive back exactly what we have given out. Unselfish love to your child comes back as love bestowed on you. And likewise a hurtful comment that wounds someone else cuts into you equally.

Some of the lessons learned are not offered so gently. P.M.H. Atwater, in her book *Coming Back,* speaks of the life review experience:

> Mine was not a review, but a reliving. For me, it was a total reliving of every thought I had ever thought, every word I had ever spoken, and every deed I had ever done; plus, the effect of each thought, word, and deed on everyone and anyone who had ever come within my environment or sphere of influence, whether I knew them or not.... No detail was left out. No slip of the tongue or slur was missed. No mistake or accident went unaccounted for. If there is such a thing as hell, as far as I am concerned, this was hell.[13]

Many near-death experiences see the life review process as deemphasizing values related to our conventional definitions of success (e.g., money, accomplishments) while stressing things like kindness, compassion, and unconditional love for others. Other research by Ring reports values that become more "human-oriented" and less focused on material possessions. In the words of one who has experienced this process, "I value people more. I don't think I value worldly goods that much. Material things seem unimportant to me now."[14]

Another reported, "Well, I don't think anybody would mind being prosperous, but I see how little it really does mean...I found out that some of these things are really laughable as far as importance. So all I need now, in my way of thinking, is to be able to comfortably survive."

Julian, a friend of mine, clearly illustrated this values shift. Julian had spent his entire life chasing after the American dream. A highly successful general surgeon, he worked 80-hour weeks while sacrificing leisure, family, and finally his health for his career. He reveled in his expensive home, cars, and boats but was never satisfied, no matter how much he accomplished or acquired. I would run into Julian at the hospital for consults and occasionally on the tennis courts.

At the top of his game professionally and athletically, I was surprised to hear of his being rushed to the hospital to undergo an emergency quintuple bypass surgery. During surgery, something went terribly wrong and he died twice on the operating table before he was finally stabilized.

Nothing builds perspective more than dying. I ran into Julian at the hospital a few months later in the doctors' lounge. "I guess you heard about my heart surgery going bad. I found out later how I'd died, come back, and died again. I guess I'm like a lot of docs who think that my M.D. somehow protected me, that we have the power to defeat death. I hadn't had a physical for 16 years when this happened. Before, I thought death was just for the next guy. Now I know doctors die too."

I was surprised at his candor as he went on, "This whole experience has changed me. I'm finished with all the competitiveness, the race to get ahead, the toys, being at the top of the heap. None of that matters near as much now. It's time I finally did something worthwhile with my life."

After his brush with death Julian took a step back and began to look seriously at his life for the first time. He scaled back his surgical practice by bringing in a partner to share the caseload, dedicated himself to trying to remedy the effects of the prior neglect of his wife and children, and began developing himself spiritually. I found out later that he joined a group of doctors who volunteered their medical talents to help children in Central America. To my knowledge, Julian never regretted these life-changing decisions.

LIFE LESSON TWO

# EXPAND YOUR SENSE OF FREEDOM AND CHOICE

Many of us don't realize the pain we carry from the covering up of our natural selves with the pretensions society demands from us. Forsaking our true feelings and needs, we assume the face most fitting to the situation. We laugh when we feel like crying, we smile when we're anxious, we feel despondent when there is no obvious reason to be disturbed. We spend so much time being who we "should" be, we forget who we are.

Remember Jackie as someone who was trapped in others' expectations. "I could never be honest about my own feelings or what I needed, even to myself. It's sad to think of all the years I wasted trying to get everyone to like me, to gain their approval. I thought if I just followed the rules, did everything that was expected of me, that I would be OK. Unfortunately, my life was never my own."

Individuals who've faced their own mortality often feel liberated; released from the "shoulds, oughts, and have tos" of more prescribed living. They find themselves less concerned and restricted by the common rules for living, giving up many of the inhibitions that limited their enjoyment of life. They cease following the "old" rules that no longer make sense in their new life.

Death has given them permission to say no to unwelcome duties, jobs, obligations, and demands put on them by other people. It allows a person to take time off to reflect, meditate, and set a new life course. Previously cherished rules of conduct don't apply or are at least questioned.

This liberated feeling is described by many who have faced death. In the movie *The Doctor*, William Hurt plays a physician di-

agnosed with throat cancer who is afraid of dying. When he im-
petuously rents a car to drive a fellow cancer patient to a concert
in another state, the friend asks him if this is something he would
normally do. William Hurt replies: "I see my tumor allowing me
certain freedoms I never allowed myself."

Jackie, who in therapy finally confronted her own end, was
similarly liberated. "Now I don't worry so much about what other
people think. If it feels good to me and I'm not hurting anyone, I
go ahead. I used to be so bound up in making sure everybody ap-
proved of what I wanted, I never did anything. I now listen to my
feelings and don't get so tied up in making everybody happy. It's
like I cut the strings and am finally deciding my own life. What a
difference."

Like children, individuals confronting imminent death respond
more from their heart, their feelings, and intuition. They are more
conscious in their decision making and do more of what they
want to do and less of what they don't. New possibilities emerge
where before there were parentally or culturally imposed rules and
limits. They feel an increased sense of invulnerability, power, om-
nipotence, and self-esteem.

LIFE LESSON THREE

# RECOGNIZE YOU'RE MORE THAN WHAT YOU DO OR OWN

Coming close to death brings about a greater acceptance of self.
Individuals with an NDE report an enhanced sense of self-worth,
more assertiveness, and personal strength. In most cases, they simply like themselves more. They recognize their faults, yet can be
more accepting of themselves as a whole.

Jack had always been shy and timid. Coming from a physically abusive family, he learned as a young child to fear anger and confrontation. "All I remember growing up was my father getting drunk and yelling and screaming. When my mother or older sister ever said anything, he'd hit them. I learned early just to keep my mouth shut and stay out of the way."

As a result, Jack lived his life hiding in the shadows, retreating from any situation that felt threatening or uncomfortable. Quiet and soft-spoken, he had become a social chameleon, blending into the background to assure his survival.

I met Jack on referral from his company. After almost being killed in a convenience store robbery, he was first terrified, then angry. "I'll never forget that robber holding a gun to my head telling me to pray before he killed me. Then he just grabbed the money and ran. Afterwards, I was shaking; I've never been that scared. Then later I was furious, angrier than I can ever remember. It made me mad that someone would do that to me, to anyone."

He now knew no matter how meek or mild-mannered he had been, or how hard he had tried to avoid conflict, he would still have to face people who might hurt him. From his near-death encounter, he began to feel and channel his anger for the first time in his life. By constructively confronting his repressed anger at his father, Jack became more assertive, learned to set limits, and expressed himself more honestly with others.

Psychologist Kenneth Ring, in his interviews with those who have been near death, reports several examples of this change.[15] One woman who survived an illness-related death experience expressed her change in self-concept very pithily: "I think it's enriched me. I think I'm a stronger person." Another woman seriously injured in an automobile accident had been very depressed and prone to suicidal thoughts prior to her accident. After her accident, she reported, "I don't have many, or any, of those passive feelings that I wished that I could die. I'm much less afraid. I'm much more able to be close to people.... I'm much more comfortable with myself. I'm not as depressed. I'm less anxious."

We often confuse who we are with what we do and own. As a result, we become inordinately stressed by threats to our career, bank account, or any number of external attributes, believing "I am my career" or "I am my physical appearance."

You are not your beautiful body, the balance in your bank account, the car you drive, the home you live in, or your successful career; you are only the core essence of your self. If you draw a line around your *self*, all other things outside this line are not you; they vanish and you will still exist. Though it's true, many have difficulty accepting this as fact.

Death strips us naked. When we face our dying, pieces of our self-image begin to fall away. Our sexual identity, status, work, our role as boss, father, spouse, and friend are all called into question. Death takes us down to our bare essentials, our essence, yet we're still whole in our humanness. When we overidentify with our roles and possessions, our freedom to be who we are diminishes as we become hopelessly entangled in our own self-definitions.

Consider Harry, formerly a kind, gentle man, who was experiencing a reoccurrence of prostate cancer and could no longer work. His illness progressed and he was unable to drive or help around the house. As he became bedridden, he grew increasingly frustrated and angry, becoming agitated and aggressive with his wife, Jennifer, and their children. Neither Jennifer nor her family could understand these dramatic changes in his temperament.

Since Harry was dying, the family avoided any confrontation with him at all. They were afraid to address Harry for fear of upsetting him. This angered him even more as he felt increasingly disengaged and patronized.

Harry's family asked the hospice social worker to become involved. She pointed out the connection between his annoyance
and his loss of control. With the social worker's help, the family
started calling Harry on his grouchy mood and irritable disposi-
tion. They started including him again in family decisions and asking him for advice and comfort. Harry's mood improved as he
made the difficult adjustment to feeling valued outside of his for-
mer roles and activities.

You are more than what you do or have. A structured disidentification exercise offered by James Bugental makes this point in a
powerful way, often catalyzing change.[16] The procedure, outlined
in Chapter 7, is straightforward and generates in the participants
strong emotions that mirror those of people facing death.

These powerful feelings, often spontaneously generated in
those who face death, can create dramatic changes in our perspective. This disidentification process creates a personal
paradigm shift, providing us with the opportunity to transcend
the social and material attachments and to reinvest in the core
of our self.

LIFE LESSON FOUR

# DEVELOP GREATER LOVE AND ACCEPTANCE OF YOURSELF AND OTHERS

As reflected in earlier accounts, people who confront their own
extinction experience greater feelings of self-worth, confidence,
and personal security. Just as often, death survivors develop a
deeper acceptance of, and caring for, others as well. Close encounters with mortality help us conquer our fears of intimacy.

Suddenly able to overcome the most common fears in being closer to others, they drop much of the judgmentalism they had once erected to separate themselves from people. Many people are only able to let go of their fears and resentment when they are near death. Dying or the threat of dying has a way of tearing away everything that stands between us and those we love.

I have seen this change in both individual and group counseling. I recall my friend and colleague Carolyn, when asked, openly shared her feelings about her illness with her patients in group therapy. People facing death achieve deeper levels of vulnerability and intimacy than they had ever known. As they become vulnerable, their openness invites deeper involvement from those they touch.

They sense the commonalties among people, focusing more on similarities and less on the differences dividing us. They are more open, spontaneous, and direct in their communications, somehow more willing to take emotional risks and less fearful of rejection.

These individuals cultivate love for themselves and others, a more accepting and *unconditional love*. The usual social boundaries and categories, sex, race, age, status, and so on, are removed, and the inherent equality of all people is recognized and affirmed. Along with this, many report a lessening of judgmentalism and prejudicial attitudes. When the mind becomes free of any thoughts of judgment, then and only then can we know things as they truly are.

As one survivor put it, "How can one friend mean any more than another when everyone is your friend and there are no strangers? Every child becomes your child. Every man your husband, father, and brother. Every woman your wife, mother, and sister. Boundaries and bloodline, barriers and taboos cease. For the survivor, there are no more divisions, races, religions, nationalities, or separations of any kind. Love has expanded outward and it doesn't quit growing."[17]

In addition to greater acceptance, concern for others deepens. Selfish needs abate, replaced by an expanded desire to help others. One survivor suggests "fulfilling yourself with love—by giving."[18]

People experience more empathy, compassion, patience, tolerance, understanding, and greater satisfaction in relating to others. When there is less concern for what others think, spontaneity and playfulness blossom.

LIFE LESSON FIVE

# CREATE A NEW APPRECIATION FOR THE ELEMENTALS OF LIFE

Nearly all near-death experiencers share one basic truth: count your blessings. This is simple yet profound. How often do we focus on what we have and not on what we don't?

Tom, after his heart attacks, found new joy in playing with his children, traveling on the weekends with his wife, hitting a tennis ball with his buddies. "Before, taking time for myself and my family wasn't satisfying. It wasn't them, it was me. I was so stressed with deadlines and deals, obsessed with making more money and beating out my competitors, I couldn't appreciate the simple things. I can't count the hours I wasted on things that meant absolutely nothing to me—drinking with my buddies, listening for hours to the same news, watching boring television shows. Then my family seemed unimportant, insignificant to me."

We must learn to attend to what we do have. As in Tom's life, small joys were lost while he searched for the big ones. Our blessings slip out of awareness, only to be replaced by petty concerns and threats to our status. By keeping our mortality in mind, we pass into a state of gratitude and appreciation for what are the "givens" of our life.

People who have encountered the end report a new zest and appreciation for life and all its simple wonders. In touch with life's essence, their feelings and senses pulse with new awareness. Psychiatrist Fritz Perls has preached, "Lose your mind and come to your senses." We pay an enormous price for losing touch with our senses: Our world is diminished. We must reawaken our senses to reawaken our lives, to feel the richness of life and its possibilities.

This reorientation involves a deeper appreciation of the changing seasons, wind in the trees, the sound of surf on the beach, laughter of children, and a hug from a loved one. Many find themselves more reverent toward animal life, nature, and the ecology of the planet.

One woman who was revived from a coma caused by a severe automobile accident spoke of these feelings: "Afterward, I enjoyed being with people more. And I enjoyed the outdoors. Nature, and trees budding. I still have a thing for spring. And it was where everything started coming alive. And I enjoyed it.... I used to take the spring for granted. But I have the feeling that I'm looking more and more and seeing life. It's really nice."[19]

People who face down death are reborn psychologically and begin their new lives much as young children do, with amazement and wonder about the simplest experiences. They reacquire the innocent eyes of youth and find they are never the same afterward. Life is no longer stable, predictable, and pedestrian. Each day they see what was once mundane as remarkable; routine as pleasurable.

One effect of this realization is living life in the present moment, understanding that life cannot be postponed. Death halts the forward and backward movement of time. Many cancer patients report that they live their lives more fully in the present moment.

They learn that the only life possible is in the present. There is a new urgency for living every moment to the fullest.

In *A Christmas Carol*, Ebenezer Scrooge's transformation consisted of a reversal of misdeeds of the previous day: He tipped the caroler he cursed, donated money to the charity workers he spurned, embraced the nephew he scorned, gave coal, food, and money to Cratchit whom he had tyrannized. Having seen a life review, he began to live his life differently and changed himself from that present moment.

People who have faced death see their life can only exist in the here and now and resolve to live it to the fullest. They have a sense of being renewed and reborn. From death, comes new life.

LIFE LESSON SIX

# FOCUS ON THE IMPORTANCE OF PURPOSE IN LIFE

We have seen that most people who have faced their own death undergo a significant shift in their values, beliefs, and behavior. Once people seriously evaluate what is important in their lives, they often find many of their previous activities, pursuits, and relationships no longer provide their life with the same degree of meaning as before.

Tom found himself volunteering for Habitat for Humanity, his first effort at community giving. "I've been very fortunate in my life and want to give something back. Since I know real estate, I'm enjoying sharing what talent and knowledge I have by building homes for those less advantaged than me. It's been much more satisfying than I ever expected. It's felt great seeing the faces of people walking into their first home."

Life is a blank slate on which we script the meaning we choose. Many survivors open their eyes and see new purpose in their lives. They are more determined than ever to define and fulfill their raison d'être. A sense of renewed purpose manifests itself as a driving force, energizing and altering life's direction.

People who are dying begin to *live* the meaning they find rather than endlessly deliberating on it. This can sometimes involve making major alterations such as changing careers, completing a stalled divorce, or returning to school.

Sometimes the changes are smaller. Virginia Woolf reminds us, "What is the meaning of life? The great revelation...never did come. Instead there were little daily miracles, illuminations, matches struck unexpectedly in the dark."

The belief that life could be cut short intensifies risk taking and the willingness to take chances. One man who almost died of a high fever said, "It changed my philosophy in life. From being a kind of passive person to a more assertive person. It made me look at things differently...I became restless. I wanted to do everything at once. That's the only negative thing. Now I want to travel. It's got to be now. I want to go back to school and finish my degree. I may not have much longer."

The search for meaning often takes people away from the social and material worlds. Seeking to know the reason for living, they search for a deeper understanding of the nature of life and for a higher consciousness to penetrate to the hidden significance of all things. They acquire an inner drive for understanding and the attainment of knowledge.

Searchers may become more involved in personal growth experiences, religious and spiritual activities, community-giving projects and organizations, and academic pursuits. Some express this newfound quest more quietly within the confines of their own family and network of friends. Each individual tries to fully actualize their own potential while also giving more of themselves to others and the world.

## CREATE A GREATER APPRECIATION FOR RELIGION AND SPIRITUALITY

Studies show near-death experiences have a profound effect upon attitudes toward physical death. Freed of their anxiety, those who have faced death come to accept that they will die, and they live their lives more fully as a result.

Having conquered their fear of the annihilation of consciousness, they view death as a mere fact of their existence. Survivors report, "I'm not afraid of death at all," or "I'm not afraid of dying and I used to be hemmed in by my fear." With this decreased fear of death comes a corresponding increased interest in religion, spirituality, and the afterlife. Many religious worldviews not only provide answers to life's deepest questions; they also encourage hope in facing the terror resulting from the awareness of our mortality.

Recall Roger's experience overcoming sexual diversion and, more directly, his fear of death. "Now that I've faced my fear of dying, it doesn't control me anymore. Though I've always been religious, I've found myself becoming more spiritual lately. I still enjoy going to church with my family, participating in services, and reading the Bible, but something's different. It feels more real, a part of me, like I'm really living what I believe. I'm more accepting of others and their beliefs than I used to be."

Interestingly, most who confront death don't increase their participation in more formal religious observances. Rather they experience a heightened inner spiritual feeling, often expressed as a

closer feeling with God more than a church; they are more prayer-
ful and privately religious.

One individual I spoke with illustrated this shift by her comment, "My faith that there is a higher power that is somehow controlling my life has been heavily reinforced." Another person
shared, "I felt closer to a God, a feeling I had not had for years. I
was an agnostic. I didn't know. I feel much closer now that I know.
I find myself praying sometimes to an unknown Force."

Overall, these persons seem to experience an increased tolerance for all forms of worship. They embrace a broader spirituality
that at its essence is a search for the truth of our existence. From
this point of view, there is no "true" or superior religion or set of
beliefs; rather, all religions are different expressions of a single
truth. One client of mine stated, "I believe in the truths of all religions. They are all connected as far as I am concerned." This is
an expression of a spiritual universalism. It includes not only the
traditional Western monotheistic religions but also an increased acceptance of reincarnation and Eastern religions.

A strong generalized value reorientation results, stressing the
importance of love and the role of spiritual values in everyday
life. In essence, people who have faced their own demise tend
to become more spiritual than religious, as seen in the conventional sense.

When you think about it, it is quite natural for those confronted with their mortality to ask the question, "Where do I go
after I die?" One of the more dramatic findings in research on
people who have confronted death is their increased belief in and
conviction about the presence of an afterlife. Near-death experiencers testify to this consistently and unambiguously. A woman
I met who suffered a heart attack said of her experience, "I believe that beyond any question there is something beyond this
life."

Many interviewed dramatically altered their view of life after death. A man who had a heart attack during surgery reported, "I would say—and not being religious at all—that there must be something after death, which I never believed in before. I always believed that when your were dead, they put you in the ground and you stayed there. But I'm not too sure about that anymore."[20]

The voices of those who have confronted death tell of wisdom accessible to everyone. The dying escort us to the answers we are seeking, to the essential lessons about life that we can use to enrich our lives.

Death's message is one of hope, love, and meaning, for it points us to a path for the very fulfillment of life, not to its diminishment. As death begins to influence our lives in more positive ways, we no longer fear an enemy but embrace a friend to guide us to the next level of living.

How can we create this change in our own life? Can we meet and befriend our own death in order to flood our lives with passion and purpose?

# CHAPTER FOUR

# The Ultimate Wake-Up Call

*Freedom is what you do with
what's been done to you.*
—Jean-Paul Sartre

Each of us hears life's whispers. When we listen closely, our dreams, anniversaries, kids and parents aging, friends passing, all tell us our time is limited.

Shaken by signs of time's passage, many feel compelled to reevaluate their lives, to ask the big questions. How do I wish to spend my life? Am I living the life I want? These questions contain within them an intense yearning, a deep hunger for greater peace, happiness, and meaning.

Karen, a critical care nurse, was startled by the news of her cancer. "My life's been turned upside down. I'm 32 years old with a good career and a family. A few months ago I was told I have breast cancer. Even though the doctors have given me a good prognosis and I think I'll be all right, my life will never be the same. There's something missing. This diagnosis has made me ask myself, Is this the life I want? I need to know now. Who knows how long any of us has?"

Greg's life suddenly hit a turn in the road. "I used to think I would live forever. Since my near-fatal car accident last year, I haven't been the same. The belief in my immortality was shattered along with my BMW. I was in a hospital bed for two months and had time to think about my life. It's been difficult at times; I still feel confused and depressed. But I'm determined not only to get my life back, but to make it better than before."

Bill was stunned by the loss of his son. "My 6-year-old son drowned in our backyard pool two years ago. Deborah and I couldn't deal with it and just got divorced. I don't see my daughter as much and miss both my kids terribly. My whole life has changed. I'm not sure what to think or do now. I've wondered why I go on living. Sure, I'm working and trying to go on with my life, but I don't know where I'll go from here."

In each of their lives, tragedy had flung open the door to change. By facing life's fragility, Karen, Greg, and Bill all recognized a need to redirect their lives but were stuck, uncertain how to go about it. Though they found the will to change, they lacked the direction to make their lives better. Many of us who have not had such a revelation are also stalled, left to discover both the will and direction.

How can the idea of facing our end save us? The philosopher Seneca tells us, "Rehearse death. To say this is to tell a person to rehearse his freedom. A person who has learned how to die has unlearned how to be a slave."

There are many ways to find peace with our limited time on this earth. We cannot engage in the myth of tomorrow, for to deny the reality of some end point we not only freeze our fear but freeze our life as well. If we intellectually rationalize life's impermanence, make a mental truce with it, we also sacrifice full, joyful living. Not knowing how much time we truly have is what makes our end the ultimate stranger.

We must confront the stranger every day in all kinds of change and loss. Perhaps your job is changing, your child is leaving home, your close friend is seriously ill, or your body is aging. Each of these changes in your life provides you with another opportunity to befriend this passing stranger. For nothing awakens us more to life than the thought of losing it.

## NEW AWAKENINGS

We must decide whether our awareness of time's passing undermines or enriches life. A full awakening experience is only an opportunity for growth, not a promise it will occur. We have to seize this chance to live more mindfully or retreat into a world of seclusion and denial.

We have wake-up calls every day. Our pet dies, we hear of a friend who is terminally diagnosed, we're involved in an automobile accident, we have another birthday, children leave home, our hair grays, and knees creak. Each experience announces our vulnerability, revealing our lives as fragile and precious.

Are you prepared to awaken more fully, to embark on a challenging journey? First, there are a few things to pack for this trip. You will need courage, imagination, and self-awareness. Courage involves a willingness to be uncomfortable. If the thought of your end frightens you, we will confront your fear. If you are not prepared for the journey, then honor your hesitation. By preserving your denial, you purchase a ticket for a later trip.

For those with the courage to begin, accept that this will be a bumpy path fraught with anxiety and uncertainty, yet one that ultimately leads to a new level of psychological and spiritual integration. By challenging our firmly held beliefs, we invite a true existential crisis, bringing with it the opportunity for change. We move to the growing edge of uncertainty. Having experienced this journey and shifted levels of consciousness, we will learn *it is the quality of life that determines its worth.*

As we've seen in others' experiences, an enhanced awareness of our end catalyzes important life changes. The idea that our time is limited helps and heals. It only requires our receptivity, a willingness to learn from those who have knocked on death's door. As one survivor told me, "It's possible to gain all of the knowledge a person learns when they die, without dying. You don't have to die to get there."

But you will need both imagination and courage to challenge your most cherished beliefs and assumptions. Just as Heidegger and others have suggested, we must have the nerve to live out our end to move to the next level of consciousness. It requires using these "urgent" experiences to question and then shatter our most fundamental belief about our immortality, that we will live forever. For this to occur, we must experience our finiteness on two levels. It is not enough to read and abstractly consider such thoughts. Simple armchair reflection of some abstract concept leaves us short of the experience.

There's a big difference between the thought of an apple and the taste of one. You must bite the apple, savor the flavor in your mouth, feel the juice run down your chin, drenching yourself in the experience. To shift to the next level of living, we have to stretch beyond the mere thought of death and truly experience *our* end on a visceral, emotional level.

Charles Darwin illustrated the important difference between rational thought and actual experience. He provided a firsthand account after witnessing a devastating earthquake in February 1835 that killed more than 5000 people in Chile. He wrote in his memoirs that the earthquake in "one second of time has created in the mind a strange idea of insecurity, which hours of reflection would not have produced."[1]

I've witnessed more change occur after a serious tragedy than through dozens of hours of psychotherapy. We have all had this brought home by the tragic events of September 11, 2001. These traumatic events forced us to stop our busy schedules and reflect on our lives. And from this pain and deep reflection, seismic changes occurred. There is no substitute for these kinds of experiences in learning life's most important lessons.

What makes such experiences such a potent catalyst for change? Just as with the traumatic experience of September 11, to take such quantum leaps we have to tap the power of the experiential mind to create significant changes in our fundamental beliefs and then in our feelings and behavior. Such urgent events provide an emotional encoding, creating a potent form of sense memory. Only then can we use our gift of self-awareness and conscious imagery to powerfully drive the desired changes in our behavior.

I ask clients caught up in their obsessive worry about a promotion, relationship, or other immediate concern to stop and close their eyes. As they relax, they imagine themselves on their deathbed reflecting on the importance of their immediate concern. How important is the concern in this larger context?

Clients either see their concerns vanish or put them in a broader perspective and approach them more constructively. With this perspective in place, they may resolve to talk to their boss or find another job, drop their petty jealousy, take the vacation they'd put off for years, or simply worry less. But in any case, they drop their concern and *do* something. Change occurs.

I've used other kinds of visualization exercises, such as imagining a 50th wedding anniversary, financial setbacks, divorce, or retirement, to help clients shift their perspective. These exercises often help us see our lives differently. They provide opportunities to stand back and ask hard questions about our priorities and focus. We are suddenly able to open our eyes wider and recognize new possibilities.

*Using the Awakening Exercises*

A concentrated set of exercises will awaken you to your own life. In my office and in my workshops, participants take several hours to several days to work through these awakening exercises. In the workshop, I ask you to set aside the time to sit and reflect, to allow your mind and heart to open to the experience you are about to create, and to let these thoughts and feelings radiate through you.

I suggest you begin a personal diary or journal to record your experiences with this practice: how you felt, what insights and thoughts came to you, your actions and how they may have felt different than before. Simply observe; do not judge your experience.

You may decide to tell those closest to you about this process. Change doesn't come easily, either for those attempting it or those close by who are affected by it. Since you are early in your discovery, I usually advise caution in sharing until you reach a firmer decision or new direction.

As you work each exercise, begin by finding a comfortable place in your home where you will be uninterrupted. Create a quiet environment. Close your eyes, take slow deep breaths, and visualize the exercise images as clearly and vividly in your mind's eye as you can. Let the image linger in your consciousness for as long as possible, even if this is uncomfortable. The deeper your experience, the greater your learning.

Remember, creating a life you love takes courage and hard work. As you go through these exercises, you may want to space them out, perhaps engaging in one a week over a month or so. You may want to just skim over them and let the ideas simmer there in your mind for a while. Or you may decide to skip over this section for now. However you proceed, respect your feelings and draw from these exercises that which is most valuable to you.

It's time to begin. I am the usher beckoning you to sit in the front row of your experience.

### EXERCISE ONE: THE DIAGNOSIS

*Imagine you have just come from your doctor's office. He has in-formed you that he has discovered an inoperable brain tumor that cannot be treated effectively by any other means. You go to several specialists who confirm his diagnosis and offer no hope for improve-ment. They tell you that you have, at best, six months to live and that you will become incapacitated only in your final days. The best predictions suggest you will not suffer pain from your condition. What will you do with the time you have left?*

*Next, imagine you have three months to live, then one day. Compare your first response and second and third. Write down your thoughts and plans for each scenario.*

Karen, Greg, and Bill had all been seated in the front row of their near-death encounters. Though you may not have had their exact experiences, you can still benefit from these exercises. In the preceding exercise you use the equivalent of a magnifying glass, then a microscope, then a neutron microscope, to examine what is most important to you. Let's see how Karen, Greg, and Bill each worked through these steps.

Karen had already been diagnosed with breast cancer. She had given this some thought and was beginning to sort out how she wanted to spend her time, for the first time questioning how long she had to live. Karen refused to be a victim of her circumstances, deciding instead to make something positive come from her diagnosis.

She first responded to the exercise's six-month limit by imag-ining herself saying good-bye to her favorite patients and leaving her job. Never having traveled outside of Florida, Karen had al-ways wanted to see the Great Smoky Mountains. She planned a two-week trip with her two daughters and close friend to spend time at a cabin in North Carolina. Afterward, she saw herself quickly getting her affairs in order by drafting her will and saying good bye to her dearest friends. Karen then dropped many of her extraneous commitments to devote more time to meet with her minister and church.

When Karen considered she only had three months to live, she made the same decisions. On her last-day scenario, she planned to spend the entire time with her daughters talking about their lives together, reassuring them, and saying good-bye. She would ask her minister and closest friends to be present for comfort and solace.

Greg approached the challenge differently. He had never considered this question and at first was uncertain how to respond. "I've chased away anyone who ever loved me years ago," he said candidly.

After carefully thinking about this, Greg just saw himself planning to leave his law firm and take his girlfriend, Susan, on a trip to visit his family. He saw how important it was to renew his relationship with his brother and parents from whom he had been estranged for years. He intellectually knew this was something he "should" do, but he could tell it was out of a sense of obligation and not from his heart.

Next, Greg thought about his decision to ask Susan to marry him. Having dragged his heels on commitment during their six-year courtship, Greg wanted to show her how much he wanted to be with her. After years of being fiercely independent, staying in control, keeping his emotions in check, he realized she was really the only person he had let get close to him. He felt anxious even thinking about this step, but he was sure he wanted her to be his wife. Greg also made plans to renew contact with two old friends whom he hadn't spoken with since college.

When reflecting on briefer times, Greg changed his priorities and made plans to marry Susan, and then planned to see his family and friends. They would take two weeks to honeymoon in Tuscany, a place they both loved to visit. On his last day, he hoped he would spend it in the presence and comfort of Susan.

Bill was very clear in his decision. He thought first of spending as much time as possible with his daughter, Jane. The first plans he made were to take her to Disney World, somewhere she had always wanted to go. He had so much that he wanted to tell Jane before he died.

It was very important she remember him as a kind and loving father, someone who would always be there spiritually for her. He then decided to rewrite his will, execute a living will he had been putting off, and set up a trust for his daughter's schooling. Bill planned to spend whatever time was left over fishing, seeing his friends, and visiting with his sister and elderly mother.

As Bill considered a three-month time frame, he considered his plans to spend more time with his daughter and with himself. He wanted some time to get his spiritual life in order and began to talk with a friend and priest. He saw his last day being spent with Jane and his sister and mother, saying good-bye.

*EXERCISE TWO: THE LIFE REVIEW*

*Near-death experiencers undergo a life review process where in a moment they go back over their entire lives and see all they have experienced. In this review, they feel all the good they have done to others as well as the bad. Conduct your own life review. What have you done in your life that you are most proud of, most ashamed of, or would do differently, change, or correct? What were the highest and lowest points and the learning that came from each? What would you like to repeat or leave out? Think of all the important people in your life and whether there is something you need to say to them or do to make amends. Make a list of these people and commit to finishing any "unfinished business" in your life. Decide from this what has been and now needs to be most important for you.*

Karen thought about all the good she had done in her life. Growing up in an abusive, alcoholic family, she learned early to please her father in hopes this would keep him sober and calm. She quickly learned that anger and conflict were dangerous and usually resulted in someone getting hurt. Karen knew her very survival depended upon her ability to please those around her.

Karen recalls often feeling embarrassed by her father's drunkenness and having worked to keep her friends away from her family. She vividly pictures in her mind hiding in her room with her little sister to escape her father's vengeance. She now regrets and is ashamed of having allowed her father to have such a negative influence on her life. Karen never discussed these feelings or experiences with anyone in or outside of her family.

She was proud of her work as a nurse and of her two daughters who were doing well. As she reflected, Karen realized she was still afraid of her father and of angering others in her life. Without knowing it, she personified the well-established relationship between cancer and suppressed emotion. I recommended she read Bernie Siegel's book *Love, Medicine & Miracles*.[2]

She wanted to learn how to take better care of her own needs, forgive herself and her parents, and be able to assert herself in her marriage and in her other relationships. She vowed to somehow make amends with her father and mother and show her daughters how to take better care of themselves in their relationships.

Greg realized his regrets over a lost childhood and the pain he had experienced in his family. He was the older of two sons and had become solely responsible for caring for his brother and ailing mother. He never understood why his mother was always sick. His father was a busy executive who often stayed at work, leaving all of the responsibility to Greg. When he did see his father, he recalls never being able to do enough to please him.

He remembers as a young boy having to stay home while his friends were off playing in the neighborhood. He felt sad and alone, often dreaming of being able to go out and play with the rest of his buddies. As he grew older, he fantasized about running away from home.

For years, Greg was a model son, a well-behaved straight-A student who followed all of the rules. Greg didn't realize it at the time, but his anger and isolation eventually exploded into fiery adolescent rebellion. He skipped school, drank heavily, smoked pot, fought with his parents, and was eventually caught stealing cars with his friends. After his arrest, he decided he had to find some way to leave home.

He began to work hard in school with the idea of going to college and escaping his mother's smothering dependency and his father's perfectionistic demands. Once he decided on his plan, Greg never looked back. He channeled his anger into action, made the dean's list, and was awarded a scholarship to an Ivy League school.

He excelled in college, graduated, and attended a prestigious law school. Consumed by his drive to succeed, he focused on landing a top job at one of the more distinguished law firms. He single-mindedly followed his dream and was right on course. Nothing could possibly get in his way.

On conducting his life review, Greg realized how angry and isolated he had been most of his life. He saw how deeply he resented his mother for her dependency and his father for his absence and irrational demands. Greg felt sorry he'd deserted his younger brother in his own hurried liberation from the family.

Now he was able to recognize how he'd allowed his drive to succeed consume his very life. Bitter and lonely, Greg had become an island unto himself. He had no friends, a long but distant dating relationship that he couldn't commit to, and his work. He deeply regretted how lopsided his life had become. Greg vowed to correct this painful imbalance.

He'd become partner in his law firm in record time and was making a mid-six-figure income. Greg was proud of his accomplishments. He had a beautiful oceanfront condo, a BMW, Armani suits, jewelry; he traveled and ate in the finest restaurants. Having developed quite a reputation as a fierce trial attorney, he was well on his way to developing a national presence. He was the master of his fate, having realized his dream of becoming successful, independent, and widely respected.

Bill found this exercise easy. He had plenty to feel bad about. He felt badly about how he had treated a long list of friends over the years and vowed to set things straight. Bill could also list and appreciate the many contributions he made to these people as well. He was proud of what he had accomplished in building his legal practice.

He felt good about his original family. His mother was a homemaker turned accountant and his father had retired after working as a college professor. Bill seemed oblivious to his father dying of a heart attack shortly after he retired. Bill was still close to his older sister and they visited whenever they could. He believed they were a tight-knit family and openly talked about how much they cared for one another.

Bill focused mainly on his guilt and regrets with his own family, especially recognizing the time he missed with Jason before his drowning. He now admitted he drank too much and was seldom home. He talked about how his wife, Deborah, saw him as tense, impatient, and angry much of the time, wanting to be the "boss" at home as he was in his business. "I remember Deborah telling me I used to order them around just like I ran the place. I never thought about that again until now. She used to say my drinking made it worse."

He regretted blaming Deborah for the accident. He was ashamed about his drinking and his involvement with another woman. He regretted the divorce and saw himself as primarily responsible for the marriage ending. The weight of "unfinished business" he carried, coupled with the tragedy of Jason's death, sat like a mountain on his shoulders.

### Exercise Three: Final Scene

*Find a quiet place and begin the journey. Close your eyes and simply concentrate on your breathing. Clear your mind and set aside thoughts of your schedule, work, family, and friends. As you feel more relaxed, imagine yourself on your deathbed. You have only minutes left to live. Your loved ones are gathered around you. Look at each of their faces and recognize who is there with you. What one message would you want them to have from you? Write down your dying words. Say these words out loud.*

At first, Karen found herself anxious at the thought of this exercise. I had originally met Karen on a referral from her family doctor. She was suffering from depression following her cancer diagnosis. Like many other cancer patients I've seen, it became clear that Karen had become exhausted emotionally long before her diagnosis. She worked hard in treatment and had recovered well from both her cancer and depression. Still panicked at the thought of her cancer recurring, she was eager to learn how she could make her life better. Though experiencing frequent nightmares, she never consciously allowed herself to consider the possibility she would die. Karen was afraid thinking about death would somehow cause it to occur. Nonetheless, she couldn't stop thinking about her future demise.

We went through the visualization in the session together. After the first few moments, she relaxed and clearly imagined herself in what would be her final moments. She found herself immediately comforted by the presence of her loved ones around her.

I said, "Tell me who you see around you."

Karen replied, "I see my husband and my two girls very close, holding my hand, comforting me. My mother, sister, and my three dearest friends are there too."

I probed further. "Tell me what's happening; look at their faces. Are they saying or doing anything?"

Karen hesitated briefly, seeming momentarily lost in her experience. "They are all very focused on me, attentive. My mother, sister, and the girls are crying. My close friends are all there. I can feel their love for me. It feels very warm. My husband, Frank, is standing somewhere in the background." Karen was clearly imagining herself in the experience.

I asked her, "What would you like to say to each of them?"

"I want to tell my friends thank you for being in my life and I love them very much. I want my mother to know that I am sorry we haven't been closer over the years and I love her and everything will be all right. I would tell my sister to take better care of herself and leave her husband who abuses her. I'm not usually that direct, but she's too good a person to allow anyone to hurt her like he has. Most of all, I want my girls to know how special they are, how much I love them and will miss them." She began crying. "I begged my girls to tell people how they really feel and to speak up for what they need. I want to tell Frank to take good care of our daughters. I told everyone to wake up and to use the time they have wisely."

Greg had come to see me at the suggestion of his law partner. Still dazed and confused months after his near-fatal car accident, he wanted to sort out what he wished to do with his life.

When we began, Greg related a very different experience with this exercise. Reluctantly, he had already begun to accept the fact that his time was limited. He immediately relaxed into his imagery and became very settled, vividly creating the image of his deathbed scene.

Greg completed the exercise on his own and brought his journal to a session to discuss his feelings. "It was a rush. I could really see myself there, and felt that I was in my last moments of life. It was scary to think that, but after a few minutes my fear seemed to subside and I felt more comfortable.

"The whole thing sent a shiver down my spine. I saw my girlfriend, Susan. She looked sad and concerned; she was crying quietly. It felt so good to have her there for me. I didn't expect how important it would feel that someone would be there, caring about me," Greg replied, seeming surprised. "I knew she loved me, but her love was so strong. It felt so comforting and intense. I don't ever remember feeling that from someone. Nothing else could have felt that good."

"Was anyone else there?" I asked.

"No, I really haven't kept up with my friends or family over the years. I guess I also realized how much time I've spent working and how little time doing anything with my relationships. I felt sad about that."

It was encouraging to see how Greg had already begun to realize how he had used his work to avoid emotional intimacy in his life. "What did you say to Susan?"

Greg continued. "I apologized for not taking more time with her. I told her how much I regretted not spending more time traveling, getting to know more about her, taking time to be with her friends and family. I would have liked us to have made time to just enjoy each other more, to get to know her family better. I told Susan I wished I had let her be closer to me. Now I see I held her at arm's length all these years. I was scared to let her in. I hugged her for a long time and told her I really loved her."

Bill's life changed dramatically after the drowning of his son. At first he blamed his wife, then himself. He was riddled with guilt, grief, and regret. Bill always planned to spend more time with Jason after he grew his legal practice and sold it. Now there was no time; Jason was gone.

Bill became sexually involved with a coworker immediately after the funeral. This affair continued over the next year, only increasing his confusion. Bill and Deborah divorced after 17 years of marriage and he temporarily lost contact with Jane, his 3-year-old daughter. Bill drank more heavily and spiraled into a deep depression where even suicide became an attractive alternative. He was alone, confused, and lost.

Fortunately, Bill reached out to a doctor friend and came to me wanting to put his life back together. Through these exercises, Bill continued the process of awakening begun by Jason's death. "I really felt a lot with this exercise," he told me. "It was hard to stay with it and not run away. When I imagined myself in this final scene, I realized that my family was there. It was very hard to see Jason, Deborah, and Jane together again, the whole family together. It brought back a lot of feelings that I thought were gone."

"What did you say to them?"

"I told Jason I was sorry and that I should have been there to save him. I held him and just kept saying I loved him and never to forget that. I miss him terribly. I apologized to Deborah for my affair and blaming her and not being able to work it out. I spoke mostly to my daughter, Jane, and wanted her to know how much I cared for her. I told her family was the only thing that really mattered and to please remember that when she grew up and had her own family."

"Anything more?" I probed, noticing Bill seemed to still have a lot on his mind.

"My mom and sister were there. I held them each and told them how important they had been in my life. I told everyone to live the life they have and not get distracted by money and things. I don't want them to postpone their living like I did, thinking that other things, like more money, would be a substitute."

### Exercise Four: The Memorial Service

*Imagine your memorial service in detail. Who would you wish to deliver your eulogy? Write two eulogies, one that you prepare for yourself as you would like to be remembered and one that someone else would write as they now know you. Remember a eulogy captures the true essence of the person. Compare the two. Are they different? Is your perception consistent with how others see you?*

*Imagine walking into the room where your service is held and find a place and sit quietly in the back row. As the ceremony begins, listen to what is being said about you. Observe who is present and how they are reacting to the ceremony. Listen to your eulogy and comments people are making about their memory of you. Pay attention to how you feel as the ceremony is completed.*

*After the ceremony, walk with them to the graveyard. Read the epitaph on your grave marker. What does it say? What would you want it to say? Watch the people's faces as the ceremony is conducted and completed. Write of this experience and what you have learned, the feelings and thoughts this exercise created in you,*

In her own eulogy, Karen spoke of her devotion to her husband and children, her willingness to give of herself, and her unselfishness with others. She had difficulty in stepping out of herself to write a eulogy from another perspective and so asked a close friend to offer her feedback as to how others see her.

Like so many other cancer patients, she had lived a life pattern of self-denial. Her friend talked to Karen about how difficult it was to really know her because she was so focused on other people's needs; she never asked anything for herself.

Karen was surprised to hear this and asked other friends for additional feedback. All of them said the same thing. Her best friend, Connie, said, "I could never really talk to you because you were always so focused on everybody else. I don't even know who you are aside from what you do for others." Karen never realized how her selflessness limited her relationships with her friends and family. Her role as "pleaser" left her feeling empty, exhausted, and alone.

At she listened in on her imagined service, she realized that part of her discomfort was due to her never having received this much attention. She was also uneasy because everyone said things that were so complimentary. Karen was always very uncomfortable with compliments.

As Karen continued to imagine her memorial service, she observed the friends and family who attended, appreciating for the first time how much she meant to those who knew her. She watched as different people cried and she listened attentively to comments made about her. One friend said, "I wish Karen had asked more from life."

Some of the comments she heard were disturbing: "Karen, I wish you had let me be more a part of your life. You were always there for me, but you never asked or let me be there for you." "I wish you had let yourself live life more and not worked so hard to please everybody." She had never seen herself in this way.

Feeling loved by those people who attended her ceremony, Karen learned she was cared for by those most important to her— her friends and family. More importantly, she discovered they cared more about who she was than what she did for them. Karen saw how her being so unselfish had in many ways actually stunted her relationships with the people she loved the most.

Greg talked with me in the office after completing this exercise.

"This was hard. I would ask Susan to deliver my eulogy, because she knows me better than anyone," he said with certainty.

"If not Susan, who would you have to deliver your eulogy?" I asked, wanting Greg to consider who else might have a close knowledge of him.

Greg hesitated for a moment. "I don't know... I don't know who else I could ask. It's hard to admit but no one else really knows me for who I am. Sure, I could ask someone, but I'm afraid it would just be superficial, empty words."

"How do you feel as you say that?" I was aware Greg had been stunned by the realization of his isolation from others.

"I think I feel sad, yeah, I feel really sad my world is so small. I guess I don't let people get close to me. Even Susan hardly knows me," he said more quietly.

I read Greg's eulogy and then the eulogy that he expected would be written by his girlfriend. Greg's eulogy was short and described him as a successful, respected lawyer and a scratch golfer; it listed many of his other accomplishments. His girlfriend's eulogy was in marked contrast. Susan's eulogy read:

Greg was a good provider and a caring man. You all knew him as a respected, capable attorney, someone who worked hard and put himself fully into his profession. He was a dedicated professional, a man who loved his work. The man you didn't know was a man who cared about me and his family. Although he had difficulty showing it, I never questioned how much he loved me. I knew his hard work and providing well for me was his best expression of his love, and that was his way of letting me know he cared. Although he didn't stay in close contact with his family, he talked about you and I know he missed you. I loved Greg with all my heart. I will miss him. He would appreciate so much your being here today. Thank you for coming.

As I finished reading I asked Greg, "How do you feel about what she said about you?"

"It hurts. It hurts to think that the only way Susan knew that I cared about her was my working all the time. I didn't realize I had become so preoccupied with my job, making money, and getting ahead. I talked to Susan about this and she reluctantly agreed. I know now how much she would miss me."

I could see Greg beginning to recognize how he had used his work to avoid dealing with other important areas of his life. He appeared anxious to go further. "Tell me about your memorial service."

"It's not funny, but thinking about this made me realize that I've been such a horse's ass that I may have to be cremated."

"Why is that?" I asked.

"Because I don't think I have enough friends to carry my casket," he said with a subdued laugh.

"Tell me about the memorial service," I asked again.

"It was devastating. The only people I saw in the church ceremony were Susan and my family. A few other people showed up from work, probably more out of some sense of obligation. A couple of golf buddies came, that was it. The only people that seemed at all emotional about my death were Susan and my family. I was a little surprised my family was that affected, given I haven't seen or talked to them in years. It seemed everyone else was distracted, looking at their watches, and wanting to leave."

"You seem sad." I noticed Greg's eyes were teary and his breathing was becoming irregular.

"I am, I never realized how much I was wrapped up in myself. I haven't let myself get close to anyone. If it wasn't for Susan, I'd be all alone." As Greg talked, he began sobbing, realizing his loneliness.

Bill was at first reluctant to imagine this exercise. He tried to do it on his own but found himself avoiding it. He came to my office declaring he was stuck. "I did write my eulogy," Bill said, "but that's as far as I've gone. I can't make myself look at the funeral service thing. I don't know why, but I want to do it and just keep putting it off."

Bill went on: "I wrote my own eulogy first. I said I was a hard-working, successful, conscientious person who tried his best. I loved my family and always wanted to find time to be with them, although I seldom did. I was a person who found out too late what was most important in life. I had much more to give people than I have ever taken the chance to express."

"You sound as if you are filled with regret," I offered.

"I am. I want another chance at life, to make up for all the things I missed out on. I want to look at this memorial service thing and find out what else there is I might learn to take forward."

Bill seemed ready. "Then let's begin. Close your eyes and just begin by focusing on your breathing. Breathe slowly and deeply. Notice yourself feeling more relaxed with each breath you take. Now, see yourself walking into the back of the church."

Bill began crying quietly. "Now I know why I didn't want to see this. It reminds me of Jason's funeral. It's so painful to remember him there, in the casket, lifeless. It's still hard to be there."

"Take your time, let yourself experience your sadness."

"I'm OK," he said, now sobbing. "I can see now that Jason's death and this exercise help me look squarely at my own. My ex-wife, Deborah, is crying hard, says good-bye and asks me to forgive her. She leaves a red rose on my chest. My daughter, Jane, is there;

she's in the back and is crying, although I don't know if she understands what has happened. My mother and father are crying and saying they love me. My sister holds my hand, kisses me on the forehead, and tells me she'll miss our times and talks together. I want to say something to them."

"What do you want to tell them?" I asked, knowing Bill had much to say in his effort to make amends.

"I want to tell my ex-wife I don't hate her and I forgive her. I hope she can forgive me for being such a jerk after Jason died. I would tell Jane I love her and will miss her and that I will always be with her. I want to say to my mom I'll be OK and not to worry about me."

### EXERCISE FIVE: YOUR LEGACY
*What is your legacy? How will you be remembered by others, those close to you and others who know of you? What have you left that others will carry into their own lives? What of you will last? Write a short summary of what you want to be most remembered for—perhaps your kind and giving spirit; your generous, caring children; or some contribution that will benefit future generations. Take the time here to consciously choose exactly what you want to leave behind, your own footprints in the sands of time.*

Karen decided from the previous exercises and her therapy that she wanted to leave a legacy beyond her own generosity of spirit. She wanted to develop a better sense of self, more confidence, and to model self-love for her children. "I know my girls will remember me as a caring person. I want them to see also that I thought enough about myself to take care of myself. I've made myself sick worrying about what everyone thought about me. I wouldn't wish that on anyone, especially my girls. I can say that, but I want to show it by just being who I am every day."

Greg clearly defined his legacy. He recognized what he had missed in his life and wanted desperately to learn how to love and show love. "I want to develop deeper relationships with those I love, and balance my life with people. I'd like to have people remember me as someone who was caring, concerned, and that I was something more than a good lawyer. It really bothered me to know Susan only saw my caring expressed by what I gave her materially. I don't want to be defined just by what I do and have."

Bill spent time to consider the legacy he wanted to leave to his daughter and the world. "I'd like to think that I can leave a daughter who is responsible, kind, and loving and who will have a family of her own. I want to feel good about my contribution to her life and happiness. I want to know that her life was made better by my having been in it. Beyond that, I want to do something more to help others; I'm not sure yet what that will be, but I want to make more of a difference in the world than I have in my past."

Now take what you've learned from these exercises to develop your own life's renewal. Your Personal Life Plan will serve as your own new reality and guide you in your life going forward. What do you want to do with the rest of today, this week, the month, your life? How will you use this perfect opportunity to make your life better?

You can use these feelings and images you created as a guiding force in living every day. These exercises provide you with a powerful focusing tool, your own magnifying glass, to examine your behaviors, thoughts, and feelings going forward from today. Now that you are clearer about who you want to be and how you want to live your life, make it come true. Keep your eye on your compass in the form of your Personal Life Plan and steer your future to reach your final destination.

By going deeply within ourselves, we tap into our most basic values and beliefs to decide what is most important. By taking the next step, writing your Personal Life Plan, you reflect on the Seven Keys and what you have learned in your awakening exercises. Let's review the Seven Life Lessons:

> *Life Lesson One: Decide what's truly important in life.*
>
> *Life Lesson Two: Expand your sense of freedom and choice.*
>
> *Life Lesson Three: Recognize you're more than what you do or own.*
>
> *Life Lesson Four: Develop greater love and acceptance of yourself and others.*
>
> *Life Lesson Five: Create a new appreciation for the elementals of life.*
>
> *Life Lesson Six: Focus on the importance of purpose in life.*
>
> *Life Lesson Seven: Create a greater appreciation for religion and spirituality.*

Now awakened, begin with your first key to next-level living by deciding the life you want today.

# CHAPTER FIVE

# How One Thought Can Change Your Life

*Everything has been*
*figured out, except how to live.*
—Jean Paul Sartre

W hen you really stop and think about it, how do you wish to live? I don't mean tomorrow, next week, next month, or next year, but now. Have you put off getting home earlier from work so you can be more involved in your daughter's soccer league? Or perhaps you've postponed biking the rolling hills of Tuscany, trading in a high-paying career for something more meaningful, reinvigorating your marriage, or coming to peace with yourself?

Tragedy, such as we have all experienced in the wake of September 11, forces people to focus on their deepest needs and priorities, to reconsider what their lives are all about. A Gallup poll conducted weeks after the terrorist attacks revealed nearly 80 percent of Americans said they had shown or would show more affection than normal to their loved ones. Nearly 65 percent said religion had become more important in their lives.

Consider what you want to be different in your own life, and decide today to bump to the next level of living. Forget tomorrow. Now is the time to set your new life's course.

## CRAFTING YOUR
## PERSONAL LIFE PLAN

We'll begin by working from the first Life Lesson: *Decide what's truly important in your life*. By doing so, you must think through your priorities carefully and be sure your behavior reflects what you believe, that your outer life is a pure reflection of your most cherished values.

Developing your Personal Life Plan is not something you will accomplish overnight. It may take many days of reflecting, writing, thinking, and revising to get to a plan you can live with comfortably. Writing, rewriting, and reviewing your plan is an essential part of the process, as it deepens your commitment to the final product. Your final plan must truly express your essence, radiating your innermost values and purpose.

Take all the time you need to craft your Personal Life Plan. An effective plan accurately reflects who you wish to be. I encourage people to consider work, physical development, play, and emotional and spiritual needs in formulating their specific goals. Each plan is different, yet all will include goals falling into three main areas: life, love, and meaning. Let's look at what Karen did in developing her own Personal Life Plan.

Notice that the goals Karen defined were positively stated, specific, and doable. They are also personal, visual, and emotionally based. Wisely, she didn't list things that she thought she "should" do or that others think she "ought" to accomplish. These are all goals she feels are important, ones she is emotionally invested in and wants to make happen in her life.

Goals need to be set in ways we can visualize and imagine every day to remind us to live the lives we wish. A Personal Life Plan is the road map that helps you remember who you want to be, how to get there, and how to know when you've arrived. It's the correction course for the rest of your life.

## PERSONAL LIFE PLAN

NAME: Karen

**LIFE: I want to nurture my body, mind, and spirit.**

*Goal 1:* I want to enjoy my every day as if it were my last. I want to learn to stay in the present moment and focus more on enjoying the simple, everyday experiences available to me.

*Goal 2:* I want to relax more by scheduling massages, reading, and going to the movies. I will spend one hour each week in my Jacuzzi.

*Goal 3:* I will exercise (e.g., walk, bike, and aerobics class) for at least 30 minutes three days a week

**LOVE: I want to respect my own feelings and needs and speak honestly in my relationship to others who care about me.**

*Goal 1:* I will honestly express my feelings and needs to those most important to me. I will say no to demands from others that do not feel comfortable to me.

*Goal 2:* I will renew a relationship with my sister. I will extend myself by calling her at least weekly, telling her about my life and asking about hers, reminding her that I love her and that I am there for her when she may need me. I will ask her for what I need as well.

*Goal 3:* I will maintain contact with my close friends, Connie, Beth, and Sue, by calling them back when they call and making plans to go shopping or have lunch together every few weeks.

**MEANING: I want to participate in activities that build my faith and spirit.**

*Goal 1:* I will continue attending my church weekly and maintain my faith and support through regular meditation and prayer. I will ask my fellow congregation members for help when I need it.

To start your Personal Life Plan, reflect on what you're doing in your present life that supports what you have learned so far. Karen began the groundwork for her Life Plan by first recognizing the importance of her work as a nurse and how her colleagues supported her positive sense of self. She vowed to continue her job despite her husband's pressure to quit. She saw the importance of her good friends and a supportive faith nurtured by her church involvement. Karen used these foundational steps to build from in crafting the goals in her Life Plan.

Take a moment and reflect on what you're presently doing in your life that helps support the higher-quality existence you want to live. Think about your life coming to an end and work backward. How do you want your life to unfold? Are you satisfied with your relationships? What experiences do you want to have? What do you want to accomplish? What mark do you want to leave on this earth?

Perhaps you already have a regular exercise program, take time to meditate, enjoy time with your children, pursue creative activities you find fulfilling, travel, or make time for reading or taking classes. In reflecting, you may discover that you have valuable human resources in close friends or family, that you feel comforted by your pet, soothed by your weekly massage, or that you honestly love your work. Reflect on the parts of your life, past and present, where you've felt most contented, fulfilled, and gratified.

Take stock and list those things you've done or are currently doing to help you feel satisfied, content, and loved:

1.
2.
3.
4.
5.

6.

7.

8.

9.

10.

Now take the time to develop your own Personal Life Plan. Think about what makes you happy, fully alive, on fire with excitement. Avoid focusing on what others expect of you or dwelling on what you haven't done, but rather look to the present. The opportunity to change your life is now. Seize this opportunity by writing your own plan in the space provided.

| PERSONAL LIFE PLAN |
| --- |
| NAME: |
| LIFE: |
| *Goal 1:* |
| *Goal 2:* |
| *Goal 3:* |
| LOVE: |
| *Goal 1:* |
| *Goal 2:* |
| *Goal 3:* |
| MEANING: |
| *Goal 1:* |
| *Goal 2:* |
| *Goal 3:* |
| Daily Whisper: |

Now that you've developed a clear vision of what you wish your life to be, we must put your plan into action. Vision without action remains only a daydream, an empty resolution. You may already be saying to yourself, "I've made some of these resolutions before, but I never follow through. What's different this time?" Good question. You need some push, a powerful daily reminder to make you do the things you know are important.

The Daily Whisper will help you to shift from passive thought to active doing. Use the thought of your limited time to generate a sense of urgency so necessary in transforming your desires into daily realities.

## THE DAILY WHISPER TECHNIQUE

Listen to a conversation between Carlos Castaneda and his teacher, Don Juan, from *Journey to Ixtlan*. Don Juan says:

> Death is our eternal companion . . . it has always been watching you. It always will until the day it taps you. The thing to do when you're impatient is to turn to your left and ask advice from your death. An immense amount of pettiness is dropped if your death makes a gesture to you. . . . The issue of death is never pressed far enough. Death is the only wise advisor we have. Whenever you feel that . . . everything is going wrong . . . your death will tell you that you're wrong; that nothing matters outside its touch. Your death tells you, I haven't touched you yet.[1]

I've said the idea of limited time has now become my frequent companion and friend. There is a way to make your end a regular ally, to wisely guide you to the life you wish to live, a friend that reminds you of what's most important in your life. We need to in-

vite this helper into our life daily, to focus us on the way we wish
to live.

Understand that awakening to our end is an ongoing process,
just as most mornings we awaken gradually, then fall momentarily back to sleep. As we awaken more often, our times of wakeful-
ness are longer and longer, and our times of sleep and forgetfulness
grow less and less.

There are many ways to be lulled back into a forgetful slumber.
Life goes on and even the best intentions get lost as we slip back
into the ordinary world. We are tempted to hit the snooze button
on the alarm of life. Anything in excess becomes a sleeping pill:
work, alcohol, food, friends, self, money, religion, pleasure, or family. We need a regularly scheduled wake-up call to keep us sharply
focused and fully alive.

Remember Mitch Albom, the sports writer who spent *Tuesdays
with Morrie*, his professor who was slowly dying from Lou Gehrig's
disease?[2] At first Mitch is living a frantic life, caught up in his successful work as a sports writer and afraid to commit to a relationship with his girlfriend. After spending more and more time with
Morrie, he begins to change his life by backing off work while becoming more involved first with Morrie and, from this, his girlfriend and life itself. Mitch Albom's deepening contacts with his
dying friend opened him up, dramatically transforming his life to
one full of love and meaning.

This change didn't happen overnight or from his first casual re-
union with his old professor. Mitch changed gradually over the
course of 18 Tuesdays, each visit having its own small, yet powerful effect, like a potent, yet slow-acting medication. Mitch needed
to regularly expose himself to his friend's pending end to awaken
himself to what was most important in his life. Like Mitch, we
must be exposed to both the fragility and importance of love and
life to appreciate their true value.

Many people shaken by tragedy have yearned to hold on to the new aliveness experienced in their awakening. They want to be able to recreate the electrifying fullness that comes from seeing their own end. How can we revisit this awakening and heightened living every day to refocus us on our most cherished goals and then on life itself?

I've devised the Daily Whisper technique to help us keep death and, more importantly, life in mind. The technique allows us to translate our keen new awareness into our daily activities so we become consciously proactive, taking charge of making our lives fuller, a process I refer to as *daily invigoration,* and the secret to the life you really want.

The Buddhists use the image of a small bird on their shoulder to constantly remind them that life is limited and to live each day fully. Is today the day my time runs out, the day death taps me on the shoulder? Am I truly living the life I want to live? Am I honestly the person I want to be?

The Daily Whisper provides us with strong counsel and daily shakes us by the shoulders, pushing us to postpone nothing in our Personal Life Plan. It is the very presence of our end point on our left shoulder, reminding us that our time is limited and guiding us to live life to the fullest. The powerful technique involves three simple steps:

1. *First, think of the feelings and images created as you responded to the awakening exercises in the last chapter. What image stirred the strongest feelings or made the strongest impression? What phrase stuck most in your mind? Think back over your exercise experience, review your journal entries, and select the one or two images or phrases having the most intense impact on you, usually images or thoughts that create the strongest feelings—anger, hurt, sadness, joy, or fear.*

*You may have a life experience that conveys the same strong mes-*
*sage—a close friend or relative you cared for while dying, a life-*
*threatening diagnosis, illness, or near-fatal accident. From these*
*experiences, clearly define and visualize the image or thought in your*
*mind. This is your Daily Whisper, a thought you can recall at any*
*time to bring back the strong feelings you experienced in your own*
*personal encounter with life's fragility and importance.*

Karen used the following as her Daily Whisper, to remind herself to follow her goals in her Personal Life Plan: "Whenever I hesitate to take time out for exercise or tell someone how I honestly
feel, I use the thought of the doctor telling me my diagnosis. That
image, of sitting there in the doctor's office first hearing the words,
'You have cancer,' is stamped on my mind for life and will never
leave me. It's what I use to keep me on track, to remind myself to
put things in perspective, to face my little fears, that it won't be
the end of the world if someone gets mad or doesn't like me. The
Whisper technique helps motivate me to take risks and stand up
for myself—to see my life as precious and not to give it away."

*2. Once you've identified your Daily Whisper, a visual image or*
*phrase, refocus on your Personal Life Plan and the changes you wish*
*to make in your life. Record your Daily Whisper on your Life Plan.*
*Remember your goals; keep them clearly focused in your conscious-*
*ness. In your mind's eye, see yourself using your Whisper or thought*
*when you find yourself falling back into your old routines, lapsing*
*into the slumber of forgetfulness, or numbing your existence.*

I suggest my clients review their Personal Life Plan and Daily
Whisper every day until they know them by heart. Some have put
them on their refrigerator, others on their bathroom mirror or
next to their bed, to look at first thing in the morning or last thing

at night. Some have posted them conspicuously on their personal organizer or computer. Several of my clients place a paper dot on their watch to remind them of their goals and Whisper.

Greg wants to learn to develop more depth and breadth in his relationships with others. He reviewed his Personal Life Plan every day at first until he could clearly visualize his goals and plan for change. Once he was more aware of the life he wanted and was able to sharply focus the specific behaviors to build that life, he thought of his funeral scene as his Whisper to spur him into action.

When you've identified at least one or two of the most powerful images, be sure you can vividly create this image or phrase in your mind.

Greg tells us, "All I have to do to get myself to follow up on my Life Plan is to reflect on that church scene with the near empty pews and people looking at their watches. It's like a laser beam focusing me on what I need to do right then. When I think of that image, I want to reach out to someone. It moved me to call my girlfriend and tell her I love her, take her off for a weekend together, give her a card or a kiss, call friends back and make time to get together, and stay in touch with my mother."

*3. Now use your Daily Whisper to motivate and direct these changes you have set forth in your Personal Life Plan. Use your self-awareness and call forth your Whisper every day to push you to live your set goals.*

For his Whisper, Bill used the deathbed scene and the statement of his legacy from the awakening excercises. "I just use the image of my kids at my deathbed and think of how Jason has given me the gift of a second chance at my life. It made me see we're all living on borrowed time. I don't want to waste something so valuable. Most people don't get a second chance. I use this image of my funeral and the phrase 'am I living my legacy?' to keep myself living the life I want to live. I've used these walloping reminders often to make myself take time with Jane, pass up a drink I don't need, keep the therapy appointments I didn't want to go to, take off from work, and let myself begin dating. I'm starting to enjoy life again. When I get tentative or complacent, I use the Whisper to jar me back to what I need to do. I'm not going to postpone doing important things anymore. I can see my life coming together for the first time in a while."

Sometimes bad things inspire better lives. Karen, Greg, and Bill used their tragedies to wake up and make significant, positive life changes. Using their Personal Life Plan as their chart and the Daily Whisper as their engine, they set sail toward a new life direction. You too must search your heart and mind to redefine and change your life's course, a change leading to a greater sense of satisfaction and happiness felt in every day.

## TURNING UP THE LIGHT: FINDING MORE LIFE, LOVE, AND MEANING

Don't be afraid of life's shadow. By learning the lessons from those who've faced their end and completing these exercises, you steer a course toward a brighter future. Use what you have learned to guide today's behavior, tomorrow's behavior, next week's, and next month's based on what is most important to you. Each day of your life, consciously decide to think, feel, and act in ways that are consistent with your Personal Life Plan.

Use the Daily Whisper technique to shake yourself out of the busyness and dull routines distracting you from your most cherished choices and goals. By keeping these pictures and thoughts in mind, you manage your daily life in a way congruent with what matters most. By carefully considering what you've learned in your awakening, you redefine your own personal definition of success and pursue it every day. No more excuses, no more illusions, no more postponement and wasted chances, no more regret.

I often use the thought of living my last day to jump-start my priorities and freshen my perspective. Things that are truly important come to the fore. I spend less time watching television and more time reading, listening to music, and writing. I bring my wife more cards and flowers, stay in closer touch with my daughters, and tell loved ones more of my caring for them. I am more patient and tolerant in traffic. Simple tasks, like washing the dishes or trimming the hedges, seem more pleasurable and relaxing. I joke and laugh more. I volunteer more time to help others. There is less focus on the "stuff" of life. When I find myself getting cross or irritable, I visit my own Daily Whisper and am guided back to serenity and happiness.

We are solely responsible for creating the life we want. As we become aware of our choices, we see old lessons and scripts we allowed to dictate our lives fall away. We decide our life every day with the thought of our end as our friend, pointing the way. As proactive people we take life by the horns, postponement recedes, and we consciously decide what we want to be and do in our remaining time on earth.

As anyone who has faced great tragedy will tell you, there are only three things that matter: life, love, and meaning. We are empowered to find a self to live with, love to share, and a purpose for being. Now awakened, turn up the light and take the next steps to deeper life, love, and meaning.

PART TWO

# AWAKENING TO WHAT IS IMPORTANT IN LIFE:

## LOVE AS THE NEXT STEP

# CHAPTER SIX

# Love Is the Cure

*Take away love,*
*and our earth is a tomb.*
  —*Robert Browning*

L ove of the self and of others brings some of the greatest and most fulfilling pleasure in life. It is the most important
ingredient of next-level living, yet many of us take the love in our
life for granted, putting off the experience of deeper love until
we're faced with the prospect of its very loss. Sometimes we need
to reminded that our time, and love, is precious.

Psychologist Abraham Maslow spoke of this purifying fire
while recuperating from a heart attack:

> The confrontation with death—and the reprieve from it—
> makes everything look so precious, so sacred, so beautiful
> that I feel more strongly than ever the impulse to love it,
> to embrace it, and to let myself be overwhelmed by it. My
> river has never looked so beautiful.... Death, and its ever-
> present possibility, make love, passionate love, more possible.
> I wonder if we could love passionately, if ecstasy would be
> possible at all, if we knew we'd never die.[1]

We all want to love and live passionately. Though yearning for
deeper intimacy, many stumble in their effort to experience

deeper levels of caring. Isolated in prisons of our own making, we remain insulated from the love around us. Our walls are within and without, blocking us from experiencing and expressing love for the self, others, and life itself. In the midst of these walls even a moment of love is a miracle.

Recognizing our time as limited furnishes the key to our freedom; the key is knowledge and the will to act on what we learn. In crossing the bridge from isolation to love, we must move through these walls of self-judgment. Our knowledge and action provide the means to experience intimacy and passion on a deeper, more satisfying level.

Many people who have faced their end describe experiencing a purer, higher form of unconditional, universal love. Less judgmental and accepting, they become more open and giving. They have moved from a "leveled down," need-based form of caring to a need-free, higher level of intimacy with themselves, others, and life itself. To develop this capacity ourselves, we must first understand the difference between the weaker, shallow expression of love and the form experienced by those shaken by death's call.

## BREAKING FREE

How then do we break free? We all want passion and love in our lives, but how do we find it? To fully understand and experience a higher love, we must first understand its opposite, separation. For it is the ability to be alone with ourselves, to love ourselves, that is the essential precondition to true love.

We suffer from a plague of isolation in our time. Despite numerous means to connect—phones, fax, computers, satellites—we often feel alone, alienated from our inner selves and one another.

Psychoanalyst Erich Fromm believed the deepest human need was to overcome separateness, to escape the prison of aloneness.[2]

Each of us, regardless of our gender, age, or culture, is left to answer the same question, the question of how to overcome this sense of isolation and achieve union, how to transcend our own individual walls to connect with our self and others.

Psychiatrist Irving Yalom describes the experience of isolation as existing on three levels, intrapersonal, interpersonal, and existential, each painful in its own way.[3] Intrapersonal isolation or alienation involves our partitioning off parts of ourselves. As we stifle our feelings and desires, we falsely accept the external "oughts and shoulds" as our own wishes. We become dependent on others, rules, and institutions for our life's direction while distrusting our own emotions and judgments. We throw away our internal compass and allow others to steer our life's ship. Having lost a part of ourselves, we are left living only half a life.

Henry, a 31-year-old engineer, was frustrated over not moving up in his firm and came to me for executive coaching. A bright and technically capable professional, he suffered from "engineer's syndrome." Henry came across as a donnish, bespectacled Magoo who never left the universe of his own head. Henry displayed no emotion whatsoever and had no idea that others saw him as cold, stiff, and robotic.

His supervisor had counseled him on numerous occasions to be more sensitive to the employees working under him, people he would typically either ignore or scold. Henry became so focused on the task at hand that he lost sight of the people involved. His major goal in coaching was to learn how to get along better with and manage his subordinates.

Henry had read all the right books on management but had never taken the time to look honestly at himself, having no awareness of his glaring emotional and social deficits. As we talked, it became evident that others in his life, most notably his wife and children, had the same complaints as his coworkers. He was, as his subordinates called him, "one big head," heavily intellectualized, machinelike, and completely cut off from his feelings.

When isolated from parts of our selves, we invariably become isolated from others. This interpersonal isolation is generally experienced as loneliness and refers to the separation we experience from other people. It is a function of many factors: geographic segregation, lack of appropriate and effective social skills, heavily conflicted feelings about intimacy, or a personality style that precludes gratifying human relationships. People who are schizoid, narcissistic, and compulsive often experience intense loneliness behind their rigid, hardened character defenses.

Henry, by his rather compulsive personality, was constricted emotionally and thereby limited in his ability to relate inwardly, as well as to people. He lacked any appreciation for his own feelings or those of others, relying rather on intellect as his exclusive means of relating. He was a prisoner of his own mind, and no matter how hard he tried he couldn't discover the key to unlock the heavy gates, locked only from the inside.

Cultural factors can often play an important role in our experience of interpersonal isolation. As mentioned, our electronic connections provide contact, yet at times actually rob our relating of its richness and depth. We substitute cell phones, faxes, and e-mail for deeper contact, when it is the quality, not the quantity, of the connection that counts. Additionally, the decline of intimacy-sponsoring institutions (the extended family, stable residential neighborhoods, the church, local merchants, long-term friends, the family doctor) has, in the United States at least, contributed to an increased feeling of interpersonal alienation and detachment.

Psychoanalyst Rollo May, in his classic work *Love and Will,* describes our society as a "schizoid world" where we have lost the foundations for love.[4] *Schizoid* means out of touch, avoiding close relationships, the inability to feel—a condition frequently seen in our technological age. It is a world in which, amid all the vastly developed means of communication bombarding us daily, actual deep, personal communication becomes exceedingly difficult and rare. May goes on to say hate is not the opposite of love; apathy is. He describes *apathy* as a want of feeling, a lack of passion, emotion, or excitement, a pervasive indifference. We experience an estrangement, detachment, alienation, and depersonalization—increasingly divorced from ourselves, others, and life. Though physically alive and kicking, we remain emotionally deadened.

He talks of the many challenges to deeper love in our technological culture:

> It is not difficult to appreciate how people living in a schizoid age have to protect themselves from tremendous overstimulation—protect themselves from the barrage of words and noise over radio and TV, protect themselves from the assembly line demands of collectivized industry and gigantic factory-modeled multiversities.

May continues:

> In a world where numbers inextricably take over as our means of identification, like flowing lava threatening to suffocate and fossilize all breathing life in its path; in a world where "normality" is defined as keeping your cool; where sex is so available that the only way to preserve any inner center is to learn to have intercourse without committing yourself—in such a schizoid world, which young people experience more directly since they have not had time to build up the defenses which dull the senses of their elders, it is not surprising that will and love have become increasingly problematic and even, as some people believe, impossible of achievement.

A third form of isolation is existential, the type of alienation tied to our very existence. Deeper than intra- or interpersonal isolation, existential isolation persists despite the most gratifying engagement with others or ourselves. No matter what we do, we are born alone and will die alone. This aloneness is inescapable, an unbridgeable gulf that exists between any other being and ourselves. How do we cope with this most essential and terrifying isolation?

According to analyst Erich Fromm, we try to overcome this uncomfortable sense of separateness in different ways.[5] Most often, we attempt to escape our loneliness through another person, either through orgiastic union, as with sex, or in highly dependent relationships.

A second means of dealing with our anxiety is by seeking conformity with a group; I am like everybody else, I have no feelings or ideas of my own. If we conform in custom, dress, and beliefs to the group, we are saved from the frightening experience of aloneness. A third way we attempt to manage our fear of isolation is through creative activity. Each of these efforts to cope with our essential aloneness ultimately falls short and we are left to face our loneliness.

We have all experienced those brief, anxious moments of feeling alone or isolated. The skier who finds himself lost on the trail, the hiker who loses her way, the driver who meanders without a map and direction, feeling ill with no one to call. However these experiences are presented, we often feel an immediate rush of dread and fear.

I recall a personal experience on an Outward Bound program many years ago in North Carolina. After having endured a number of physical challenges, we were faced with the "solo" experience. The solo involved being left in the wilderness for several hours to remain in one place, alone with ourselves in the quiet wilderness.

I remember the initial anxiety of sitting still, without any distractions, being left to myself. I first became caught up in thinking about work, what was planned in the future, and thoughts of the immediate past. I became antsy, then quickly overwhelmed by thoughts about wandering around and exploring my surroundings. I resisted the temptation, consciously forcing myself to remain still.

After a short time, I began exploring inwardly and became caught in thoughts about my life, where I had come from, my feelings and relationships, what was important to me. I began to miss my wife and children. I longed for their company and found myself looking forward to seeing them again.

As these feelings settled, I felt more attuned to my surroundings and appreciated the beauty of nature and the world. I focused on my love for those closest to me and for life itself. My time alone led me to a greater appreciation of what was most important in my life.

This experience reminded me of an ancient Japanese practice that is said to cure many human ailments: One is locked into a room where there is a toilet and very little else. Food is provided three times a day. It is said that the penitent is tired the first day, sleeps much of the second day, is restless the third day, is climbing the walls the fourth day, is nearly out of his or her mind the fifth day, can hardly remember the sixth day, and comes to a great peace and tranquility on the seventh day.

## GETTING TO KNOW YOU

This ability to be alone with ourselves is precisely the precondition to a deeper, more satisfying love. We must be able to confront our aloneness before we can turn lovingly toward others. Otherwise, the fear of our aloneness causes us to flail at others in our desperate attempt to avoid drowning in a sea of isolation. Panicked, we relate to others out of anxiety and desperation, not from conscious choice or love.

Steven, a client of mine, was driven by a compulsive sexuality. His promiscuous sexual "coupling" offered him a powerful, yet temporary respite from his underlying feelings of emptiness and isolation. He broke all the rules of true caring by using others as mere tools of distraction. Steven's relating to women was mechanical and opportunistic. He did not want to know the name of his female objects, as the real name made the contact more personal. There was no room for truly engaging them. He never concerned himself with their desire or needs. Steven had never considered how to relate to women, if not thinking of them as sexual objects. Later in therapy, he was finally confronted with the questions, "What do I do with women?" "What do I do with men?" and "What do I do with people?" He finally confronted the humanness of others while exploring a different way of relating.

Steven was terrified with the therapeutic assignment of spending time with himself without the convenient distractions of sex, work, and toys. He was not accustomed to attending to himself—his thoughts, feelings, and needs. This step, although terrifying, was critical in the process of Steven facing his "demons" and developing the capacity to know and love himself, and later others.

Being alone introduces us to ourselves, someone we may not want to know. For some, being alone is so anxiety-provoking they will do anything to avoid the experience. I have had numerous patients tell me, usually on the heels of a relationship breaking up, that they would rather be in a bad relationship than alone.

Kate, another patient of mine, once told me she did not feel she existed if no one was thinking of her. She constantly sought contact and affirmation from others to feel alive. Given her anxiety, she avoided being alone at all costs, for being alone put her in touch with her own existential fear of isolation. Kate would become involved with virtually anyone who would attend to her, no matter what the physical or emotional toll. This need led her through a series of intense, unsatisfying, and, at times, abusive relationships.

I first met Kate, an attractive 28-year-old legal secretary, after she had become extremely depressed after the breakup of a relationship. She had pleaded with the boyfriend to remain, promising to change and do anything for him to stay. She had threatened suicide, professing her "love" and saying she could not live without him. Kate only felt completed when in a relationship and panicked at the thought of being alone. She was an emotional bottomless pit, crying out for others to fill her, to save her from herself.

When I first saw her, she had not slept for three nights, was weeping and terrified by the prospect of being on her own. "I love him and can't live without him," she said in a pleading voice.

"I'm curious," I said to her, "You've told me you love Jim and can't live without him. Yet, you have only dated for two months. He was often gone and left you alone for days at a time. When he was with you, he mistreated you by calling you names and criticizing you. He had never offered any commitment to stay in the relationship and told you he didn't really care anything about you. Help me understand why you are so depressed over losing a relationship that seemed to offer you so little."

"You're right, you don't get it," Kate replied angrily. "I'm nothing without Jim. I hate my job. I don't have any friends. He was my whole life; I'm nothing without him."

"Have you had other serious relationships in your past?" I asked.

"Yeah, I dated several men over the years and have been married twice. I loved them too, but not as much as Jim," she replied, obviously irritated with my questions.

"Tell me about them," I suggested.

"Well, I dated several men. I saw Jack when I was 18 for a few weeks and we got married right away. It didn't last. He was a drinker and never worked, so I ended up supporting him until he finally walked out a few years later. After Jack, I dated a guy, Dick, for awhile. I caught him with another woman in our bed, and he left and never came back. We were together about two years and I think he slept with other women before that one. I was married a few years ago to a painter, Ed, who drank and beat me. We got divorced this year after he caught me fooling around with Jim."

"So you have had several relationships before Jim and survived each of those breakups," I pointed out. I wanted Kate to put her current circumstance in some historical perspective. I set an appointment in a few days, concerned how she would do in her current panic over the breakup. She agreed to see me again.

Kate called the next day to cancel her appointment. When I saw the note canceling our session, I called to check on her. "I wanted to see how you're doing."

"I'm OK. I met someone last night at a bar. I'm feeling much better, so I don't need to come back." She quickly declined my suggestion to meet again to talk about her relationship problems.

Kate, like many dependent individuals, is fine as long as she can attach to someone who provides the security and identity she so desperately needs. So consumed in seeking this security, such individuals have no energy left to love. They do not tolerate aloneness and will do anything to avoid it.

Many people share this fear, perhaps not quite to this extent. Yet, they are uncomfortable with being alone, with only themselves. Their behavior takes on a frantic quality as they run faster and faster to escape what they fear, themselves. To avoid this discomfort, many busy themselves with work, relationships, food, alcohol, sex, shopping, or any activity that helps distract them from themselves and their dread.

A common avoidance is relationships. When we engage others to ward off our own loneliness, we transform the other person into an object, just as if the person were so much machinery. When this occurs, a healthy individual usually knows he or she is being used rather than engaged and will leave the relationship for a more fulfilling partner. Only a person with a comparable need will stay and provide the complement in such a union.

Larry, a tall 35-year-old client and computer programmer, was obsessed with his fear of loneliness and haunted by the anxiety of never finding his perfect mate. Consumed in his search for Ms. Right, Larry spent every waking moment looking for ways to meet the woman he would spend the rest of his life with. Though he was bright, successful and attractive, one woman after another met him and, after a short encounter, broke off the relationship.

He could not understand why he was unable to sustain any relationship given his list of desirable attributes. The women were driven away by the intensity and desperation of his need for love and, I believe, their unconscious recognition he had little love to give. Highly judgmental, he rapidly and contemptuously dismissed all candidates who did not measure up to his "template" of the perfect mate. Larry couldn't see that his desperation and judgmental attitude prevented him from ever developing the self that would make him truly attractive to his suitors. He would not consider looking at himself and resisted the suggestion of spending time alone.

Sadly, Kate and Larry illustrate the tragic irony of many who so desperately seek others to complete them. Those who desperately need the comfort and pleasure of an authentic union are the very persons least able to form such a relationship. They are also unable to recognize their plight. At our last visit, Larry made it clear that he would not be deterred in his quest.

Many wise thinkers agree that isolation and loneliness must be experienced before it can be transcended. Clark Moustakas, in his essay on loneliness, states, "The individual in being lonely, if let be, will realize himself in loneliness and create a bond or sense of fundamental relatedness with others. Loneliness, rather than separating the individual or causing a break or division of self, expands the individual's wholeness, perceptiveness, sensitivity and humanity."[6]

Author Robert Hobson uses the phrase "resting in our loneliness," yet many of us writhe in our aloneness.[7] We struggle in our aloneness. Interestingly, those who are willing to confront their isolation can learn to relate in a mature, loving fashion to others. Yet, ironically, it is only those who can already relate to others and have attained some modicum of mature growth that are able to tolerate loneliness.

Therapists will often advise periods of self-enforced isolation during the course of therapy. For my patient Steven, the experience generated important emotional material and, secondly, he discovered hidden resources and courage he did not know he had. Steven's experience is common. In being alone, we learn about ourselves. Most importantly, we learn we can survive what we fear the most, our isolation.

Anyone who tries being truly alone can tell you how difficult it is. First you begin to feel restless, fidgety, and anxious. Next, in your discomfort, you rationalize your unwillingness to continue the practice by thinking it has no purpose or value, it takes too much time, and so on. If you continue beyond this point, you find your mind filling with other thoughts.

Just as I experienced in my "solo" program, you will observe all sorts of thoughts coming to mind—where you will go in the evening, all that you have to do, problems with work or children—rather than permitting your mind to be empty. Few people pass beyond this point and are able to explore their deeper feelings and sensations. When was the last time you were really alone with yourself for any length of time?

### SOLO EXPERIENCE

*It would be helpful to practice a simple exercise. Find a quiet place where you will not be interrupted for at least an hour. Sit in a relaxed position, take deep breaths, close your eyes, and clear your mind of all interfering thoughts and images. Try to center your attention on your thoughts and feelings in the moment. If your mind wanders, become aware of this and refocus your attention on what you are feeling. Spend at least 30 minutes with yourself and see what you notice. If you can, stay longer and use the whole hour. Try another time and stay longer periods and see what you discover about yourself. Keep a record of your feelings and what you have learned about yourself in your journal.*

Now ask yourself questions about your own experience of isolation and love. How do you define love? How do you know if someone loves you—how can you tell this? Who do you feel closest to? Do you trust these people with your deepest feelings and self? Do you talk openly to them about these feelings—fear, hurt, sadness, caring? Do you relate exclusively to people who provide something for you? Is your love focused on receiving rather than giving?

Do you find it easier to be loved or to love? Do you attempt to know, in the fullest sense, the other loved ones in your life? How much do you hold back in your closest relationships? Do you fear being out of control? Do you genuinely attend to or listen to the other person? When you relate to others, are you present and focused on just them? Do you care about the growth of your significant others?

To explore your own capacity for love, take the simple self-test on pages 114-115:

## LOVE SELF-TEST

Please answer these questions by circling True or False. Your first response is usually the best.

1. I accept compliments easily.                                      True    False

2. I am able to make and keep my promises
   and commitments.                                                  True    False

3. I generally feel good about the person I am.    True    False

4. I can accept and learn from my mistakes.        True    False

5. When confronted with things I fear, I will
   usually face the situation.                                       True    False

6. I find it easy to honestly express my feelings
   and needs.                                                        True    False

7. I am usually satisfied with what I have
   accomplished.                                                     True    False

8. I often do things (e.g., leisure, exercise)
   that are good for me.                                             True    False

9. I have been told by others that I am a good
   listener.                                                         True    False

10. I believe I am worthy of love and respect.     True    False

11. I am responsible for my own existence.         True    False

12. In most instances, I practice what I preach.   True    False

13. My closest relationships are based on choice.  True    False

14. I have a right to treat my values and
    convictions as important.                                        True    False

15. I am accountable for my choices in life.       True    False

16. I am usually liked and respected by people
    I like and respect.                                              True    False

17. I do things every day I find exciting
    and enjoyable.                                                   True    False

18. Most of the time, my focus is on the present
moment.                                          True    False

19. I generally know how I feel emotionally.      True    False

20. If I asked those closest to me, they would say
I am open and caring.                            True    False

21. I find it easy to talk about my strengths and
shortcomings.                                    True    False

22. People who know me best would say I am
compassionate and understanding.                 True    False

23. I find it easy to trust others, and others see
me as trustworthy.                               True    False

24. I feel connected to others and the world
around me.                                       True    False

25. I enjoy spending time with myself.            True    False

This test is to provide you with a simple way to assess your capacity for love. Questions center around issues related to your ability to love and accept yourself, share your love in close and committed relationships, and experience some joy and love for life. This is an exercise to help you better understand yourself and how you stand in these three areas. Use this information, along with what you have learned in the earlier chapters, to understand your depth in loving.

To calculate your score, add 1 point for each true response. If you scored between 18 and 25, you have a well-developed ability to love. If you scored between 10 and 17, you have a moderate capacity for love and may want to look closely at those things you could change to bring more love into your life. If you scored 9 or lower, you may find it difficult to care sufficiently for yourself, which could hamper you in your relationships and life. Whatever your score, you can see areas you may wish to consider and improve upon.

The answers to the self-test tell you about your ability to love. We are each at different levels in our capacity for caring. Your answers tell you of the quality of the love you feel and are able to express to those around you.

Are you experiencing the level of love you want in your life? How do we better understand what constitutes this deeper, authentic, more gratifying love? Just as we understand what higher love is, how can we move to this experience and feel greater fulfillment and satisfaction?

## THE HIGHER QUALITY OF LOVE

It is the quality and depth, not the breadth of love that counts. I have met a number of people who were well known, admired, and "loved" by many in their relative celebrity status who were wholly unsatisfied by this shallow love. Though initially flattered and impressed by the public's infatuation with them, they later recognized how this notoriety left them feeling empty and used. Most eventually found it more an annoyance.

So why do we postpone our love, believing we'll get back to our relationships tomorrow? When we wake up and realize we don't have all the time in the world, we suddenly begin working on and deepening our relationships—making amends, communicating our love, and more honestly risking and sharing ourselves. When time is short, it is the purity and depth of love that determines its fullness. We seek a stronger sense of connectedness, a fuller, deeper feeling of closeness and intimacy that strengthens and sustains us every day. How do we define this deeper love? In defining love, I will first describe what it is not. Many people experience a "leveled down" form of love and don't really understand what higher love means.

I see this confusion in my practice every day with people laboring under serious, painful misconceptions about what real love is. These very misconceptions become barriers to true mature love. Our misunderstandings lead us to isolation and unhappiness, to the pain of a diluted, unsatisfying form of intimacy. To reach the higher love we need, we must first break through the confusion limiting us.

The most common and ultimately painful misconception is also the very form of love many seek: a fantasized or romantic love. Romantic love is heady, intense, temporary, and usually referred to as "falling in love." People romantically involved experience a rush of good feelings, are "crazy" about someone, "head over heels," "lose their minds," and quite literally become temporarily psychotic. This type of love becomes the answer to our woes, the balm healing all our sores.

Romantic lovers fall under a spell, feeling as if the relationship makes them whole. They are completed. Their relationship, like a powerful drug, briefly cures their loneliness and isolation. They have met their perfect match, the one person who can meet all of their needs forever. This is the stuff of enchanted fairy tales. As in the tremendously popular romance novels and television soap operas, romantic love is idealized, not real, fantasy not reality, illusion, not life.

I feel sad for the people I meet daily caught in the throes of romance, fully believing they have found the love they have always sought. Sam came to me "in love for the first time" in his life. Approaching 50, he had met a woman 20 years his junior at a trade show and was sure she was "the one." Spurred by a recent heart attack, he knew he was at a crossroads, compelled to choose a new direction for his life.

A successful businessman, Sam had scaled the heights of his career in publishing and was seeking a new frontier. Married for 27 years to Patty, he complained how their relationship had grown distant and stale. Patty had become increasingly involved in her own social and volunteer interests while taking care of her elderly mother. Their four children, now all grown, had moved on to their own careers and families, leaving them alone to contemplate their empty relationship.

They shared little together and, when they did speak, talked mostly about the children and her family. The sexual relationship had years earlier become occasional and routine, more recently dying a quiet death. Sam knew he was bored with his work, stuck in his marriage, and uncertain about where he wanted to go. He knew he needed a change, any change, to breathe new life into his existence.

"I don't want to live the rest of my years like I'm living now. There's got to be more to life. My heart attack tells me I won't be here forever," Sam said. What he did not recognize was the extent of his unhappiness and depression.

Not surprisingly, he met Marsha, who proved to be the tipping point for a marriage teetering on dissolution. Marsha was bright, attractive, and successful in her own right. Recently divorced with two teenage boys, she had returned to her career in public relations. Sam saw Marsha as perfect. She was everything he wanted in a mate—interesting, exciting, fun, and most importantly, she adored him. He was intoxicated by her constant attention.

They spent hours talking about everything, at times endlessly into the night. He couldn't remember feeling this alive since he was a teenager. Sex was stimulating and better than he had ever experienced in his marriage. She was everything he had ever wanted in a woman. Sam felt they both were totally accepting of one another, describing Marsha as his "soul mate." Like many, Sam feasted on the perfect love of a near-perfect stranger.

He had decided he would leave his marriage and marry Marsha. His only hesitation revolved around his concern for his family, the children's reactions, and the potential financial meltdown. Sam expected Patty would be angry if she discovered his affair and, even if she didn't find out, would take him for "everything" in a contentious divorce.

Sam "loved" Marsha and was convinced he knew her. He was certain the hours they had spent together over the past few months let him know her better than anyone he had ever met. He knew how he felt, and his feeling was right.

Yet, as we talked, he realized he had not met her two children, parents, siblings, or even her friends. Sam knew little of her past marriage or life. He would not see any faults or shortcomings or expect there would be any. Despite his feelings and encounters thus far, he did not *know* Marsha.

Sam admitted his closest friends had cautioned him to proceed slowly and it was at their insistence he sought counseling. Yet he was determined to throw himself fully into this relationship. He was like a starving man suddenly seated at a table brimming with food. She had become the unattainable; Sam's most intense joy was not in the having, but in his desire to have. He was caught in the throes of what I considered a temporary "romantic psychosis."

Though his marriage was, for all intents and purpose, over, Sam had never been alone. He had never stopped long enough to reflect on what he truly wanted or needed for himself or in his life.

He had been desperately lonely, emotionally and physically starved, for a number of years. "I can't remember ever feeling loved by Patty. We got married in college after she became pregnant with our oldest. We never even thought about not getting married. I'm not sure we ever loved each other. We were Catholic so we kept having children. Don't get me wrong. I love my kids. After a while, I felt trapped and just put my energy into working and taking care of my family. Patty was focused on the kids and her social obligations, not me. Over time, our marriage became a sad joke."

"Did you and Patty ever talk about your relationship or your unhappiness?" I asked.

"Not really," Sam replied. "I did ask Patty to go to counseling a couple of times, but she didn't think we needed it. She seemed OK with our marriage. We never fought, so I guess she thought everything was fine. Now I can see how distant we've been over so many years. I'm sorry I didn't leave sooner."

"Do you imagine your relationship with Marsha may have problems at some point?" I asked.

"No. Marsha's nothing like Patty," Sam quickly responded. "Marsha's very loving. She can't get enough of me and I adore her. I can't imagine we will ever be like Patty and me. I love her and she loves me. That's all that matters."

Sam was unwilling to look more closely at his new relationship, for fear this examination would somehow tarnish his sacred love. He could not recognize that Marsha might be a bridge to a new life, that the relationship might not survive this transition.

Once Sam and Marsha learned the truth about each other, their relationship might not bear up under the discovery. Fantasy would be replaced by reality, disillusionment would inevitably set in, and questions about the other would surface. Marsha would likely serve as a "transitional object" for Sam and help him in eventually discovering the life he had always sought.

Though Sam would disagree, what he felt for Marsha was not love but the chemical rush of infatuation. It is, by its very nature, temporary and intoxicating. In the experience, we lose our heads. Others around us see us as "out of our minds" and no one can convince us of the danger of our position. Only when the psychosis clears do we recognize our feelings for what they are and reorganize our lives. Some people are destined to seek out this drugged state constantly. Addicted to romance, they bounce from one affair to another.

A second misconception some people have is that love is about objects or activities. Real love is not tied to objects or things, as when people "love their work," "love money," or cling to possessions and ego attachments. Real love has only to do with people and nothing to do with things.

Joan, a 22-year-old college student, was struggling with the sudden, bitter divorce of her parents. As we discussed her relationship with her mother and father, she tearfully described the emptiness and disappointment she felt in her attempts to relate to her dad. She recounted a story of her father's seeming interest in her playing on the high school softball team.

Joan became excited, hoping she had finally found something she could do to involve her dad more in her life, but that was not the case. "When I asked him to help me get ready for the several-week practice session, he gave me his credit card and told me I could get any equipment I needed," she said with disappointment in her voice. "I was really hurt by his lack of interest. I think he expected I would really be excited with this new equipment, but all I wanted was for him to take some time and throw the ball with me. He always gave me things instead of himself."

It was clear this was one of many examples of missing her father's involvement in her life as she grew up. I asked Joan if she ever told her father she needed more of his time and attention.

"Yes, I did tell him how I felt. He just was angry and told me I didn't appreciate the stuff he bought me. He got defensive and made excuses. I could tell he didn't want to give more of himself or see how other people feel. This divorce is just another example of how he has difficulty looking outside himself. I guess I just need to learn to accept that giving things is the only way he can express he cares." Joan was beginning to come to terms with what her father could provide; his expression of caring was limited to the giving of objects.

Remember Greg who spent his life focused on accomplishments, work, and the acquisition of things? He sublimated the anger at his parents into his work and his striving for success. While dampening his anger, he unknowingly diluted his capacity for love at the same time. Greg had worked 80 hours a week in his push to amass wealth and power. He was consumed in his efforts to excel and gain recognition and status, and this attitude permeated his love life as well. Before meeting Susan, he was sexually promiscuous with a number of women from whom he had remained emotionally detached. Although he cared deeply about his fiancée, Susan, he could only express it through physical gifts, not emotional connection.

Though Susan described him as loving his work, she did not see him as a loving person. Susan was able to translate his giving of things as his best effort at expressing his love for her. His love was focused on activity, objects, and self-aggrandizement, not on people. Greg had not learned that real love is for human beings.

In therapy, Greg began to recognize through his awakening exercises the limited expression of his love. "I didn't realize how I had cut myself off from any feelings except anger. Although I was vaguely aware of my irritability and grouchiness, I didn't recognize its source. I just wrote it off to traffic, work, stress, or the annoyances du jour. I now see I was loaded with rage at my parents and how they treated me. My anger was like a giant wall keeping everyone out. People were intimidated, scared, or had just decided not to fool with me. Now I understand how lonely I felt, how isolated I had become."

I asked Greg how he had handled his sense of isolation. He replied, "I didn't see it at the time. I now can realize all this energy got focused in my need to succeed. As long as I could wrap myself up in my competitiveness, winning, and doing well, there wasn't time for anything else.

"I had to be the best, have the best; it was my reason for being. A lot of my colleagues and friends encouraged this; they liked me taking them out for expensive dinners, buying them nice gifts, taking them on trips, earning big fees for the firm. Sure, I kept score by buying myself stuff and later buying Susan things I thought she would appreciate and be impressed by. I could never figure out why she wasn't more appreciative, though now I understand."

Greg had learned important lessons from his near-fatal car accident and deep personal reflection. He now recognized he was more than what he did or earned, and could begin to see he had value beyond any possession or thing. Greg was struggling to experience his feelings and to express his love for his true self and those important people around him. His love of objects and things had left him feeling empty and unsatisfied, yearning for something substantial and filling. Death is often the teacher, clarifying and bettering our love.

A third misconception is that love is sex. Love is not lust and libido. As is often the case, sex may be mixed with other forms of love—romantic, object, dependent—yet it's not authentic or higher love.

Sam's relationship with Marsha is one example of love based largely on sex and physical attraction. This form of love usually fades and leaves the relationship wanting. Sex apart from true love becomes empty and vapid over time; we are alienated from our own feelings and those of our partner. We become erotic machines without emotion.

The sex act is the most powerful enactment of connection imaginable, for it allows for those few moments a sense of true union and relatedness. It is a potent yet temporary escape from our loneliness and separation. Sex without emotion may be exciting, pleasurable, and recreational; it may temporarily soothe our loneliness or salve our wounded ego, but it is not love.

Kathy was an attractive 16-year-old client brought to me by her mother. Though a bright young woman, she was failing school, fighting with her mother, drinking, and violating curfew. Her mother was concerned that Kathy might drop out of school or become pregnant. At first resistant, Kathy slowly warmed to her therapy.

It soon became evident Kathy was reacting to her parents' recent divorce. Her father had been discovered in an affair and had left the home several months ago. Consumed in his new relationship, her father had dropped out of her life. Hurt and angry, Kathy began acting out her feelings by drinking, skipping school, defying her mother, and becoming sexually promiscuous. She felt rejected by her father and was seeking his lost love in the arms of anyone who would have her. Kathy felt "loved," ever so briefly, while physically embraced by the men she had sex with, confusing sex with love.

I asked Kathy how she felt after having sex with her various partners. She replied thoughtfully, "I don't think about it. I just know for those few moments I feel better. When someone's holding me, I feel like everything's OK." After several therapy sessions, she was able to say, "I guess when I do let myself think or feel anything, it doesn't feel good. The guys don't call me afterwards, and they talk about me at school. I know they don't care about me or they wouldn't do that. I guess I just miss my dad and they're kind of a replacement."

Kathy was able to see she was using sex as a means to feel loved. As she recognized her feelings about her father leaving, she later contacted him and reestablished a relationship. Her acting-out behavior subsided, and Kathy later developed a caring relationship with a boyfriend.

A fourth common fallacy is emotional dependency masquerading as love. Love is not dependency or fusion where our very survival and identity are symbiotically linked to the presence of another. Dependent people seek fusion, the giving up of the self to merge with another. They submerge their own needs; they seek to find out the other's wishes, and then frantically make those wishes their own.

Dependent people choose safety and fusion over individuation and self. When asked, they often say they feel like children in a world of adults. They are not capable of mature love, for their love is self-sacrificing and depleting. Dependent love is controlling and possessive and encourages the subversion of the self.

Remember Karen who struggled with love in her life? Though on the surface, Karen's giving seemed a loving gesture, it was not. Passive-dependent people are "givers" who do things for others for their own reasons. Whatever we do for someone else is to fulfill a need of our own. Their giving is not freely chosen, nor is it responsive to the needs or growth of the receiver.

Also remember Karen's friends feeling slighted by her inability to offer a two-way relationship? They did not feel her giving as a loving gesture, but as a reflex precluding her openness to their reciprocation. Karen mistakenly assumed she was responding to others' needs, when in fact she was responding to her own. Her friends needed to support and care for her, but Karen could never receive their love, for she did not feel she deserved the love of others.

Dependent people's motives in doing things are usually to cement their attachment, to avoid conflict, or to gain the accept-

ance and approval they so desperately need. Their giving is not
done freely or by choice, any more than an alcoholic chooses to
take the next drink. Karen's giving had its genesis in fear and guilt,
not choice or love. Karen had never learned how to express her
own needs.

The inner emptiness and fear Karen felt was the direct result of
her parents' failure to fulfill her most basic needs for affection and
love as a child. She was never able to develop an inner feeling of
being valued and appreciated. It was no wonder she felt compelled
to focus on satisfying everyone, before ever attending to her own
needs and feelings. It took her cancer diagnosis to awaken her to
a higher quality of loving.

This subjugation of the self occurs most often in individual relationships, though it can occur in groups as well. We see this same
dependency-fusion dynamic in people's immersion in causes,
cults, countries, and projects, where the sole aim is to erase our isolation by radically eliminating our self-awareness. We give up our
identity to be like everyone else; we conform in customs, speech,
dress, and beliefs while sacrificing any independent thoughts or
feelings that make us different. The person becomes totally devoted to the cause, project, group, or divine being, without any
sense of self-awareness. The "I" becomes lost in the "we."

Thus fused, the group or cause will not allow this dependency
to be undermined or threatened. That is why a cult isolates the
individual in an effort to maintain their control and dominion.

The hated enemy of fusion and conformity is self-awareness.
For to begin asking self-defining questions such as, What do I
want? What do I feel? What are my goals in life? What do I have
in me to express and fulfill? liberates the individual from the "we-
think" and separates him or her from the group. These questions
are actively discouraged, because they disrupt the stranglehold of
dependency and control.

True love involves two people who choose to be together. Individuals must learn to relate to another without giving way to the desire to relinquish the self. The true recognition and acceptance of a separate human being is an essential building block in the foundation of higher love.

If romance, lust, yearning for things, and dependency are not love, then what is? What, then, is the nature of a higher or mature love? I define deeper love as *a commitment to actively promote the betterment of another or ourselves through respect, acceptance, and honest confrontation.* This being said, I am fully aware any definition of love offered is woefully inadequate to describe this complex, mysterious state. Let us explore this definition further.

Most experts agree a relationship, at its best, involves individuals who relate to one another in a need-free fashion. Yet how is it possible to love another just as the other and not for what that other provides for the lover? How can we love without using the other, without a quid pro quo, without a heavy dose of infatuation, lust, admiration, and self-service? Many wise thinkers have pondered this question and suggest how we can create this mature form of love.

Fromm in *The Art of Loving* clarifies certain common misconceptions about love. He tells us love is an active process requiring both effort and knowledge.[8] Most people think the problem in love is in *being loved*, rather than in *loving* or in developing the capacity to love.

Fromm draws a distinction between romantic love and mature love. Mature love is a positive act, not a passive affect; it is giving, not receiving, "standing in," not "falling for." Individuals with a hoarding or exploitative style will feel depleted and impoverished by giving, cheated by giving and not receiving. They keep score and guardingly watch their gifts to be sure they are ahead of the game.

The mature "productive" person gives as an expression of strength and abundance, the expression enhancing one's aliveness. Fromm states:

> When one gives, he brings something to life in the other person, and this which is brought to life reflects back to him. In truly giving, he cannot help receiving that which is given back to him. Giving makes the other person a giver also and they both share in the joy of what they have brought to life.

Mature love implies other basic elements: concern, responsibility, respect, and knowledge. We must be responsive to and respect the needs of others, fully learn and know them, which is only possible when we are able to transcend our self-concern and see others for who they really are. We have to listen and experience others empathetically, to enter their private world, and sense their life and experience.

Abraham Maslow, a humanistic psychologist and author of *Toward a Psychology of Being*, offers a second view of love.[9] He proposes that a person's fundamental motivation is oriented toward either "deficit" or "growth." Neurosis, he says, results from a deficiency or a lack of fulfillment, beginning early in life, of certain psychological "needs"—that is, safety, identification, belongingness, love, respect, and prestige.

Individuals who have these basic needs satisfied are growth-oriented; they are able to realize their own innate potential for maturity and self-actualization. Self-actualization refers to our ability to realize our full human potential. Growth-oriented people, in contrast to deficiency-oriented individuals, are far more self-sufficient and far less dependent upon their environment for reinforcement or gratification.

Growth-oriented and deficiency-oriented individuals have different types of relationships. Growth-oriented people are less dependent, less beholden to others, less needful of others' praise and affection, and less anxious for honors, prestige, and rewards. Such people do not require continual interpersonal need gratification. In fact, they prefer their privacy and may at times feel hampered by others' presence.

Deficiency-motivated people, on the other hand, relate to others from the point of view of usefulness and utility. Their relating is purely need based and tied to what others can do for them. Those aspects of the other person not responsive to the perceiver's needs are either overlooked altogether or regarded as an irritant or a threat.

Maslow suggests love then becomes transformed into something else, resembling our relationships "with cows, horses, and sheep, as well as with waiters, taxicab drivers, porters, policemen, or others whom we use." This type of love is similar to the relationships we saw in the lives of Steven and Greg.

Growth-lovers are more independent of each other, more autonomous, less jealous or threatened, less needful, more proud of the other's triumph, generous, and altruistic. Growth-love provides self-acceptance and a feeling of love-worthiness, enhancing the person's continued growth and development.

Many of the attributes seen in near-death survivors resemble the same characteristics described in Maslow's growth-lovers. They are both more altruistic, independent, self-accepting, generous, and growth-oriented. They have developed a greater capacity for love, are more open to experience, alive, spontaneous, self-transcendent, and democratic in their thinking.

Many of the death survivors and self-actualized were capable of the highest form of love: *agape*, a universal love devoted to the welfare of others, as is the love of God for man. They shared a capacity for a fuller love, one more satisfying and enriching.

## NEXT-LEVEL LOVE

To love authentically means to be actively involved in promoting the growth of self and others. When we study what mature, higher love is, we see it includes several critical components.

### Commitment First

Mature love cannot occur without certain conditions being met. Biology is no guarantee of love, romance is no assurance love will occur, and promises fade with time. Commitment to loving is the first and necessary step to constancy and trust, the foundation of a caring relationship.

Greg could never form strong attachments given his fears of fully committing himself to a relationship. He held back, often hiding in his work and pursuit of success. He was stuck on an emotional first base—crippled by fear and unable to open himself to true intimacy and connection. Without this full commitment or true covenant, love eventually withers and dies.

In my work with couples, the first thing I assess is the partners' level of commitment to the relationship. Are the individuals truly invested in maintaining and improving their relationship? Their emotional stake in the relationship is of paramount importance, for if it is missing, no degree of effort can make the relationship work.

Sally and Jeff came to me to save their marriage. Together over 20 years, they talked about their long history, their two teenage children, and the pressures they each felt from family to hold their relationship together. I immediately sensed something missing in their relationship.

Sally spoke about how she had become increasingly independent of Jeff over the past several years after returning to her career as a physician. She had developed new friends, interests, and confidence, much of which Jeff resented and tried to undermine. A high school teacher and frustrated writer, he was threatened by Sally's autonomy and expressed this by his attempts to control her.

This had led to frequent and intense arguments. These conflicts continued to escalate until Sally finally decided not to argue anymore. Instead, she began physically and emotionally distancing herself from Jeff. Her commitment to Jeff and the marriage gradually eroded, creating a giant chasm no one could repair.

By the time we had met, Sally had already left the marriage. Though physically present, she was emotionally divested from Jeff and the relationship. The only feelings she had left for the relationship were anger and resentment. Sally's only reasons for staying married had do with her concerns about her sons and her family's reaction.

There were certainly problems in the relationship—communication, the way the couple handled conflict, and numerous differences, to name a few—but without commitment, these problems could not begin to be resolved. Despite Jeff's vehement protests, Sally had already exited stage left.

For Sally, my office was simply a brief stop on the way to her attorney's office. They were divorced a short while later. The bond or glue holding their love had disintegrated from years of neglect and hurt. Without investment and commitment, there would be no chance to recover their lost love.

### Give Fully and Freely

Caring fully for another means to relate in a selfless way, without the thought, "What's in it for me?" No longer so focused on the commerce of relationships, we are committed to relating completely. We step outside ourselves, momentarily leaving our feelings

and needs aside. Relating selflessly involves listening completely in
the moment, with your whole being. If part of you is somewhere
else, you have failed to relate.

Our attention conveys our love. To give fully, you must offer
all of yourself, the most precious thing you have: your life, joy, interest, understanding, knowledge, humor, fear, and sadness. In this
deeper giving, you enrich the other by sharing your aliveness. Caring is reciprocal and what is given is reflected back to you.

Recall Joan's hurt with her father's difficulty in sharing himself.
Though he tried to convey his love by giving material things, she
felt cheated by his shallow gifts. Joan did not care about the base-
ball equipment he so generously provided, she wanted her father's
time and attention. She wanted him.

Giving fully is difficult. We let ourselves become distracted by
the demands of the day, somehow believing that everything else
is so important. Think of the times you've related to a loved one
while focusing part of your attention elsewhere. Perhaps you were
preoccupied with work, watching television, reading the newspa-
per, anticipating some upcoming golf game, or simply glancing out
the window. In splitting our attention, we dilute the connection so
vital to love.

Often when I meet with couples I ask how much time they
spend together talking or sharing. Invariably, they spend little time
together alone as a couple and when they are with one another,
their attention is often directed elsewhere. This lack of focus and
sharing gradually drains their passion, sucking the very life out of
their relationship. To timidly hold back, to ration our involvement,
is to risk eventual distance and pain.

Part of giving fully involves sharing parts of ourselves that create friction in a relationship. At times confrontational, true love
does not judge, demean, or intentionally harm the receiver. Loving
involves saying no, setting limits, and disciplining—often the

harder part of caring. I see this often with couples and parents who are unwilling to speak honestly of their needs and wants. They "can't" say no to a spouse or child for fear that person will become angry or hurt. They tremble at the thought of someone not liking or approving of them.

I've often told couples that if you can't tell your spouse to "go to hell," then what kind of marriage do you have. No loving relationship worth its salt is limited to the positive or excludes constructive conflict. Purely supportive relationships are limited and superficial, lacking in the depth fostered by more honest communication. When conflict is excluded, the relationship becomes surface and polite and passion and intimacy dies.

Sam and Patty couldn't communicate openly. They were proud of the fact they had not had a fight during their 27 years of marriage. However, their inability to talk honestly about their feelings led to greater distance and, ultimately, to their divorce. Sam would not confront Patty with his true feelings for fear of hurting her. Not coincidentally, it was these very feelings that caused him to begin his affair with Marsha and eventually leave the marriage. Love involves open, honest communication—which by its very nature includes constructive conflict.

To love deeply, we must give freely and fully of ourselves. This, too, is a core component of love.

*Love Is Accepting and Respectful*

Love is listening, understanding, and caring about the feelings, needs, and wants of others, helping them become fully alive in the moment of your encounter. It is respecting the unique individuality of others, allowing them to grow and unfold as the persons they are and not whom we wish them to be.

Sally wanted to return to work to satisfy her need for autonomy. A bright woman, she missed the intellectual challenges offered by her profession. Jeff, caught in his own insecurity and career frustration, felt threatened by her need for growth and independence. Though Sally at first tried to work through their differences, Jeff could not allow her to grow and tried his best to stifle her efforts. His attempts to control Sally inevitably resulted in the demise of their relationship.

Authentic caring involves stretching beyond our own needs and feelings to better appreciate the other's experience. We must listen well to truly know the other. This accepting presence develops trust and safety and encourages greater sharing and vulnerability by the other.

### Love Is Action

Love is a verb. Caring is active and easily seen in our behavior.

The act of loving and being loved is observable and clearly perceived and experienced. Love is not a feeling, but an action. How do you know you are loved? You know by your experience, which is based on others demonstrating loving actions over time.

It is not simply a word, a promise, or a statement of our devotion. Love is work. Loving involves risking and extending ourselves by what we do in our relationships. Nowhere is this dichotomy seen more dramatically than in abusive relationships.

Candy spoke of her prior husband, Hank, loving her while also physically abusing her. Though he would frequently profess his devotion and love after an abusive episode, his behavior was not that of a loving partner.

Hank's actions were controlling and possessive, clearly demonstrating his inability to offer mature love. Candy's recognition of this contradiction between her husband's words and actions helped her to end her destructive marriage.

In working with couples I will frequently ask, What does your partner do that lets you know he/she loves you? Just as often, they

sit staring at me not sure how to respond. This is usually a difficult question to answer. Think for a moment how you know you
are loved by someone.

As you reflect I believe you will discover your feeling loved is
based on very specific actions or what I call "caring behaviors" that
you have observed over time. Among couples, we see a lot of these
caring behaviors in the early courtship. Usually, in this stage of the
relationship, we are bending over backward to show our love.

Think of how you let people know you love them. Telling
someone is one way, buying gifts is another. More importantly,
love is *demonstrated*—by giving flowers, cooking a special meal or
dessert, calling and asking how the day is going, rubbing feet or
shoulders, giving a kiss or hug as part of a greeting or good-bye,
listening attentively, making chicken soup, visiting a bedside when
someone is sick, or sending a card to say get well.

In each example, real love is expressed by small, oftentimes
daily, actions. Our behavior paints a picture of our love for all
to see.

### Love Is a Choice

Love is volitional and offered freely. Mature caring comes from
richness and growth, not dependency or need. We do not love to
escape loneliness or to complete some missing part of ourselves.
We care because we want to, because we choose to.

The act of loving and being loved breaks down the walls separating us from others and allows us to overcome our sense of separateness while retaining our personal integrity. It does not
diminish the lover nor ask him to sacrifice himself in the deal.
Love, as Fromm suggests, presents the ultimate paradox where two
beings become one and yet remain two.

Kate was incapable of offering love freely. Bound by her own
dependency she desperately flailed at one relationship after an-

other to save herself from a stormy sea of isolation. She did not *choose* to be in a relationship; she *clung* to them out of her fear of independence and isolation. Relationships were a refuge to be purchased at the price of her autonomy.

This is also seen in relationships based on guilt and obligation. Louise, a 32-year-old architect, saw me for problems she was having with her mother. Her mother demanded she call her every day and would become angry if Louise failed to do so. Louise, busy with work and family, tried her best to satisfy her mother. She had learned from prior experience that failing to do what her mother asked resulted in criticism of her as a selfish, uncaring daughter. Louise allowed herself to be controlled by her mother's criticism.

Louise found herself becoming more depressed over the situation, knowing she would never be able to satisfy her mother's demands. As we talked, she better understood her feelings of guilt and that the anger she felt for her mother she had channeled to herself.

I asked her, "Other than guilt, what do you feel toward your mother?"

"I love her," she said without hesitation.

"Tell me why you love her," I said, pushing Louise to delve deeper into her feelings about her mother. I could tell many of her emotions revolved around her effort to be the dutiful daughter and escape the painful criticism and guilt.

"Well, she is my mother. Beyond that, I don't know why I love her. I just know I should feel love because she's my mother," she said, confused about my question.

"If she were not your biological mother, is she someone you would seek out to spend time with?" I pushed further.

"No. I don't really like her as a person. It's hard to even be around her. She's always been critical, negative, and demanding. No matter what my brother or I did growing up, it was never enough. If she wasn't my mother and I didn't feel guilty, I would-n't have anything to do with her. My brother doesn't call or see her at all," Louise said with conviction, beginning to express her resentment for the obligatory nature of their relationship.

As we scratched the surface, we saw that relationships with her mother were based purely on duty and obligation. Louise's relationship had become just one more responsibility, just like paying bills or washing dishes. There was no joy or caring between them, only the grudging fulfillment of some childhood obligation. This was not a loving relationship, volitional and chosen by both parties.

Louise was able to work through her guilt and resentment and relate more out of her own needs and feelings of caring. Though they had less contact, Louise was able to feel more comfortable and at peace in the times she spent time with her mother.

Love is a choice.

### Love Is Enriching

We are enriched, altered, and fulfilled by loving. Love is self-enhancing and replenishing, supporting and nurturing of our growth and development. It is not demeaning, depleting, and hurtful.

Love builds and strengthens us. Mature caring rewards us, alters us. Yet as these rewards flow from genuine caring, they do not instigate it. Analyst Victor Frankl says it well—the rewards ensue but cannot be pursued.

Karen again presents the example of someone who believed she was loved and loving. Yet, this love was depleting and hurtful. The more she gave to her husband, the less he returned. There were few rewards for Karen as she could not allow herself to be replenished and nurtured by others. She drained herself by giving in a way that did not allow reciprocity, leaving her depressed and empty.

Stronger love is enriching because it requires commitment, involvement, acceptance, action, and choice. As we seek a deeper love, we must work to create these conditions, which are the essential building blocks of a higher love.

I believe we are incapable of loving another before we first are able to love ourselves. The capacity for loving the self, others, and life is one and the same, inseparable and indistinguishable from one another. To develop one is to develop the other, as each go hand in hand.

## LOVE: THE IMPERFECT ANTIDOTE

I recall returning from a run one summer morning. As I approached my home I saw my cat, Teger, observing a young sparrow lying on the ground apparently having fallen from its nest. It was covered with down and sat very still, unable to fly, helplessly flapping its half-grown wings. Teger was slowly approaching it when suddenly, darting down from a tree close by, a dark-throated sparrow fell like a stone right before his nose. All ruffled up and terrified, with pitiful cheeps, it flung itself twice toward Teger's face and jaws.

This mother sprang to save its nestling while its tiny body was shaking with terror. What a huge monster Teger must have seemed, and yet it could not stay on its high branch out of danger.

My cat stood still, observing first and then drawing back. Clearly, he recognized the force he was facing. I picked him up despite his protest and walked away full of reverence for the scene I had observed. I felt respect for the tiny heroic bird and for its demonstration of love; love is stronger than death or the fear of death.

I understand that the bird's experience was not what we human beings usually call love. I recognize the danger of being overly sentimental about the relation of love and death. It is too easy to glibly mention love as the solution to all of life's problems. Yet love is a solution, because it moves us into deeper caring and connection.

Love is an imperfect antidote to our fears of death and aloneness. No relationship, with others or ourselves, can eliminate our separateness or isolation. Each of us is ultimately alone in our journey. We must bear this aloneness with courage and resoluteness. Yet aloneness can be shared in such a way that love compensates for the pain of isolation. We must use love to cope with this pain and to make life bearable and full.

## TAKING OUR MEDICINE: BREAKING DOWN THE BARRIERS

As we face our end, we recognize that it is the investments in friends and family that come back to nourish and comfort us. In the end, our love is our greatest legacy and lives beyond us in those we touch. It is the only way a part of us remains behind after we have gone.

Take what you have learned and break down the barriers to deeper love in your life. You must first explode any misconceptions and truly understand what deeper love is to experience and express it to yourself, those around you, and in your life. You must face your isolation and end, to find the will to love completely.

People who have neared death's door tell us of a love more mature and true. Trauma survivors who have faced life's fragility become committed to bettering their relationships, giving more of themselves, and actively showing love. They're more open, caring, and accepting of themselves and others. When the end draws near, prejudices and judgment fall away as people experience a greater connection to all living things. The simple thought of mortality cleanses and purifies the experience of caring, barriers are ripped down, while love becomes unconditional and universal.

Our friend death helps us in our conscious commitment to actively love others and ourselves. In his last days before dying, Morrie Schwartz, Mitch Albom's mentor, personified how death opened him up to the preciousness of life and love. We can each benefit from this example and use the next chapters to extend our love further.

How can we move to a higher level, deeper experience of our love? How can we make our love more authentic and satisfying? We will learn more about deepening our own experience, to fall back in love with ourselves, each other, and life.

# CHAPTER SEVEN

# The "I" Equation

*If you bring forth what is inside you,*
*what you bring forth will save you.*
*If you do not bring forth what is inside you,*
*what you do not bring forth will destroy you.*
　　　　　　　　—*Gospel of St. Thomas*

"It took me 42 years and a plane crash to finally look at myself," said Robert after having survived a downing in his private plane. "All these years I've focused on the wrong things—competing, winning at any cost, succeeding in my career." But along with his no-holds-barred success as a fund manager came an attitude that he looked back upon with regret.

"I was spoiled and arrogant, used to getting my way. After my accident, while lying in the hospital, I could barely lift my fork to my mouth, and my daughter had to feed me," he recalled. "That's when I let go of my ego. I became less demanding. Now I see it was all to prove I was worthwhile, something I never believed inside. I just want to come to peace with who I am before it's too late."

Tragedies such as this often remind us that no love is more important than the love for self. How we feel about ourselves affects our every waking moment, influencing our ability to be happy and relaxed, how well we work and play, the quality of our relationships, and our peace of mind.

Psychologist Nathanial Brandon tells us, "There is overwhelming evidence that the higher the level of self-esteem, the more likely one will treat others with respect, kindness, and generosity. People who do not experience self-love have little or no capacity to love others."[1] Healthy self-esteem involves understanding, accepting, and loving ourselves for who we are and is fundamental to our ability to experience deeper connections with others and life.

## WHAT IS SELF-LOVE?

Many are confused by the terms *self-esteem* and *self-love*. When I speak with patients, they often associate self-love with selfishness or conceit. They are afraid of becoming narcissistic and egotistical. Feeling good about ourselves has somehow become confused with bragging, arrogance, boasting, and selfishness.

These behaviors are not signs of too much self-esteem, but of too little. People who feel good about themselves are not braggadocios or boastful. It is the low self-esteemers who must talk about their accomplishments, wealth, or other attributes to prop up their sagging sense of self-worth. They are compelled to prove themselves, to show they are better than anyone else.

Many people also confuse self-esteem with ego. People are said to have "big egos," thinking this is synonymous with self-love. People with swollen egos do not necessarily have positive self-esteem. In many cases, like narcissists, they use their fragile, inflated sense of self-importance to cover their underlying sense of inadequacy.

Many who shun positive self-esteem actually suffer from an unhealthy self*less*ness. Their sense of self has been neglected, ignored, and starved almost to the point of nonexistence. Their love for themselves has shriveled and died, like a dead flower.

We know it is harmful to have too little self-esteem. Is it possible to have too much self-esteem? The simple answer is no.

I view self-love or self-esteem as a three-factored equation. The first factor is self-respect, the belief that you are worthy of respect and happiness. Factor two is assertiveness. Assertiveness is feeling entitled to express your basic needs, feelings, and wants. The third factor is self-efficacy. Self-efficacy is having confidence in your ability to cope well with whatever life may throw you. It is trusting in yourself and your capacity to effectively handle the challenges of living. Let's examine these three factors in more detail.

Self-respect is the belief in our own value. It is not a delusion that we are superior, "perfect," or greater than anyone else. In fact, it is not competitive or comparative at all. It is simply the conviction that we are worthwhile and our well-being is worth supporting and nurturing. Self-respect is based on the notion that we deserve the respect of others. We are who we say we are, we show integrity—as our words and actions match. People who have self-respect take care of themselves, protect their legitimate interests, and accept their honest achievements.

Assertiveness, the second component of self-esteem, involves honoring and appropriately expressing your feelings, needs, and wants. It means standing up for yourself and being comfortable with who you are—to live authentically. This is not to be confused with timidity, where we become a doormat and allow others to take advantage of us. Nor is assertiveness being aggressive, where we gratify our needs at the expense of those around us. Assertiveness is a healthy balance where we are able to have our needs met while respecting others in the process.

The third component of self-esteem, self-efficacy, is perceived competence. Can we effectively manage our lives? Competence shows that we have confidence in our ability to handle ourselves and the world. We know we can cope and are resilient despite life's inevitable storms and setbacks.

Self-respect, assertiveness, self-efficacy—this is the essence of self-esteem. We need all three factors in order to establish a sense of inner security and stability. Take one or two factors away, and the equation becomes nonsense. Many live their lives figuring with false factors and equations that don't make sense, constantly trying to balance themselves and pretending to appear confident. Yet, their uneasiness is apparent to all.

The benefits of loving ourselves are incalculable. Solid self-esteem not only makes us feel more comfortable, but also helps us live our lives more effectively; it is a necessary building block for positive health and relationships. Our level of self-love impacts every area of our life—our work, relationships, ability to handle daily problems, and ultimately, our happiness.

In contrast, inadequate self-esteem cripples and deforms our lives. We see this every day in dead-end careers, poor mate selection, frustrated marriages, promising ideas later sabotaged, destructive drinking and eating, harmful habits, negative self-fulfilling prophecies, an insatiable hunger for love, and unfulfilled dreams.

Can we actually see self-love at work? How do we observe self-esteem in ourselves or others? Self-love and self-loathing are easy to distinguish. People who have self-love are comfortable giving and accepting compliments, consistent in their words and actions, honest in revealing shortcomings and strengths, open to constructive criticism, able to say no, capable of taking care of themselves, and flexible and adaptable in handling changes in their life. We see confidence even physically in an easy, relaxed posture, purposeful walk, and direct eye contact.

People with low self-worth are obvious in their self-hatred. They are racked by fear, anxiety, and despair. They stumble over

words, do not look you in the eyes, and are timid and shy. Individuals who detest themselves are self-denigrating, show prejudice
and hatred, and bristle at the slightest hint of criticism.

Tense and unhappy, they often engage in self-defeating behavior such as substance abuse, poor work performance, and destructive relationships. Low-self-esteemers brush off compliments and
have trouble accepting the positives about themselves and their
life. They feel they don't deserve love and acceptance and create
negative self-fulfilling prophecies to prove it.

In many cases, people with low self-esteem try to mask their
feelings of inadequacy. They present a veneer of assurance and
poise while distracting themselves and others with a well-mani-
cured appearance, material acquisitions, sexual exploits, status, or
popularity. These impostors have spent their lives perfecting their
outer facade rather than an inner sense of confidence. Though appearing strong and capable, they often tremble inside, fearing others will discover their private sense of inferiority. I am convinced
positive self-love is essential to good health.

How do you honestly feel about yourself? When was the last
time you really looked at your own sense of self-worth? No, I
don't mean the false props we all use to feel good about ourselves—the fancy clothes and cars, the corner office, the slender
body, the big home or bank account—I mean the stripped-down,
basic version of you. I mean *just* you, the person. Ask yourself
what you love about you? Can you come up with a list of things
you truly value about yourself, and say them out loud, and more
importantly, believe them? How do you really feel in your gut
when someone compliments you? That's a gauge of your own
self-worth.

It's so easy to get caught up measuring our worth by external
yardsticks as we lose our way with false promises or quick fixes
for our lack of self-love. The road to our selves is lined with

sideshows and glittering attractions, all screaming for our attention. Lighted billboards advertise the circus just ahead with instant
gratification—bars, cults, infomercials, corporate offices, "wild
man" weekends, all promising the ultimate in fulfillment. Many
of these common detours involve attempts to find worth through
something outside of us.

Yet, when we base our worth on externals, we're never
enough, and this drive to measure up and to attain some impossible goal goes on to infinity. It's always one more sexual conquest,
one more promotion, one more raise, one more company, a nicer
car, larger home, fatter bank account, new relationship, another
award or title—yet the void within us remains unfilled. No matter how hard we try to use things to boost our sagging sense of
self-esteem, we are doomed to fail.

Just like Robert's plane crash, sometimes it takes extreme situations, traumatic experiences, to make us take a hard look at ourselves, to embark on the challenging journey to inner peace and
acceptance. And yet there are few journeys more fulfilling.

David had all the trappings of success and fame. A prominent
businessman and civic leader, he enjoyed a substantial income and
prestige, a loving family, and a secure future. David was striking in
his appearance. An exceptionally tall, powerfully built gentleman,
everything about him exuded confidence.

He belonged to all the better clubs, attended the right
church, shopped in the best stores, and ate in all the finest restaurants. A philanthropist who did good works, he was loved by
many. No one would have ever imagined him to be other than
what he seemed—a self-assured, successful business owner who
had it all.

Beneath this well-polished facade, David did not like himself.
Highly critical and judgmental no matter what he accomplished,
he was never good enough. His interior life was filled with fear,

loneliness, and depression. David was anxious he would be "discovered," that someone would finally see behind his mask and recognize his inner feelings of inadequacy.

With this fear, he could never reveal his true needs and feelings, even to those closest to him. Instead of developing self-respect and compassion, his energy had been channeled into supporting the image of success and competence. Despite all of the people who loved him—his wife, his children, his friends—he despised himself. All the admiration of his associates and the community did nothing to assuage his feelings of worthlessness.

In his 40s, he had gone in for a routine cardiac stress test only to find he had major blockage in his coronary arteries. He immediately underwent quintuple bypass surgery during which he almost died while on the operating table and was revived. After surgery, he became significantly depressed and was referred to me by his friend and cardiologist. David's doctor knew his depression left him with increased risk of further heart problems.

"I'm here because my doctor told me if I didn't deal with this depression, I probably wouldn't live long," David said as he walked into my office. At first reluctant, David continued our meetings and quickly realized the basis for his emotional plunge.

Unable to work, lying in bed physically and emotionally weakened, he was stripped of his normal distractions. He was suddenly left without many of the usual props to support his fragile sense of self-worth. The importance of his things, roles, and responsibilities had fallen away, leaving him psychologically naked and exposed.

David's doctors warned him he could eventually build up further blockage in his coronary arteries and his condition required periodic monitoring. Since his confrontation with death, he felt he was living on borrowed time. He began seeing himself and his life in an entirely different way.

"I think it's time I look at the fact that I've been living a lie," David said. "I don't want to keep wasting my life holding up this mask and feeling so empty inside. I've always felt like a fake, hiding who I really am. If there's one thing I learned from my surgery, it's that life is fragile. It can all be over in a finger snap. I want to come to peace with who I am."

He was realizing that living a lie, in the long run, was harder than living truthfully and that all his focus on externals had left him exhausted. The ultimate source of self-acceptance could come only from within him, for to live authentically, David would have to confront his inner emptiness. In listening to David's struggle, I was reminded of Anne Morrow Lindbergh's observation in *Gift from the Sea*, "The most exhausting thing in life, I have discovered, is being insincere."[2]

How does one develop healthy self-esteem? Research tells us one of the best ways to build good self-esteem is to have been fortunate enough to have grown up in a nurturing home environment. This is an atmosphere where our parents raised us with love and acceptance, provided us with consistent structure, reasonable rules, and appropriate expectations. These same parents believed in our essential goodness and competence and conveyed this attitude to us through their behavior.

What if we were not so fortunate to have had this early nurturing? Are there other paths we may take to this end? In cases where this parenting did not occur, how else do we develop positive self-love?

Fortunately, some of us are able to engineer emotionally corrective experiences through other nurturing relationships in our lives, repairing some of the early damage of neglect and abuse through later positive, caring interactions. Similarly, successful psychotherapy helps dissolve many of the fears and obstacles blocking the development of a solid, positive sense of self. Urgent life crises often can facilitate this same process.

We want a way to become more caring and compassionate toward ourselves, yet we need a push to put us on the path leading to healthy self-love. Otherwise we put it off, thinking we will take better care of ourselves tomorrow. But sometimes, as we put ourselves on hold, time runs out. A client recovering from cancer once told me, "I've lived with this nagging self-doubt all my life. I'm determined not to take it with me to my grave."

What do you do that strengthens your own positive feelings about yourself? For example, do you exercise, meditate, volunteer your time, help your kids with their homework, or make time to be alone? All these things can help us feel more caring, compassionate, and calm—just a few positive steps to a stronger sense of self-worth.

You can choose each moment how you wish to feel about yourself. You are the holder of the key, only you can control your self-perception. Once developed, self-esteem is within you—nobody can give it to you and nobody can take it away.

Deeper self-love involves the same components of other-love discussed in Chapter 6. We must be committed to loving our person, willing to give freely and fully to ourselves, accepting and respectful of who we are, and allow ourselves to be enriched by this caring. Otherwise we're caught on an endless treadmill, chasing after poor substitutes, forever trying to find something just beyond our grasp.

Greg was caught in this very trap. He worked harder and harder to accomplish more and more. He was on a never-ending search for the right job, car, home, woman, trip, award—believing that if he could achieve his goal, he would finally discover peace and happiness.

"There was a voice inside of me always saying, 'Not enough, I'm not enough.' After awhile, I wasn't enjoying my successes as much," Greg told me. "I felt this pressure to always have to prove myself. I remember thinking just before my car accident, how do I ever get off this treadmill? In that sense, it took almost dying to finally give up the race."

What can awaken us from this numbing sleep and put us on the path to healthier self-love? Tragedy taps us on the shoulder whispering Life Lesson 3: *We are more than what we do or own.* We confuse our personal identity and worth with what we do or what we have. You are not your career, your bank account, appearance, athletic ability, automobile, or sexual performance. You are so much more. I confront patients every day with this fact, some gently and others very directly, yet only a few can hear my words.

Stop for a minute and ask yourself, Who am I? What is your first answer? Your second, third, and fourth? Commonly, when asked this question, we begin by describing our roles: home-maker, accountant, mother, boss, churchgoer, sister, son, civic leader. These are descriptions for what you do, not who you are. These labels say nothing to describe your inner qualities, strengths, hopes, dreams, fears, vulnerabilities, or what makes you special as a person.

Sometimes we lose sight of who we really are. Extreme situations, life-threatening experiences force us to go deeper in our reflection, to shed the superfluous layers covering the essence of our being. So ask yourself now, who are you outside of your roles and role expectations? Who are you beneath all your things and responsibilities? When we divest ourselves of all that is not our core, we move to who we really are, the first step to self-love. Trauma reminds us time is short, pushing us to find our true self.

Take a few minutes to complete a structured disidentification exercise developed by James Bugental that is often used with cancer patients.

*STRIPPING DOWN*

*Set aside 45 minutes and find a quiet, comfortable place to write. You will need a pad of paper or eight three-by-five cards. Start by listing on each of the eight cards your response to the question, Who Am I? As you complete your responses, review your answers, and then arrange the cards in their order of importance, putting the least important on the top and most important or core responses on the bottom. Study the first card and think carefully about what it would be like to give up that attribute. What would that mean in your life? After several minutes, go on to the next card, and so on until you have divested yourself of all eight attributes.*

*How did it feel to let go of the less important parts of you? The more important or core attributes? Notice what you value in yourself, the relative importance of each attribute, and how it felt to divest these aspects. When done, go back and reintegrate by going through the same process in reverse. See what you consider your core self— the essence of your being. Write your feelings from this experience in your journal and reflect on what you have learned.*

Urgent life crises strip us naked, leaving only our bare essence. Whether a busboy, attorney, housewife, executive, or cook, all are affected the same way. People going through serious life-threatening experiences dramatically transform their values and focus. No matter what their station in life, they no longer strictly define themselves by their work, roles, or possessions. These survivors transcend material and social values while shifting to core values and activities, such as love, knowledge, and meaning.

When will you face this question? If you are only what you do, and then you don't do it anymore, who are you? I have seen individuals shaken violently when robbed of their roles: mothers with grown children, harried executives facing sudden retirement, healthy people suddenly ill, active individuals unexpectedly crippled. Their entire identity had been tethered to their work, parenting, caregiving, civic involvement, or physical condition.

Yet inevitably we all must face such losses in our lives and, if not careful, can drown in a flood of self-pity accompanied by the question, "Why me?" We wonder why we, and not someone else, were afflicted by this dreadful tragedy.

"I can't understand what I did to deserve this. At first I was angry with my neurologists for telling me I had cancer. Now I'm just pissed at God for ruining my life," shared one client who had lived fully through his roles. Roles expire, leaving us facing our true selves.

In psychotherapy I help people develop love for themselves, discovering a healthy level of self-confidence and esteem. I am convinced this work involves several distinct steps, specific internal changes people create and practice that lead them to feel more worthwhile. These steps involve developing greater self-awareness, clearing the mind of negativity and muddle, opening up and accepting our emotions or disowned parts of ourselves, and being willing to openly express our feelings, needs, and wants to others.

To get to this higher level of self-love, we must look honestly at how we think, feel, and act. Let's begin by looking at our mind.

## A LOVING MIND

Trauma survivors often discover their self-worth does not reside in what they have or do. Their self-esteem does not depend on what they know, their physical appearance, work, others' opinions, or their possessions. They don't postpone feeling worthwhile until they have reached some seemingly important goal—a big promotion, the first million dollars, a college degree. They cherish their very existence, and in their eyes all people are inherently affirmed and worthwhile.

If we were to peer inside a trauma survivor's head, we would see a mind cleansed of judgment and negativity. The perceptual filter has been scrubbed of many of the cognitive distortions blocking our acceptance and love. How do we cleanse our minds of those thoughts contaminating our capacity for love?

Yogi Berra, in his wisdom, once said, "Half the game is 90 percent mental." More than half of love is mental. The way we evaluate ourselves every day determines our true capacity for love. Our beliefs and thoughts set love in motion or stop it dead in its tracks.

Our beliefs become our thoughts, thoughts the beginning of all feelings, feelings the driver of all action, action the beginning of character, and character determines our life. Our beliefs and thoughts form the bedrock of the self. We must first examine and change those perceptions standing in the way of our love.

## CLEAR THE MUDDLE: THE MENTAL ROADBLOCKS TO LOVE

Imagine someone close to you judging and criticizing your every thought, feeling, and behavior. No matter what you did, your friend tells you your performance is subpar, calls you names, frightens you with worst-case scenarios, compares you unfavorably with others, and makes sweeping negative generalizations about your behavior.

Now stop for a moment and look in the mirror. Do you speak to yourself this way? Are you your own best friend or worst enemy? Are you your own greatest critic? How much of your life's precious time and energy do you wish to spend judging yourself and others? Most would respond "none," yet they spend hours every week doing just that.

If you listen to yourself closely, you're likely to trip across your own hidden criticisms. Have you ever thought or said, "That's just not right," or "What's wrong with you?" Do you catch yourself asking a lot of "why" questions, for example, "Why did you get your hair cut that way?"—which is just another way of saying it looks lousy.

If you meet survivors, you'll be struck by their calm acceptance and loving openness to their own and other's experience. You won't hear critical, judgmental voices condemning themselves and those around them. It is as if the reality of death has somehow cleansed their minds of negativity.

Listen to your own muddled mind, your inner voice. Observe how you speak to yourself. The way we internally communicate with ourselves largely determines our capacity to love ourself and others. Are your words kind and reasonable, encouraging and supportive, loving and nurturing? Or are they critical and cruel, unreasonable and demanding, and laden with negative value judgments? Does this buzz of fears, worries, and anxieties circle your head like a swarm of hungry mosquitoes?

This voice you live with every day is one of the most powerful influences in your life. Listen carefully, for this inner voice dictates how you think, feel, and live in this world.

How did you develop your critical inner voice? To change this voice, it often helps to first recognize whose voice it is. Is it your parents? Uncle Harry? Your sixth-grade English teacher? In many cases we adopt the voice of significant others in our life: parents, teachers, bosses, and friends. These opinions are incorporated as our own as we constantly replay them in our head. Now is the time to question these disrespectful voices and quiet those standing in the way of our happiness. These familiar voices are often the primary obstacle to love.

We each have habits of thought we use to interpret reality. Negative cognitive patterns demolish our self-esteem and dampen our mood and energy. The critical mind adopts a number of methods to block us from seeing ourselves and life as it is. Our mental filter becomes clogged with negativity.

These cognitive distortions take many forms—the tyrannical *should*, overgeneralization, negative labels, merciless comparisons, perfectionistic expectations, dichotomous or polarized thinking, and mind reading, to name a few. We must be willing to confront and challenge these messages to create a more reasonable, loving communication.

Can you recognize the muddle in your mind? Let's review briefly some of the cognitive clutter keeping you from greater love and happiness.

## Tyranny of the Should

Positive self-esteem is a product of your evaluation of yourself and the extent to which you believe yourself to be a capable, worthy person. In many cases, the only things blocking you from enjoying the gifts of self-confidence are your own judgments about yourself.

This is a *personal* judgment and can be based on truth or distortion, on reality or imagination. Of all the judgments we make, this is the most important.

Many of us muddle our mind with erroneous thinking and harsh judgments, distorting our perceptions and damaging our self-esteem. One of the most common distortions is created by the *should*. The words *must*, *have to*, and *ought* are also offenders.

Trauma survivors are grounded in reality, in the way things actually are and not how they should be. I have seen more unhappiness caused by this simple word than by many things outside of our control.

I frequently hear these unreasonable expectations: "I should be happier." "I shouldn't feel hurt about this." "I should have left this job a long time ago." If you listen, you will hear these expectations spoken frequently in the dialogue of the perfectionist, the guilt-ridden, and the procrastinator. Many people struggle in accepting themselves and the world as they are, desperately attempting to pretend otherwise.

To find self-love, we must learn to accept ourselves and the world as they are, not as we think they should be. We may not like that we are 10 pounds overweight, that our boss doesn't treat us as we think he should, that our husband is not very affectionate, and that there are hungry children in the world. But our not liking these realities or feeling angry or guilty about them does not alter these facts, it only amplifies our misery. Complaining, finding fault, pretending, and judging do no good and separate us further from our love. An old English proverb states, *Faults are thick where love is thin.*

By first accepting that these realities exist, we can then consciously decide whether we wish to do anything about changing these facts or not. Telling ourselves we should does not move us to constructive action; rather it only leads to destructive guilt and paralyzing self-condemnation.

We must first accept ourselves for who we are before we can go about the business of change. Accepting who we are does not mean we like something or approve of a behavior, only that we recognize where we are in order to move forward. Acceptance becomes the solid platform from which choice and change occur.

Christopher constantly harped on himself for not sticking with a career. Having inherited a family fortune at a young age, he could never find the motivation to stay with a consistent vocation. He was bright and had attended several different universities and started up small companies only to become distracted with a new home, boat, or child.

Chris consistently criticized himself for not doing more with his work, echoing his father's reproaches over his "wasting" his life.

It's as if he had to be whipped and punished to perform. Fifteen years of self-flagellation had not produced one bit of career accomplishment nor provided any distinct direction for his life.

When I met Chris he was awaiting his third child, dabbling in some minor real estate deals, boating, traveling, and spending time with his family. The fact was, whether he or his father thought he "should" work or not, he did not have to. When faced with the choice of attending a class or studying, he usually opted to play with his children, go boating, or work on his latest project. Aside from his own stinging self-criticism and the occasional embarrassment not having a job would cause, Chris was for the most part comfortable with his life.

He was not lazy, for his time was spent productively with his family, hobbies, projects, and friends. He was very involved in those things he enjoyed. After working with him to discover the motivation and structure necessary for an occupational direction, he decided consciously to return to his life as it was. At this point in his life, he had no reason to change his behavior.

Over the next months, Chris was able to give up his internal name-calling and destructive assaults on his mood and self-esteem. He accepted that he was not ready to make this change in his life and stopped the self-punishing tirades over his lack of a formal career. From this self-acceptance, if circumstances shifted, he could go on and make a change in his life.

Interestingly, I ran into Chris a few years later and he had started his own computer consulting business. He had taken a hobby he really enjoyed and then began selling his services to help small businesses address their technology problems. This work allowed him the freedom to continue to spend time with his family and other interests, while satisfying his need to feel productive.

To develop greater self-esteem, we must liberate ourselves from the "tyranny of the should." Trauma survivors have freed themselves by focusing on and accepting themselves as they are. Harking back to the increased freedom and choice discussed in Life Lesson 2, they lose their concerns with others' unreasonable expectations and demands and steer their lives by their own internal compass.

*Overgeneralizing*

Overgeneralizing involves taking one example or fact and making it a general rule. If you happen to be late for a party, you tell yourself you're never punctual or you're always late. If you make a mistake at work, you're a loser. All men are deceitful, all women are flaky. Everyone is cruel, no one is friendly.

This type of global thinking distorts our reality and contaminates our experience. You can detect this distortion with the use of absolute words such as *never, always, every time, everybody, nobody, all,* or *none.*

After her relationship with her father, Karen felt no man could ever be trusted. She fully expected every man she met would eventually hurt her, this belief blocking her from ever developing a positive, emotionally corrective intimate relationship with a man. Overgeneralized negative beliefs and statements foul our perceptions and interfere with out ability to deal with the world.

If you, like Karen, are guilty of this mental error, erase these absolute terms from your vocabulary. Begin to use specifics instead of generalities. Check your evidence before drawing expansive conclusions and indictments to use against yourself and others.

Accepting yourself means becoming aware of and ridding yourself of the self-denigrating thoughts that damage your self-love. To start, track and eliminate negative labels, dropping words like *stupid, fat, lazy, ugly, dull, mean, pushy, skinny, dummy, needy, bitchy,* and so on. If you must, use specific terms to describe the behavior you do not like and then resolve to change those behaviors you feel are important.

*The Negative Filter*

In this case, your perceptual filter is negatively slanted where you see and accept only negative information and dwell on it exclusively. This distortion colors your view of yourself and the world, causing everything to appear darker than it is. This filter blocks out any positive feedback because affirming information would only contradict your distorted sense of reality.

Positive experiences become disqualified, as you figure out some reason "they don't count." The person paying you the compliment "just doesn't know" you, or perhaps there is something wrong with him or her for seeing you in a constructive light. By denying the positive, you are able to maintain your negative perception regardless of contradictory information.

Life isn't an audition for some later performance. This is it. Mortality teaches us our time is short. Open your arms and take the positives given every day.

To clear this filter and develop a more balanced perception, you must begin to recognize your positive attributes as well as how you discount yourself. This is difficult to change by yourself. You must drop your camouflage and openly share your negative self-perception with those closest to you, thereby allowing them to repeatedly confront your habit of discounting their positive feelings and perceptions.

David believed everyone in his life only cared about him because of his position and status. "If I didn't do something for all the people in my life, they wouldn't care about me at all." As we talked, David was able to recount several friends and family members who had expressed their love to him through both words and actions, yet he could not accept their love. "Well, they may say they

love me, and even act that way, but I still don't believe them. They
don't really know me, for if they did, they wouldn't feel that way.
I don't feel I deserve love."

David had taken a brave and critical step. We first must have
the courage to honestly admit our feelings of unworthiness to
ever get beyond them.

## Comparing: The Loser's Game

Another way of muddling your mind and damaging your self-esteem is through the loser's game of comparing. Most people who
compare themselves to others come out on the short end of the
stick. When you play, your self-esteem is on a roller coaster, flying
up and down depending on what you happen to be measuring at
the moment.

Is the person next to you at the office taller, smarter, better
dressed, wealthier, more articulate, funnier? Are you usually flawed
by comparison?

Greg was always competing with those around him, making
sure he was "better" at everything. If someone seemed brighter,
friendlier, was driving a more expensive car, dating a more attractive woman, or had a lower handicap—Greg was determined to
outdo them. He had to be on top or he was nothing. Trapped by
his fiercely competitive spirit, he was in a race he would ultimately
lose. Someone eventually outdid him.

Stop comparing and focus on your strengths and positive attributes. Find things you feel good about and like about yourself.
Work on believing you are worthwhile just as you are. Affirm
your right to be yourself. Celebrate your uniqueness and value.

## The Curse of Perfection

A fifth damaging belief is that we must be perfect to be loved and
accepted. David's perceptual filter was filled with distortions that

hurt him and those around him. He constantly labored under his own perfectionistic expectations. Though seeming self-confident and "having it all," David was a walking paradox.

The goals we endorse heavily influence our self-esteem. William James, a brilliant American psychologist, pointed out over a hundred years ago that self-esteem is linked to the ratio of expectation to successes.[3] A person may develop low self-esteem because he sets his goals too high or achieves too few successes.

So it is not necessarily true that someone who is accomplished will have high self-esteem. Since David's goals were unattainable, he could never reach a level of contentment or satisfaction.

David came by his perfectionism honestly. Raised in a strict Catholic family as the oldest of three children, from a young age he was expected to be responsible for his younger sisters. Like many wealthy children I have seen, he grew up pampered, pushed, and inwardly tortured.

Though seldom home, David's father was a strong presence and president of a third-generation manufacturing company. His mother was heavily involved socially in the community and was often away pursuing her many volunteer activities.

Pushed by his own father, David's father had high expectations for his son, grooming him from an early age as the heir apparent to succeed him in the family business. David attended the best schools, his friends were hand picked, manners and behavior meticulously groomed, and his every move carefully scrutinized. He was to be the perfect young man. For the most part, David followed his parents' lead, never questioning their demands. Over time, their expectations became his own.

Because of this upbringing, David grew into living what most would see as the perfect life. As an adult, he had succeeded his father as president of their large family business. He was highly successful, well educated, and married with two beautiful children.

David was involved in many civic and social activities and admired as an upstanding member of the community. Looking from the outside, it seemed David lived a charmed life.

What was not evident, however, was how David felt about himself. David had lived his life trying to measure up to his parents' expectations. He knew he could never do enough to please them or himself. He was lost. He had few close friends and did not feel he could trust anyone. Though personable and seemingly friendly, he kept everyone at a distance, fearing they would learn his inner secrets. David was constantly busy, trying to meet his many responsibilities. Often exhausted, he took little time off, with the exception of an occasional golf tournament or social engagement.

When he began to feel unhappy, David felt guilty and quickly squelched his misery. He would often question himself, "How could I be so unhappy? My life looks perfect." David had planned to continue his life according to his prewritten script, had he not bumped into death, and then his life. He decided he would change, no matter what the cost. He was determined to learn the reasons for his unhappiness and then work to create a fulfilling life.

What we usually discover between ourselves and full awareness is fear. If we open our heart to feel deeply, to feel all our feelings, our life will change. There is danger in facing our inner truth, in honestly asking ourselves what we love and want. "Fear of knowing," writes Abraham Maslow, "is very deeply a fear of doing." How much do we want to know if knowing forces us out of our comfort zone?

"I'm afraid if I really did what I wanted, I'd blow my life up," David told me. "I do know my responsibilities are suffocating me. Admitting that scares me." David was beginning to reveal how much he disliked his life and that he could only see two ways to deal with his dilemma. In his dichotomous view, he either had to stay and do exactly what he was doing or chuck it all and run away to a remote South Sea island. David could not yet envision changing his life in any other way.

"Before my bypass, I just figured I would go on like my dad and do this until I die. That's what he did. He was obsessed with his work, power, and importance and thrived on how others saw him. Everyone looked up to my father. He was respected and admired; yet I know he wasn't happy. I don't want to live his life. I have to get to where I feel better about myself. I'm not going to live forever, and knowing that, I'm willing to take some risks I wasn't willing to before."

It's only when we've nearly lost everything that we're free to do anything. Confronting his catastrophic expectations that people would reject and criticize him if he were more himself, David committed to take the risks of authentically expressing who he was.

He, like so many others, feared revealing his humanness. David was embarrassed by human traits like ignorance, confusion, jealousy, and sadness. He had learned to show the world his happy, confident face while deep inside being tormented by his inadequacies and doubts.

Life's much too short to toil under the heavy yoke of perfectionism. Know and accept your true feelings and needs and let go the pressure of living up to others' expectations of you and your life.

### Dichotomous Thinking

The sixth negative cognitive pattern to listen for is polarized or dichotomous thinking. You may catch yourself using this "all or nothing" perceptual style where everything you see is good-bad, right-wrong, or black-white. You are either wonderful or worthless, brilliant or stupid, beautiful or ugly, great or awful.

Bill was caught in his own guilt and regret after his son's drowning. He blamed himself, thinking he was responsible for all that was wrong in his life. He "screwed up" his marriage, neglected his kids, fumbled his business, and caused Jason's death. Believing he had done everything wrong, he felt terrible about himself.

Bill was guilty of all-or-nothing thinking, believing he was a villain, all bad, totally to blame for all the negative events in his life. The fact was, he was responsible for some of these problems—he could have invested more in his marriage, family, and the business—but this did not make him solely to blame for all that happened. He was neither sinner nor saint but, like each of us, a combination of both.

If you think in polarities, look for shades of gray. People are too complex to be simply categorized and labeled. We each fall somewhere along a continuum and deserve more understanding. Think in percentages, appreciate the differences in yourself and others, and use descriptions instead of labels.

### The Mind Reader

The last mental roadblock of the muddled mind is mind reading. This is the tendency to believe everyone thinks and feels the same as we do. We assume we know what others are thinking and feeling. Consequently, we expect others to view and judge us as we view and judge ourselves.

David assumed his wife would judge him as childish if he told her he missed her and wanted to spend more time in her company. He didn't ask her directly, for he knew how she would feel and expected her to be rejecting. Ironically, others seldom make as big a deal of our faults as we do. In many cases, our imperfections often go unnoticed.

I recall speeches I have delivered where I fully believed I had performed below par, only later to find my audience was extremely complimentary. Are you aware of doing this? If so, do not assume anything. When in doubt or if you find yourself guessing what others think or feel, stop and ask. Directly checking out your assumptions can save you a lot of pain and sorrow.

Each of these negative thought patterns can clog your perceptual filter, keeping you from developing greater love for yourself. Aaron Beck, a cognitive psychologist, addresses many of these mental errors in his book *Love Is Never Enough*.[4] Pay close attention, and if you notice these cognitive roadblocks, clear them away to pave a path to greater happiness and peace.

## FOCUS ON THE POSITIVE: PATS ON THE BACK

We often become so focused on our negatives that we lose sight of the positive aspects of ourselves. Our filter becomes clogged with negative thoughts, strangling out the perceptions that encourage, support, and inspire our confidence.

Many people struggle as much with the positive sides of themselves as they do with the dark side. We are uncomfortable with affirmation and approval, compliments, and joy. We can be as frightened of our assets and strengths as our shortcomings and weaknesses. We can refuse to accept our positives and affirm our basic right to happiness, peace, and serenity.

To feel good about ourselves, we must take time to appreciate our strengths and assets, and recognize what is working and going well in our lives. When time is short, gratitude grows. Our mortality begs us to be kind.

How often do you take the time to reflect on your positive qualities and acts? When was the last time you took a moment and patted yourself on the back, remembered something you did to help someone, an accomplishment, a kindness extended to a friend or stranger? When did you last appreciate the love others feel for you—your child, spouse, parent, or friend?

Think of the last time you were complimented by someone or did a favor for a neighbor. If you can allow yourself to feel good about these thoughts and experiences, you let your self-love flourish. Use these thoughts to your advantage, to feel better about yourself and your life. Come back to these thoughts often by trying the following exercise:

### PATS ON THE BACK

*Find a comfortable place where you won't be disturbed. Close your eyes, breathe deeply, and relax. Go back in your life and imagine a moment where you felt successful, loved, and confident. Stay focused and experience everything about that time: the tastes, sights, sounds, smells, and feelings. See how you looked and how others appeared in the scene. Hear the confidence in your voice and the praise from those around you. Let yourself feel the self-acceptance and confidence. Now anchor this experience in your mind to your body by touching your right thumb with first finger of the same hand. Touch it firmly as the image rests in your mind. You can touch your right thumb and finger at any time to recall this feeling of success and confidence. You can do this whenever you need to counter a negative feeling or anchor on a positive feeling in yourself.*

David had difficulty attending to the things he did well. Always focused on his impossible standards, no matter what he did, he came up short. Believing he was never good enough, he politely declined others' compliments and congratulations. He knew he didn't deserve them.

Painfully at first, and with practice, David uncovered and talked about his positive attributes. With repetition and feedback from others, he started at least intellectually believing his positives. Over time, with much encouragement and support, he gradually accepted he had true worth and value as a human being.

We each have to go through much the same process. First we have to be able to intellectually recognize and accept our talents and strengths, as well as our shortcomings. Then we have to test our impressions in the world and get feedback as to their validity. Lastly we're left to sort out and incorporate what is true, accepting both positives and negatives as who we are.

Where are you in this process? Can you accept the positives? As we've seen, many people find it difficult to believe and repeat, even to themselves, affirmations about their inherent worth or value. They feel uncomfortable, hesitant to agree to or accept their right to be loved or happy.

Read the following statements reflecting positive thoughts and self-worth and see how you feel. If you were in your last days, wouldn't you want these inner thoughts and beliefs to be with you? Like a coat, try them on for size. Do they fit? Can you accept them intellectually and, more important, emotionally?

- I am lovable.
- If someone doesn't happen to reciprocate my feeling toward him or her, it may feel disappointing or even be hurtful, but it is not a true reflection of me as a human being.
- I am admirable.
- I have a right to accept and honor my feelings and needs and treat them as important.
- My reason for existing is not to live up to someone else's expectation; I can choose my own life.
- Those people who I respect and care about will usually like me.
- I have a right to make mistakes and will use these errors to grow and learn.

- I am worthy of happiness.
- I do not sacrifice my best judgment or convictions to gain the approval or acceptance of others.
- I express myself honestly and directly and in a way appropriate to the situation.
- I am responsible for my choices in life.
- I accept my feelings, behaviors, and thoughts, although I may not like them.
- I keep my promises and commitments.
- I show compassion and forgiveness toward others and myself.
- I choose my relationships voluntarily.

It's important to maintain a set of beliefs that enhances our positive sense of self. Make your own list of positive affirmations and say them every day. Use the above list to begin. Remind yourself of your inherent worth every day.

## LOVING HEART: OPENING TO FEELING

Our first focus was on changing the thoughts that ultimately affect our feelings and behavior. Death tells us to accept *all* of us. Let us now look more closely at knowing and accepting another part of ourselves, our emotions.

The second biggest obstacle to happiness and success in life is blocking our emotions. How do you feel about your own feelings? Do you cherish and embrace them or lock them away like some dangerous animal?

Many believe that by closing our heart we protect ourselves from pain, not realizing instead that we isolate ourselves even more from joy. I have come to believe that the opposite of happiness is not sadness, but the numbness of a closed heart. Joy, love, and happiness are only available when we are willing to go through our fear, pain, and grief to get there.

So to unblock the fountain of love we must learn to accept and transcend our fear and negative emotions. This is impossible until we realize that no one makes us happy or scared, excited or sad. Our emotions don't happen to us as much as we choose them. In fact, our own thoughts, emotions, and behaviors are the only things we really do control in our life.

I am reminded of an Eastern tale that illustrates our locking away parts of ourselves. It is a story of a poor man discouraged by life. He lives in a tumbledown cottage and barely scratches out a meager existence on the small plot of land surrounding his home. One day a mysterious stranger arrives on his doorstep.

"You live in a vast mansion," the man tells him. "You just don't realize it yet."

The man laughs. Anyone can see his house is small. But the stranger persists.

Slowly, with the guidance of his new friend, the man begins to discover hidden parts of his dwelling. First, he finds a forgotten room, then another, and another, until entire lavish suites are revealed. In the end the man becomes proprietor of a thousand-room palace, the same that he had once mistaken for a single dilapidated room.

Often I feel like the mysterious stranger, guiding others to discover and reclaim their lost rooms and, by doing so, the fullness of their person. We cannot see our mansion if we lock the doors to our feelings, all the while thinking emotions are the problem. We confine ourselves to the tumbledown cottage of our mind.

We think that if we get rid of sadness, anger, fear, and frustration, our life will be better. We surgically remove these painful feelings from our awareness, banning them from our consciousness. Yet, experience shows that when we refuse to acknowledge our emotions they acquire the greatest power over us.

As you work on opening your heart, you will confront repeatedly the fearful habit of closing down to pain. We most easily recognize this suppression in our bodies. Physically, we tense muscles,
hold our breath, and generally work to shut down our affect. We
shift our attention into our head, thinking, analyzing, and judging, in order to steel ourselves against our emotions.

Notice the next time you are close to feeling something unpleasant how you control or block your unwanted affect. Fortunately, by becoming aware of how we physically and mentally
block our emotions, by attending closely to these reactions and
sensations, we can also free our feelings and expression. Awareness
is the key to owning and releasing our emotions.

Many share the misconception that there are only two things
we can do with our emotions. We either reactively suppress them
or reactively spit them out. By becoming aware of our emotions
we can learn to accept their presence and consciously choose how
we wish to express them.

When we cut off a part of ourselves, the entire self suffers as
we're left living only half a life, never accepting all of who we really are. But by accepting this important part of ourselves, we take
on greater strength and wholeness and open ourselves to the wonder that is life.

## FREEING THE HEART

For most, opening our heart is a frightening prospect. We are afraid
of our emotions; they are the enemy and must be kept at bay. To
accept and own what we feel is no easy or welcome task. It takes
courage to enter the fire of our emotions and risk exploring those
parts of ourselves we would rather disown.

Remember Henry, the compulsive engineer struggling in his
efforts to advance in his firm? Though a high-performing, tech-

nically proficient engineer, he lacked the basic affective and social skills to get along with and manage people. He was a man locked in his own mind, a living machine with no allowance for his or others' emotions. Henry is certainly no exception. We all know someone who is half a person, who has developed intellectual strengths while avoiding undesired emotional aspects.

The irony is the more we disown and block our emotions and the more we try to get rid of them, the more influence they exert in our lives. I recall an experience in graduate school where I was awarded an assistantship to teach psychology courses. Never having taught or spoken publicly before, I was extremely anxious in my first class. Voice cracking, legs shaking, and mentally stumbling, I struggled to survive the class while trying to preserve some shred of dignity.

As I fought my anxiety, I only became more tense. After telling my story to a few friends, I was able to laugh and accept my anxiousness. Once I accepted my fear and could see the humor in my stumbling, I began to relax. When I accepted my fear, it lessened, and I felt more comfortable.

I gradually became more confident and began to enjoy my teaching. Now, I look forward to speaking in public. We are always stronger when we accept every part of ourselves, every feeling and fragment.

## OWNING OUR FEELINGS

Most of us have been trained to live from the neck up. Our culture values intellect, knowledge, quick thinking, and solid education. But living in your head keeps you disconnected from other important parts of who you are and how you feel—keeping you from ever becoming a whole person.

Contemporary therapists know much of their work focuses on helping patients reintegrate previously split-off parts of themselves.

In one study, successful therapy patients were asked to rank-order 60 factors in therapy according to what they felt was most helpful. The single most frequently chosen item by far was discovering and accepting previously unknown or unacceptable parts of themselves.

Self-acceptance involves accepting every part of ourselves. It is a willingness to say about any emotion, thought, fantasy, or behavior, this is an expression of me. Not necessarily an expression I like or want, but nevertheless an expression at this time. If I am angry, sad, lustful—I am feeling it and it is true; I do not try to deny or rationalize it away.

This does not mean we cannot change what we think, feel, or do. But to do so, we must first accept where we are and own our experience.

I cannot overcome a hatred I cannot feel, work through a fear I try to rationalize away, or resolve sadness denied. I cannot forgive myself for a behavior I will not admit. I cannot change a part of me I insist does not exist. To change and grow, I must first accept the reality of my full experience. Stagnation comes from denial, not acceptance.

A client of mine became angry with me for pointing out a part of her experience. Margie was a most pleasant, articulate woman who immediately impressed me as being extremely polite. Meticulously groomed and attired, it was evident she paid great attention to appearances.

Having only weeks earlier lost her husband in a car wreck, Margie sat in my office, smiling, talking about her experience of the accident. As if she were discussing her luncheon plans, Margie calmly described regaining consciousness only to discover her husband's lifeless body beside her.

As she continued smiling, I found myself very uncomfortable listening to her describe the horrific scene. I asked her, "Margie,

I'm aware you are smiling as you talk about your husband's death. How are you feeling right now?"

She stopped suddenly. "I'm fine. I just thought you needed to have all the information about what happened so you could understand my situation."

I knew she was not aware of using her smile to cover up the sadness over her husband's recent death. "I appreciate what you're telling me. I was more interested in what you're experiencing as you talk right now about the accident. Take a moment and see if you are aware of how you feel."

"I don't know how I feel. Why is that important?" she asked, still smiling, yet seeming more irritated at my question. Margie was someone used to hiding her feelings and did not like others poking around behind her pleasant exterior.

"I was just concerned you may be feeling scared or sad after having gone through such a traumatic event. I know if I had gone through what you have experienced, I would be very upset," I offered, testing whether she had any awareness of her emotions about the event.

At first, Margie stiffened, then I could see her body shaking, jaw trembling, and eyes beginning to tear up as she listened to me. Her smile gradually dissolved.

"I don't like to admit it, but I guess I am sad over what has happened." Margie spoke more softly: "I've always been the strong one and my husband never liked me to cry. Ed thought it showed weakness, so I try to smile and keep it together, no matter what." She had become aware of her emotion, a part of her she had not allowed for some years.

She began crying, "I really miss Ed, I just was trying not to feel it." By accepting her sadness, she began grieving her loss and by that began coping with what this change meant in her life.

Most of us did not learn that hurt is a close cousin to happiness and to suppress one is to deny the other. We did not get lessons on how to handle grief, express anger constructively, or accept loss as a natural part of living. Instead, the whole topic of feelings and emotional development was either ignored or openly ridiculed.

This willingness to accept and express our emotions does not determine what we eventually do or how we behave. I may wake up grouchy and not want to go to work; I can recognize my feelings, experience and accept them, and then get up and go to my office. I can become irritated in traffic when someone cuts me off, acknowledge my frustration, take a few deep breaths, and offer a friendly wave.

To experience what Joseph Campbell called "the rapture of being alive," we must be willing to swim in the whole ocean of our emotions. By allowing ourselves to dive in head first and experience them fully, we know where we are and from there where we want to go. Feeling and accepting sadness, loneliness, fear, anger, or grief lets us then move on to another place.

Once we fully experience and accept our negative feelings, they usually dissipate. By accepting our emotions, they have their say and then shuffle off our experiential center stage. In owning our feelings, our essence, we become alive and strong in our wholeness.

## AFFIRMING THE TRUE PERSON

Serious life crises reawaken us to the need for self-love, of wanting to come to some peace about who we are. We learn to love ourselves by cultivating our character.

Carl Jung has said he would rather be "whole than good." Recognize and accept all of who you really are and don't be diverted by what you do or have. Tear away the inner and outer distractions preventing you from honoring your core self.

Recall *Tuesdays with Morrie* where Mitch Albom's dying professor artfully guided his shedding the distractions of his busy schedule, hollow ambition, and fear of closeness. Mitch was locked in a prison of his own making, unable to relate to himself, Morrie, and his girlfriend. His friend's dying gave him the courage to accept his feelings, cast off many of his external demands, and thereby open himself to deeper connections with himself and others.

Trauma survivors often develop greater self-acceptance and caring, the first step in sharing a deeper love for others and life. Affirm and cherish your person. Learn to pat yourself on the back. Reinforce the positive. When life is precious, there is little time for judgment and criticism, for blame and loathing.

Act in ways consistent with self-love and respect. Our behavior reflects our attitude and feelings. Are you taking time for yourself, to nourish your mind, body, and spirit? What are you doing every day to support self-love and respect?

Remember Karen's Personal Life Plan and her goals to make time to support her developing self? She set aside time for exercise, friends, church, reflection, and prayer. Greg focused on cutting back on his excessive work schedule while making time to spend with his fiancée, Susan, and close friends. Bill concentrated on developing forgiveness and compassion for himself and others and devoted his time to his daughter.

What do you do that reflects your own commitment to self-esteem and self-love?

If we followed you for a week, what would we see to tell us you value yourself? Do you make time for you—to read, meditate, pray, visit friends or family, exercise, go to a play, listen to music, get a massage, cook, volunteer your time, or watch a comedy? Do your actions support and affirm your basic worth as a person?

When time grows short, the importance of all these things becomes evident. Trauma survivors honestly recognize their shortcomings and, as significantly, focus more on their value and strengths. Their minds are clear of muddle and negativity and their hearts are open to feeling. Accepting and caring, survivors affirm their value and the inherent worth of others. Their actions demonstrate their love for themselves, telling us of their worth.

Life is important. Your time is precious. Treat yourself well. Buddha said no matter how hard we search we cannot find anyone more deserving of love than ourselves. Start with loving yourself. It makes your every day a deeper experience.

# CHAPTER EIGHT

# Quantum Connections

*There is a land of the living*
*and the land of the dead and*
*the bridge is love, the only*
*survival, the only meaning.*
—*Thorton Wilder*

Who and how we love shapes our days and provides the texture for our inner and outer lives. Yet often our attention is scattered and diffused. We have too many things on our plate and are distracted by the sheer number of commitments, relationships, and responsibilities we have accumulated. In our preoccupation with the little things, we lose sight of who matters most.

When we believe we will live forever, we can afford to waste time; spending precious days, months, even years engaged in pointless activities and empty relationships. When the end beckons, priorities shift, pushing us closer to those we love. In mortality's shadow we see the truth of who matters and what we need to do to redeem our relationships.

"Cancer was an instant cure for my bad relationships," shared Carol, a client of mine, after her diagnosis of breast cancer. "I don't waste a lot of time dealing with people who were draining me and only cared about themselves. I save my time and energy for those who have been there for me and bring joy to my life."

Trauma survivors take a hard look at what's wrong with their lives and act decisively to change what is not working for them. No more delay, no more postponement. As time becomes precious, only those relationships that are fruitful and nourishing are kept; the rest are ended or allowed to fall away.

People who have faced death often overcome the most common fears of intimacy and attachment. They become less judgmental and prejudiced, more open and spontaneous. Feelings of tolerance, empathy, compassion, and patience flow freely as survivors make quantum leaps in their ability to love and be loved.

Life Lesson 4, *Develop greater love and acceptance of yourself and others,* forms the basis for this chapter. The feeling of attachment, of being related, of caring about someone, of being cared for is critical to our existence. As social beings, the quality of our relationships greatly affects our health and happiness. Carl Sand tells us, "There is only one happiness in life, to love and be loved."

## DEEPENING OUR RELATIONSHIPS: LEARNING THE LANGUAGE OF LOVE

Once awakened to the importance of loving relationships, we sometimes lack the knowledge and tools needed to strengthen our feelings of intimacy. Indeed, much of the energy of psychotherapy is devoted to instituting or restoring capacities for normal intimacy and the social skills to maintain viable loving relationships. We want to feel closer, fortify our connections, reinforce our caring, yet find ourselves uncertain as to how to proceed. How do we carry our love to the next level?

The idea of mortality loans us the courage to be vulnerable, pushing us to risk greater intimacy. Facades drop away. Once open, we deepen our connections by improving communication, the lifeblood of relationships. By powerfully conveying our immediate feelings, wants, and needs, we move closer to those around us.

As in self-love, our communication provides the key to deeper caring. Our actions and words express the language of love.

I have spoken to many people over the years who have faced death, either their own or through the loss of a loved one. In that experience relationships intensify as the individuals feel an increased sense of urgency to connect with others, to express their feelings and the importance of their relationships.

Have you ever noticed that when threatened, your first thought is of survival and the second is of loved ones? In fact many of us would say our closest relationships are more important than life itself, yet how many times have you put off showing your love to those most dear to you?

We can speak a language that heals our wounds and those closest to us. We begin this deepening process by deciding who is most important in our lives. Once known, we must risk conveying our true feelings and needs to those we love.

With whom do we share our love? How can we change our actions and words to deepen the love we feel for and share with those closest to us? Let's address each question in turn.

## WHOM DO YOU LOVE?

Those who have stepped near death's door fully appreciate the importance of loved ones. When our time is short, we turn first to those we care most about.

You may remember the awakening exercises that asked you to contemplate what you would do if you only had a few months to live. If your time were limited, whom would you choose to spend time with? We are forced to make choices every day about who we visit, call, and take time to be with. The idea of an end point forces these decisions, making us reevaluate and prioritize our relationships.

Your time is finite. You cannot be with everyone; and every day, conscious or not, you're making decisions as to who is more important. Take a moment and reflect on the important people in your own life. Next evaluate the relative significance of the people in your life.

Karen was surprised by her friends' reactions to her cancer diagnosis. Some avoided her altogether, superstitiously believing her cancer was somehow contagious. Some gossiped about her condition. Others were intrusive, asking about every detail of her diagnosis and treatment to satisfy their voyeuristic needs.

Karen's true friends listened attentively, offered the support she needed, and respected her privacy. They put her needs before their own and were genuinely concerned about her struggle.

It's easy to be someone's friend when times are good. In good times, fair-weather and true friends act pretty much the same, so it's hard to know who really cares about you in times of smooth sailing. When you're really in trouble you discover who your true friends really are.

The real test of a relationship comes when we find ourselves in desperate need. When was the last time you were sick, broke, downtrodden, or in a dire crisis? Remember the courage it took to reach out for help and the warm feeling of loving support from a child, mother, sibling, or friend? We cherish these gifts of love, never forgetting the sacrifices made by those who stand by us in our darkest hours. In this way, crises purify our relationships.

Think for a moment of the last time you or your relationships were tested. Only the truest of friends and family stood with you, no matter how inconvenient, costly, or troublesome it may have been. Others fall away.

I listened to Karen's struggling with her friends' and colleagues' reaction to her illness. "I don't know what to do. People approach me and just start crying or they act like my cancer is contagious, like they're going to catch something. It's really upsetting to try to deal with my own problems and know how to handle them at the same time."

She went on: "I find myself pulling away, like I don't want to be around anyone. It's too painful." As we spoke, Karen was able to more clearly distinguish her own needs and feelings and what she wanted in these various contacts. She recognized her relationships would have to change and that some would have to end.

Karen decided to step away from the voyeurs, gossips, and complainers while moving closer to others who showed real caring. She made difficult decisions about her friends who drained or fueled her, decisions many people didn't understand. It was very painful realizing she had outgrown some of her relationships. Karen, in a few short months, had largely reshaped her relational world.

"I was able to learn to let other people give to me, to talk about what they could do to help me. This was difficult; I kept feeling guilty about not doing more for them. It took some time for me not to apologize for asking for something from them.

"They volunteered to help with the kids, do chores around the house, take me to my radiation treatments, or just listen if I needed to talk. I couldn't believe all they did. What really shocked me was that they actually appreciated my asking for help. I found out who my real friends were after all."

Karen allowed her illness to help her forge deeper connections with those who really cared for her. Her cancer distilled her rela-

tional world, leaving only those people who knew and responded
to what she needed most. By her conscious awareness and decisions, she improved the quality of love in her life.

You can consciously decide every day to whom you want to
give your time and energy. Commit to spend your valuable time
with those who truly care for you, who value and nurture your
being. Step back or in some cases away from those people who
drain and pain you. But first understand which relationships
are which.

Take time now to decide who is most important to you.
Which people do you spend time with and how much? Who can
you trust implicitly with your deepest secrets? Who is most supportive of your growth and happiness, and in contrast, who would
be most painful to lose in your life? Who feeds your heart and
soul? Who accepts you no matter what? Who makes you laugh? If
you consciously made decisions about your most meaningful relationships, who would make the short list? The focus is on depth,
not breadth.

### DISTILLING YOUR LOVE

*Of the people in your life, who offers you deeper love and support?*
*Who really cares about you? Review the characteristics of mature*
*love in Chapter 6 to gauge your present relationships. Which of*
*these relationships match those criteria? List the 10 closest rela-*
*tionships in your current life. Rank each from 1 to 10, 1 being the*
*most important, 10 the least. You may want to reflect on the*
*deathbed awakening exercise to help clarify their order of impor-*
*tance. Is the time and investment in these relationships reflected*
*in your behavior? Would these individuals know they were on*
*your list, that they are most important to you, and the order in*
*which you placed them? Who would include you on their list?*
*Have you communicated their importance to you? Which of these*

*relationships would you like to deepen or improve? If you were dying now, would any of your answers change?*

If you completed the earlier awakening exercise in Chapter 4, you probably noticed many of the same people appearing on your list. If you did not, carefully consider whom you would hope would be near you in your last days or moments.

Did any of your answers surprise you? If you showed your list to those you named, would anyone be surprised they were named or by their order of importance? Do you communicate their significance to you so they know your love for them?

I have used a variant of this exercise with couples who take each other for granted. I ask each partner to write a "final" letter to their spouse, assuming that would be their last contact with them. They're to be emotionally honest and communicate whatever they need to say to them, given this will be their last communication. In some cases, I suggest they read the letters out loud to one another during a scheduled quiet time. After each shares their letter, they talk about their feelings with one another. This powerful experience can deepen the level of intimacy in a relationship.

People who face endings realize the importance of communicating their love to those people most important to them. In a more dramatic example, the most common deathbed regret people experience is not having expressed their true feelings to significant others in their life.

It is not too late. Love is more than a feeling. It is action. Are you willing to express how you feel to those most important in your life? To deepen your relationships and plunge into greater intimacy and closeness, you must communicate your caring directly. Take the risk, face your fear of vulnerability, and let others know how you really feel. Say it consistently in your actions and words. Let's begin with your actions.

## ACTING OUT YOUR LOVE

Action confirms our love, yet we often forget to let others know how much we care. We live with the assumption people know how we feel about them. We may love our spouse, children, friends, or siblings, yet without telling or showing them, how would they know? Our behavior, even more clearly than words, conveys our feeling.

Unfortunately, sometimes it takes the threat of divorce to awaken couples to the need to renew their love. These withered relationships have suffered from years of indifference and apathy. Like a garden never tended, the flowers have died and the soil has dried and been overtaken with weeds. Although neglect and inattention have taken their toll, often all that is needed is a heavy dose of tender, loving care.

When our relationships are new and fresh, we shower our loved one with actions of great caring. We tend our romantic garden every day. Everything is exciting and fresh. We talk and listen attentively for hours about the smallest of things, celebrate with candlelit dinners for no good reason, pick fresh flowers, soak in steamy tubs, take long walks on the beach, hold hands, hug often, and cook special meals for our love. We see these behaviors frequently in courtship, with these actions undeniably conveying our attention and the other's value.

Over time these behaviors thin as our energies become diverted to work, children, friends, hobbies, and ourselves. We may say we love each other, but where is the visible evidence to confirm our words? What has happened to our loving actions? As our energies become diverted and this thinning occurs, love slowly becomes buried under layers of indifference, resentment, frustration, boredom, or anger.

How does your garden grow? Tending love and gardens takes work. We must make the time and effort to demonstrate our car-

ing every day in small ways, consistently conveying the importance
of those closest to us. We mustn't assume they know of our feelings
or that we'll come back to them tomorrow. We can't afford to
postpone our love, for without this daily attention, our caring relationships, just as the neglected garden, shrivel and die.

Caring behaviors are simple, positive, specific, and doable in a
day. These small acts convey potent messages to our loved ones,
unmistakably communicating our love. Commit today to do one
loving act toward someone you care about—whether it be your
spouse, daughter, father, or a close friend—and savor the response.
Throw your arms around your child and give him or her a big
hug and kiss and watch your child bloom. It's never too late
to start.

Bill had always believed his son and daughter knew how much
he loved them, yet he seldom told them or showed this love. After
Jason died, Bill was racked by guilt and regret over not having
demonstrated more of his caring for his children. Do your loved
ones know you care? If you wonder at all, have the guts to ask
them, and when they say yes, ask them what you do or have done
specifically that let's them know. If they hesitate or can't name anything, you have your answer.

You likely have intense feelings about those people closest to
you. Are there important things you have not said to them? Is
there anything you want to share with any of these people? Is
there any misunderstanding or hard feeling you wish to clear up?
Is there something you wish to write down or record in some way
about your life?

The following exercise will help you express your caring to
those who count. You may want to review your responses to the
Life Review awakening exercise in Chapter 4, determining if
there is anything else you need to include as you complete this
exercise.

## LOVE LETTERS

*Time to screw up your courage and say the things you've meant to convey for years. Sit down and write a letter to each of the three most important people on your list. Be honest about your feelings, what you admire or love most about them, any "unfinished business" you may not have dealt with, or anything else you believe is important. You may have questions you wish to ask. What have you learned from them? How have they contributed to your life? Do not censor yourself or hold back. After you finish each letter, think about sending it to the person. Do you have any hesitation to communicate your feelings directly? If so, what is your reluctance? Will the person be surprised by anything you have to say? Assume this to be your last contact with each one. Be sure to convey whatever you need to say to prevent later having to live with the guilt and regret of not having done so.*

Karen discovered she had a recurrence of cancer, now having spread to her spine. At first stunned by the news, she quickly recovered and became even more determined to fight her illness. As a nurse, she realized her chances of surviving had decreased tremendously since her original diagnosis.

Karen stopped working. She talked with Frank and her children about her condition. She began addressing problems with her husband, making definite plans, and developing a legacy for her daughters. "Even though I plan to beat this, facing my end has given me the confidence to speak up and tell people what I feel and need. I'm asserting myself with Frank, and though he balked at first, he's become more responsible in helping me around the house and with the kids. He's scared too, and we both see how my illness has actually brought us closer."

When I spoke with Karen about this exercise, she had already determined who was most important and had written letters to her husband, daughters, family, and friends. She actively communicated to each how much she cared, and she worked to resolve any unfinished business and to answer any lingering questions.

Greg realized from his auto accident and the awakening exercises how superficial his relationships were. In developing his Personal Life Plan, he saw his relationship with Susan as the most important in his life. How could he have let all their surface conversations pass for intimacy when there were so many important things to talk about? Although he was frightened about opening up, he was determined to learn how to develop closer contact with her and other people in his life.

Russian author Dostoyevsky wrote of this pain, "I am convinced that the only Hell which exists is the inability to love." Greg, like many others, had come to see relationships in terms of *getting* something to fill the vaguely understood emptiness within. He had given love only on the condition that he got something for it, whether sex, praise, security, or comfort.

With all the energy he had put into developing his image and career, he had spent little time cultivating his capacity for emotional closeness. "I'd been so caught up in my career and success I never gave myself time to explore myself or my relationships," Greg said.

Endings and loss push us to finish unfinished business. Often we feel compelled to tie up loose ends, to tidy up our emotional house, yet often we wait until some distant tomorrow.

David, too, had "unfinished business, things he had feared doing and had put off doing for years." Having grown up in the family business, he liked speaking in business terms. David talked about his near-death experience: "I felt like I was going out of business." Taking this same metaphor, we spoke of all the things he wanted to do to take care of loose ends before "shutting his doors."

This meant, David, like all of us, had to confront those very things he feared. "I don't know if I'm ready to tell people how I really feel about them," he said. "I've never been very good at expressing my feelings. I've just expected my family knew how I felt, given I've provided for them well over the years. That's how my father showed he loved us; he would buy us things."

David continued, "The only thing getting me to consider this is nearly dying on the operating table. I don't want to die, like my father, never having told my wife and kids how much I love them. It's this thought that drove me to write these letters and to risk exposing my feelings. I don't know why something so simple seems so difficult."

"What's so frightening about telling those closest to you how you feel?" I asked, wanting David to look more closely at his fear of vulnerability.

"They may confirm my basic sense that all they value is what I give to them, that my true worth is what I provide and not who I am. That really scares me. They could confirm my worst fear." His voice shook as he talked about his fear.

"You could also discover the opposite. Your wife, kids, and friends may also tell you how much they care about you apart from your money. Wouldn't you have preferred your father had taken this chance and told you how important you were?" I asked.

David hesitated a moment, lost in thought. "Yes, I would have. It would have meant a great deal to have heard him tell me he loved me. He never said it, and I live with that every day, wondering how he really felt." Pausing again, he reflected on his words. "I don't want my kids to have to guess about my feelings for them. I am going to give out the letters and then talk to them about wanting to change our relationship. I want to do more with my wife and kids. I'd like to take more time to see them and have fun. It's not too late to change."

Do your loved ones have to guess how you feel about them or do you tell and show them each and every day? Will you be remembered as a kind and loving person by your survivors?

David used these lessons to become more involved with his children. He cleared the slate, so when the time came, he could "close the doors" on his life feeling clear and content.

Karen, Greg, and David all decided who was most important in their lives and began to act in ways to deepen their relationships. Their willingness to honestly share their feelings and needs, to become emotionally transparent, drew those around them closer. Their behavior clearly demonstrated their commitment to a stronger loving and relating.

## THE COMMANDMENTS OF LOVING COMMUNICATION

Next to our actions, our words express our love most clearly. Do your words tell those close to you of your caring? Are your actions supported by and consistent with what you say to those dearest to you?

Expressing love involves more than just saying, "I love you," or other simple declarations of devotion. Loving communication includes the words we use every day, in our every expression and interaction. Deeper love means using words to build and enhance, support and nurture, to consistently convey our tenderness and affection.

Survivors often become more loving in their communication. In my years of working with individuals and couples, I have discovered a higher quality of communication to be founded on 10 essential principals, or what I call commandments. Let these principles guide you in your verbal expression of a deeper love.

*First Commandment: Quiet Inside*

Take just one moment and reflect on how much it means to be fully understood by someone. The ultimate expression of love is listening, the first foundation for effective and intimate communication.

Listen well. If you do nothing more, listen fully to those you love. This is the most important and difficult task of loving another. Philosopher Paul Tillich reminds us, "The first duty of love is to listen."

Good listening begins with not talking, either vocally or subvocally. You cannot listen fully if you are interrupting, talking, or going over in your head all the mistakes the speaker is making or your arguments about what is said.

Concentrate completely on what the other is saying—actively focus your attention on the words, ideas, feelings, and actions. You must hear all of this to truly understand what the person is conveying.

You can listen faster than a person talks, so use this rate differential as an advantage to stay focused and on track. The rate of speech is roughly 100 to 150 words a minute and thinking 250 to 500 words a minute. This difference provides you with more time to concentrate and think back over what exactly was said to get the message right.

This rate differential can also work against you. You have to avoid the temptations of mentally arguing with the person who is talking to you. If you're preparing your rebuttal or counterargument, you are not listening.

The idea is to clear your head and heart while listening, being fully present and receptive—essentially becoming an empty vessel. You can think and feel, but leave your thoughts and emotions aside for the moment. Try to push your ideas, fears, anger, and worries away momentarily so you can be fully engaged and present to the speaker.

*Second Commandment: Quiet Outside*
Find a quiet place to talk. In addition to clearing internal noise, set aside major external distractions.

Don't try to talk about important topics or issues with the children present, in the company of friends or family, with the TV blaring, or while reading the paper, using the computer, writing a letter, and so on. Create a physical space where you are completely available. This allows you to offer the other your full attention.

*Third Commandment: Listen with Your*
*Eyes and Ears*
Pay attention to more than just the words you hear. Look into the other person's eyes so your attention is anchored on them and nothing else. Look at the speaker's hands, body, face, and mouth.

Remember the most important communication is nonverbal and expressed by cues given off by the body. To listen fully, you must hear the person's tone of voice, inflection, pace, and volume, while also observing how the person's body is reacting. Is he sitting on the edge of his chair, looking away, smiling, speaking quickly, or standing with hands on hips?

Body language is the subtlest, most overlooked, yet most powerful form of communication. Often these nonverbal cues give us away, projecting the true feelings in our messages. I often encourage people to pay close attention to their and others' nonverbal messages. Without knowing it, we frequently react more to the nonverbal cues than the content of the words themselves. When communicating, try to appear on the outside the way you want your partner to feel on the inside.

We will sometimes give and receive mixed or confusing messages. In some cases there is a contradiction between a person's words and actions. When this happens, ask for clarification. "Pam, you say you are angry right now, yet you're smiling and laughing at the same time. I'm confused. How do you really feel?" If the person doesn't recognize the inconsistency between words and actions, gently point it out and try to reconcile the contradiction.

In this example, Pam might be able to see the mixed message and provide a more congruent message, "I didn't realize I was laughing. I do that when I'm angry because I get uncomfortable when I express frustration. I guess I try to soften what I say with a smile. Thanks for pointing that out. Yes, I am angry at you for coming home so late and not calling." In situations where the person can't recognize the inconsistency between words and actions, simply respond to what is said while mentally logging the contradiction.

### Fourth Commandant: Be Direct

Be direct in expressing what you think, want, need, and feel. I always recommend we make statements; don't ask questions. Statements are a much more direct way of communicating than asking questions. Many people use questions having little to do with what is being asked.

For example, "why" questions are often disguised "shoulds." "Why didn't you call me last night?" could easily be heard as "You should have called me last night." This can quickly lead to the listener becoming angry or defensive.

### Fifth Commandment: Take Responsibility for Yourself

Only focus on what you can do to improve communication. Resist the temptation to blame the problem on your partner.

Take responsibility for your part of the interaction and communication. You as a sender or receiver have some responsibility in the exchange. Focus on improving your part and not on what the other person may or may not be doing wrong. You can only change your contribution in the exchange.

## Sixth Commandment: Stay in the Present

Stay present in the moment. Do not start talking about the past or future unless it is pertinent to the immediate conversation. I have seen more conversations go off track when someone suddenly shifts and brings in some past behavior to make a point or win an argument. This is deadly. Avoid it.

Keep your focus on the present feeling or thought. This will keep the communication centered and directed to what is immediate and important.

## Seventh Commandment: Focus on a Single Issue

When discussing difficult problems or issues, take one at a time. Try not to fall into "kitchen sinking," where you begin throwing in every issue but the kitchen sink.

It is difficult enough to deal well with one issue, let alone trying to sort out and resolve a number of them. Keep your conversation on one problem at a time. You can always set aside time to come back to other issues later.

## Eighth Commandment: Cleanse Your Talk

Avoid the mental as well as the verbal roadblocks discussed in Chapter 7. If you think them, they will seep into your language and others will react as negatively as you do. Try not to think them, and if you do, do not let them show up in the message you relate to your loved ones.

Let's review the common communication errors that will destroy any chance for effective, loving communication. Review this list to be sure you are not using any of these methods.

- Stop overgeneralizing. Become aware of the statements using absolutes—such as always, never, every time, all, and so on.
- Be specific in your words and expressions. Good communication is clear and precise.
- Don't use exhorting, moralizing, preaching messages, as is done with *should, ought, have to,* or *must.* Avoid giving orders, directing, or making demands. "You have to listen to me right now." "You should go to church more often." People generally do not like being told what to do. These messages often cause the receiver to do the opposite of what you demand.
- Make positive requests for things you want and need from others. "I'd really appreciate your taking me to work tomorrow" is usually much better received then "You have to take me to work."
- Drop the labels, judging, criticizing, blaming, and making negative evaluations of others. "That is very immature of you." This type of message stops communication in its tracks, with the receiver either becoming hurt, angry, or defensive.
- Make direct statements about your feelings, needs, and wants.
- Do not analyze, interpret, or diagnose. Unless requested, offering interpretations and diagnoses is usually not appreciated. "You feel this way because your mother never paid attention to you as a child." Let the other person decide what the underlying reasons or motives may be.
- Speak only for yourself.
- Unless you are a college professor teaching a class, avoid giving logical arguments and talking down to someone to try to influence or convince them of the "rightness" of your position. Lecturing, teaching, and becoming didactic in your messages is not effective.

- Do listen. And then listen some more.
- Be careful not to placate or be overly consoling or reassuring. This sometimes downplays or denies the other person's feelings. For example, a close friend comes to you to talk about the sudden death of her father, crying, needing to share her feelings, and you say, "It's OK, don't cry. You have no reason to be upset, your father is in a better place now."
- More importantly, listen and reflect the feelings you hear. Allow others to experience their emotions.
- Don't threaten, warn, admonish, or give ultimatums. This is usually telling people what consequences will occur if they do or do not do something. "If you don't start talking to me more, I may have to find somebody that will." "I'm not going to tell you again, if you do that, you'll be sorry."
- Do allow others to learn from their own experience. People need to learn for themselves; let them.
- Stop trying to "fix it." Unless someone explicitly asks, do not offer advice, provide solutions, or suggest answers to problems people bring to you.
- Do listen well. In most cases, people are just looking for someone to listen to them so they can come up with their own solutions. Set your ego aside and listen. Otherwise, you risk alienating people while responding to your need to fix their problem.

*Ninth Commandment: Be Empathic*

Be empathic; try to get in the other person's skin and think what he or she thinks and feel what he or she feels. It is difficult to move out of our own frame of reference and see a situation from another's eyes, yet this is an essential skill in high-level empathy. We must be able to identify, but not necessarily agree, with the other person's experience to help that person feel understood.

One way of building your empathic skill is by active listening—really tuning in to what the other person is feeling and experiencing in the moment. This involves clearing your mind, carefully attending to the other person, and then being able to accurately reflect back their words and emotions, thereby validating their experience. This lets the other person feel that you really understand. This skill takes practice but can pay powerful dividends.

*Tenth Commandment: Make No Assumptions*
Do not read minds. If in doubt about how your partner thinks or feels, don't assume, ask! This one error, of thinking if people really knew or loved us they would know what we think or feel, is responsible for more emotional suffering than any other. When you are unsure whether someone understood you, clarify your message. On the other side, if you are guessing about what someone said or meant, stop and seek clarification.

Now let's put some of these principals to the test. Sit down and read through the following exercise with a loved one. Read it aloud and then go back and try the exercise itself, keeping in mind what you have learned. The test is whether at the end of the exercise, both of you feel understood.

## MIRRORED REFLECTION
*This is a tried and true communication exercise best done with a friend or loved one who is interested in learning how to communicate more effectively. Sit comfortably in a quiet place and plan to spend 10 to 15 minutes paying attention to how you speak and listen to one another. Decide who will start as the sender and the receiver of the message. You will reverse these roles later. The task for the sender is to send a brief message, one or two sentences, using all you have learned in this chapter. The message will be neutral or positive in content and begin with an "I" statement, preferably*

*stating a feeling or preference. Remember to keep the Ten Com-*
*mandments in mind in formulating the message.*

*As the receiver, the listener, your task is different and perhaps*
*more difficult. This is the active listening we referred to earlier.*
*You are to be a mirror and reflect back what you hear. There are*
*two parts of the message to listen for and reflect back to your part-*
*ner. The first and easiest is the content of the message. For exam-*
*ple, you would reflect back by paraphrasing the message, "I hear you*
*appreciate my taking you to dinner last night." The harder part*
*of mirroring involves hearing and feeding back the feeling part of*
*the message. This is seldom directly stated and may be interpreted*
*by nonverbals, such as tone of voice, inflection, pace, volume, or*
*body posture. If the feeling part of the message is unclear, ask*
*for help. As the listener, do not respond with your thoughts or*
*feelings without first asking the sender whether you understand*
*the complete message. Only then can you change roles and send*
*your message.*

*If you're interested, take your communication to a deeper level.*
*Using the same process you just learned, begin talking about some-*
*thing important to you that you've never talked about before. Then*
*have your partner do the same, allowing your conversation to*
*progress in depth and intimacy. As your talk deepens, symbolize*
*your increasing intimacy by touching your partner lovingly. If for*
*some reason your partner is reluctant to talk about something, don't*
*press. Stop where you each feel comfortable.*

Let's look at a successful example of this process. The sender
will begin the dialogue using the principals of reflection.

Sender:    "I really appreciated your sitting down with me
last night after dinner and talking about your work
situation."

Receiver:   "I hear you appreciated my taking time to talk to
            you about the problems I'm having at my job. You
            seem to like that I talked to you."

Sender:     "Yes, that's what I said. I feel like you understand
            me."

This simple exercise practiced daily can help you and your loved one communicate more effectively. Effective communication is not easy, but by learning potent ways to verbally communicate with others we deepen our emotional bonds and strengthen our relationships.

Take these tools to craft a love that knows no tomorrow. To deepen our relationships, to leap to the next level of love, we must have the courage to risk our vulnerability, to surrender ourselves by speaking and acting in ways that powerfully convey our caring. We will smile more, laugh more, touch more, listen more, for at this next level our every action and word shouts who we are and the importance of others in our lives.

So ask yourself, who is truly important to you? Whomever you claim as significant, show this by your undivided attention, for that person will feel your love only when you make him or her the center, the focus of your life. Once we awaken to the impermanence of our precious life, all there is left to do is to love, and love well.

## REACHING OUT: JOINING COMMUNITY

Life's tragedies drive home the critical importance of belonging to something larger than ourselves. If you long for high-quality relationships and quantum connections with others, developing a strong sense of community becomes an essential next step.

Community makes us whole by serving as a place of awakening to a deeper sense of who we are. It challenges us to be authentic, teaches us to love, and heals our emotional wounds. At its best, communities help us overcome our fears, tell us the truth about ourselves, and provide the safety necessary for us to thrive and grow. Everyone yearns for this sense of community in some way.

Trauma survivors sometimes find their emotional and social ties initially shattered by their traumatic experience, only later reconnecting to those important relationships available to them. A loving, supportive community is an integral part of healing and a high-quality life. Beyond your individual personal relationships—such as family, friends, neighbors, colleagues, and coworkers—expand your embrace to include others.

Can you reach out beyond your immediate family and friends? Are you open to other relationships that can provide you with nurturing and care? If you can be open enough to notice, community lives and breathes all around you.

Every being we encounter holds his or her own unique expectations, dreams, desires, and demands, which enrich the texture of our lives. The person who does your hair, delivers your mail, serves you lunch at your favorite restaurant, your family doctor, priest, massage therapist, dentist, all play an integral role in your life. These people add a sense of familiarity, support, and belonging that's easily taken for granted.

Karen, after first being diagnosed, was not receiving the emotional support she needed from her husband. Initially afraid to share her condition with her daughters, parents, and friends, she turned to a breast cancer survivor support group for solace. The group helped her initially adjust to her condition and gain the courage to speak openly to her family. She still maintains contact with a few of these group members when she has questions or needs their special presence. She also turned to her church for their prayers and spiritual guidance.

Being in and drawing from a community of others is an inescapable part of a full and meaningful life. Gathering to observe ceremony, ritual, festival, parade—these are the ways we share the rich cycles of both life and death, the deepening of the experience of life together.

Assess your own support system. Do you have the people in your life to provide for your physical, emotional, mental, and spiritual needs? If so, be appreciative. If not, reach out to others—whether they be extended family, new friends, church or spiritual partners, support groups, clubs, or social service organizations—to respond to your needs. Open your arms wider to a community of loved ones.

# CHAPTER NINE

# Burning Life Brightly

*If we really want to live, we'd*
*better start at once to try. If*
*we don't, it doesn't matter,*
*but we'd better start to die.*
         *—W .H. Auden*

All of us die, yet not all of us live.

Are you living your life fully? Or are you just existing, getting through another day? When did you first fall out of love with life? How did we move from childlike wonder and joy to the deadening cynicism of adulthood? At what point in your life did your feelings dull and life lose its color?

If you are like most people, you are aware of only a small fraction of your potential feelings and sensations. You possess sensations of pleasure and excitement only waiting to be explored. As psychologist William James suggests, "We are only half-awake. Our fires are damped, our drafts are checked. We are making use of only a small part of our possible mental and physical resources. You have a host of positive feelings—like joy, warmth, wonder, and enthusiasm—that you rarely experience, yet reside within you."[1]

Many are dulled to their experience. Remember Roger, caught in the quagmire of his own sexual compulsivity, desperately searching for a way to "feel" anything? Emotionally anesthetized, he clung to sex as the only way he knew to feel alive. Numbed by alcohol and his cocoon of defenses, Roger found himself cut off, isolated from those things that make life worth living.

Yet there are different kinds of life-threatening experiences, some obvious, some subtle. Thoreau described the most common life-robbing existence as one of "quiet desperation"[2] where we are blocked from living life fully. Many of the same walls we build for protection keep us from living our life more vibrantly. What stands in your way?

Do you use the "being tough" wall, the "denial" wall, the "work" wall, the "too busy" wall, the "food" wall, the "holding it all together" wall, or the "alcohol" wall to stifle your vitality? These are the same barriers separating us from ourselves and those we love. The thought of death demolishes these obstacles, leaving us wide open to life.

Keeping your mortality in mind, recall Life Lesson 5, *Create a new appreciation for the elementals of life.* Survivors live every moment fully, each day as if it were their last. Senses are sharper and attuned so color is brighter, smells more pungent, feelings heightened, and sounds wondrous. Being psychologically reborn, survivors see everything with fresh eyes, hear with young ears, and feel with tender hands. Life is new and exciting, a wonder to behold.

Like a criminal facing execution at dawn, a brush with death powerfully concentrates the mind. Even simple chores take on new pleasure, mundane tasks a different joy. I recall a cancer patient telling me, "Since surviving cancer, it feels like I've gone from seeing the world in black and white to color. Everything's different. I see and experience everything more intensely. It's like when I was a child, seeing and touching everything for the first time."

Those who appreciate life's impermanence provide us with powerful lessons on how to live with greater vitality and passion every day—if we are willing to listen. They offer glimpses of the insights people gain as they face the loss of all they've ever known. By keeping our end in mind, each moment takes on new importance and meaning.

We learn to more fully appreciate and experience life. Go back to the awakening exercise where you were diagnosed with cancer and have only a few months to live. As you contemplate your short time on this earth, write down all the reasons that you wish to stay alive. What are you most thankful for? You might put down hundreds of things—love for your friends and family; having new experiences; your wish to fulfill old dreams, learn more, meet your grandchildren, belly laugh, meet new people, make love, cry, travel, or enjoy nature.

We want to grab all life has to offer us, to drink it in until we are intoxicated by the experience. These are the experiences, some lasting only minutes, that made you feel most alive. If you were to take the time to reflect, choose the one moment of your life you would want to live over again. What would it be? The answer reveals the essence of your experience. Savor this essence.

Contrary to popular belief, the best minutes of our lives are not passive, receptive, and relaxing—though these too are enjoyable. The most intense moments of our lives occur when our bodies, minds, and hearts are stretched to their limits, often in the most trying of circumstances.

These experiences are not necessarily pleasant when they occur. The marathoner's muscles aching and lungs exploding as he crosses the finish line, a pianist trembling at a concert's climax, sobbing at the loss of a loved one, the wonderful pain of childbirth, a first sexual encounter, the surgeon sweating as he saves his first patient—these optimal experiences demand our full involvement in the moment.

Yet how much of your time and energy is devoted to the very activities and experiences you list as so meaningful? Even if you do participate in these experiences, are you open to enjoying them fully? When they take the time to notice, many people are bewildered by the fact they can't quite taste, can't quite touch, can't quite smell, can't quite feel, can't quite hear, and can't quite see. With our bodies numbed by the dizzying distractions of our busy minds, our perceptions and senses become the poor cousins of our experience and are blunted and tamped down.

We process our lives secondhand, through our minds, by thinking and not experiencing. Our experience is further diluted by films, television, computers, and radio—living in an alternative or virtual reality. We are spectators, sitting in a darkened audience, watching our life as if it were a movie, one step removed from our existence. It is like we have cotton in our noses and ears, fogged glasses, and our skin is wrapped in gauze. All is dulled, artificial, stale—we are numbed to our experience.

David spoke of losing his zest for living. "Before my heart surgery, I was too rushed to live. My schedule was packed and I was rushing around just trying to keep up. Looking back now, my whole life just seems a blur." He was realizing how much of his life had been devoted to managing his myriad responsibilities, having taken little time to simply savor the living of it.

"Sure, we have been to some of the finest restaurants, traveled to wonderful places, played on some great golf courses—living what many believe to be the finest of lives. The funny thing is, I never took the time to really enjoy any of it. My mind was usually on my business, my civic obligations, or what I had to do when I finished what I was doing."

Like many of us, David had lived what, from all outward accounts, was a full life. In fact, most people who knew him envied his lavish lifestyle. He wanted for nothing. Yet given his push to have more, to continually focus on higher goals and achievements in the future, he never enjoyed what he did have. His experience of his wonderful life was dampened by his drive to have and do more.

To wade in the stream of life, we must take off our shoes and socks. To live fully, we must shed the layers of intellect, analysis, and judgment blocking us from our experience by slowing the mind. Quieting the mind means less thinking, worrying, fearing, judging, hoping, calculating, trying, regretting, controlling, and distracting. When we reflect on our greatest moments, we see our mind is as still as a glass lake.

Nietzsche, an existentialist, expresses this shift in a beautiful passage:

> Out of such abysses, from such severe sickness one returns newborn, having shed one's skin, more ticklish and malicious, with more delicate taste for joy, with a more tender tongue for all good things, with merrier senses, with a second dangerous innocence in joy, more childlike and yet a hundred times subtler than one has ever seen before.[3]

There are two secret skills to falling back in love with life. First, you, like the inner child you've long ago abandoned, must return to your senses, to the very roots of your experience. Rip away the intellectual filter clouding your perception. Get off the ropes and into the center of life's ring. Standing in the center, you are able to experience life directly, firsthand, and there learn the second skill—living fully in the present. For it is only by rediscovering our full sensual experience in the moment that you can fully embrace what you love.

## EMBRACING LIFE:
## COMING TO OUR SENSES

Psychiatrist Fritz Perls said, "Lose your mind and come back to your senses." It is time to embrace life through our senses, our connection to the world around us. The emphasis in this chapter is to regain our love for life by focusing on our feelings and sensations and less on our mind and intellect.

Though our intellect is invaluable for analytical tasks involving rational problem solving, it can block our feelings and experience. As we discussed in Chapter 5, our mind can impair our emotional functioning, dull and dampen our emotional fires, and blur the richness and color that is life. Awareness gives us the power to resuscitate the senses so often numbed by the mind.

I recall the one lazy spring afternoon watching my cat, Teger, preparing to pounce on an unsuspecting bird. He was a lesson in full concentration. Effortlessly alert, he crouched, gathering his relaxed muscles for the spring. No thinking about when to jump, nor how he would push off with his hind legs to attain the proper distance; his mind was perfectly still and focused on his prey. There were no thoughts of what would happen if he missed his mark. He saw only bird. This beautifully natural process was only interrupted by my last-minute intervention.

End-point encounters often shock the mind and body, opening new ways of thinking and feeling in the world. Survivors frequently report experiencing a new awareness of their senses and emotions, having their childlikeness restored after years of mental confinement. Years-old defenses crumble, egos fall away, pretense dissolve, leaving a only freshness and newness. Liberated, survivors practice a new self-forgetfulness.

Recall Robert, the arrogant fund manager who battled back from a serious plane crash. "If anyone had ever told me that I could get so excited over simple things like walking on the beach or playing catch with my daughter, I would have laughed in their face. I feel like a kid. Everything is new and fresh. My new attitude has opened a whole new world to me."

Trauma survivors frequently report heightened perceptions and sensation. You, too, can sharpen your senses with some focusing and practice, making you more alive to the world around you. At first you may experience the benefits of one sense at a time. As you practice the following exercise and become more attuned, you'll become aware of your total experience. Do this exercise and take in your total sensations as you go about everyday activities such as washing dishes, cooking dinner, playing with the kids, or walking your dog. All these simple tasks can become tremendously exciting if you treat them as sensory escapades.

### SHARPENING YOUR SENSES

*Find a quiet place where you will not be interrupted. Sit in a comfortable chair or on the floor. Close your eyes. First be very still and listen closely to the sounds around you. Listen to them one at a time and then all together. Don't try to judge or identify them, just listen. You will hear an ever-changing symphony of sounds that is always there for you to enjoy. With your eyes still closed, shift your attention to your sense of touch. First feel the air against your skin, the texture of your clothing, then anything within your reach. Next, slowly stand up, open your eyes, and move around the room, touching things in the room, fully attending just to the feeling of the things you contact.*

*At another time find someone who is willing to help you in an experiment. This would involve a close, trusted friend or family member. Close your eyes and let that person lead you through the house, introducing you to different things to touch, smell, taste, and hear. Continue this blind exploration outside. Go to a tree, a rock, the lawn, water, a face—all new experiences when you are blind.*

*You will likely feel a bond of trust develop as you continue this exercise. If your partner wishes, trade places and lead him or her on the same experience.*

Other activities help you tune into your senses. Howard Lewis and Harold Streitfeld offer a number of sensory-centering exercises in their book *Growth Games.*[4] When we open to our senses, we appreciate the simple pleasures of life. A toothy smile, a cool summer breeze, slow dancing, the warm sun on our face, a sensual massage, spitting seeds from a sweet watermelon, a fish striking our line, the sweet smell of a bouquet of flowers, a steamy shower, or stroking the soft fur of our cat.

Death survivors open their arms to embrace life. By focusing our attention, we appreciate the elementals of life, cherishing life's most simple pleasures. Joseph Goldstein reminds us, "The receptive quality of love allows every experience to enter us, to touch us. It allows us to be touched by the wind and sun, by other people, and by each part of ourselves, by the trees, the birds, and all of nature. It is the practice of intimacy with all of life."[5]

What moves you? What feeds your heart and makes you feel deeply? Is it your child's laughter, a spectacular sunset, great music, or ecstatic dancing? Maybe it's those moments when things just seem to go well and you're filled with gratitude. Pay attention to the things that shake you up, send chills up your spine, tickle your funny bone, move you to tears, or make the hairs on your neck stand up. These are the things that fill your heart and soul.

Enliven your existence each day by doing the smallest things more slowly; eating a peach, for example. First hold the peach in your hand firmly with your eyes closed, sense its temperature and texture, its shape. Is it perfectly round, can you feel its contours? Touch the flesh to your face, your hands, and your arms. Get to know the smell by breathing in the fragrance. Now run your tongue slowly across the skin. Cut the peach in slices while listening to the sounds. Hold the pit in your mouth and feel the texture, then spit it out. Take one section and eat small bits slowly while savoring the flavor. Eat one slice at a time and, if possible, feed someone a slice slowly, and then let that person feed you. Do the same kind of exercise with any little thing any day.

Tune in to your senses to rediscover the pleasure and joy in your life. Let yourself experience the biggest pleasures from the smallest things. As you do, you will also recognize how much of this ability is linked to how well you stay in the present moment.

## LIFE IS SHORT: MAKING EVERY MINUTE COUNT

Life is but a succession of single moments. If we can't live single moments, we can't live life.

We run too quickly through our lives, missing out as we rush toward the next important thing we have to do. Or we make the opposite mistake by living in the past, constantly reviewing what could have been. Are you searching desperately for the handbrake in order to halt your dizzying schedule and reclaim your life?

Steven Levine, in his book *A Year to Live,* suggests the practice of "taking a day off."[6] In this interesting and at times frightening exercise you contemplate the world without yourself in it. Like George Bailey, the affable main character in the film *It's a Wonderful Life*, you would walk the streets as though you are not there, as though you had died yesterday. You focus on a world without you. From this exercise our worries and regrets fall away as unimportant.

If you recall the movie, everything George Bailey wants from life—money, travel, career—seems to elude him. In an act of desperation, George prepares to leap into the icy waters but is saved by a cherub who allows him to gaze at his life outside of time. Only when George is allowed to glimpse the pattern of his life as a whole do his isolated actions add up, revealing the meaning and connection from seemingly random acts. Saving his brother from drowning, taking over the family business, marrying, having children, helping friends, working in the community—all seem to be ordinary occurrences. Combined, these ordinary events take on great meaning, becoming a chronicle not of regret but of a wonderful life.

The degree to which we torment ourselves with future worries or past regrets keeps us from living life now. We get stuck dwelling in the past or panicked about the future while losing our sense of the here and now. And every moment thrown away or wasted is one more moment taken off our all too brief life. When you add them up, how many of these moments, days, months, or years have you squandered?

Pay attention. How often do you wholly experience what you're doing at the moment? Your focus is divided. You're in conversation with a dear friend yet find yourself thinking about a missed deadline. You take a quiet walk in the beautiful countryside but obsess about problems you left behind in the city. You have a romantic candlelit dinner with your spouse and find yourself distracted by the dirty dishes you have yet to do.

Being present requires emotional acceptance—standing still and feeling it. In the simple act of slowing down and becoming more aware in the moment we allow ourselves to interact with our senses and the world. We can ground ourselves in the present moment to become totally immersed in our experience.

When was the last time you did something for the final or only time? Do you think you would approach your next meal, conversation with your child, round of golf, or lovemaking session differently if you knew it was your last? What would happen if you entered each moment, each meal, each conversation, each prayer, each romantic encounter as though there would never be another? When was the last time you paid attention to something as simple as your breathing? If you've ever choked or couldn't catch your breath from running, you know the feeling of panic. Yet we take such a simple act for granted. But if your breaths were numbered, how would you experience the breath you're taking right this moment? Breathing would instantly take on a whole new importance.

A tale is told of two Zen monks on a pilgrimage to a distant monastery. Walking through the wilderness for many days, the monks arrive at a river. Here they observe a beautiful young woman sitting by the water's edge.

"Excuse me," the woman says to the monks. "I don't know how to swim. Would you be able to help me cross this river?"

"Of course I will," says the first monk and without hesitation lifts the maiden up and carries her to the other side.

The two monks walk the rest of the day in silence, finally reaching a place to stop for the night. Over the evening meal the second monk says to the first, "You know the rules of our order forbid us to have any contact with women. It was wrong of you to talk to that young girl, let alone pick her up and carry her."

"Oh, her," says the first monk. "I put her down back by the river. You've been carrying her all day long."

Like the monk, we carry thoughts or desires along, dividing our attention. Your mind is split and focused on a thousand different things. Many people pride themselves on being multi-taskers, able to do several things at once. In fact, in counseling Type-A executives with their cardiac-prone behavior, one of the targets of treatment is what we call polyphasic behavior.

Polyphasic behavior is where an individual carries on several activities simultaneously. He is listening to the television, reading the paper, shaving, and talking to his wife, all at the same time. This level of mental and physical activity, though arguably efficient, is highly stimulating and stressful. These individuals are time pressured, trying to fit more and more activity into less and less time.

Though this ability can perhaps make you more productive, it keeps you from slowing down and simply enjoying the moment. We rush through our lives trying to cram more stimulation into every minute, all the while enjoying each moment less. The sign of a healthy mind, an integrated person, is the ability to do the opposite of multitasking, to be fully in the present. This ability is seen in a *single-experience focus*, where your full attention is anchored in the present moment.

In this age of perpetual noise and stimulation, we must learn to concentrate our attention to achieve this single-experience focus. This involves training ourselves to slow down, to stop and attend to the current moment, clearing away the din of internal and external distractions. We are bombarded by these distractions every moment—our own worries about the future, regrets about the past, other's expectations and demands, the babble of news items, and other largely irrelevant information.

Greg lived a life of rising expectations. Working harder, accomplishing and accumulating more and more, he found himself less and less satisfied. The problem arose not from his escalating goals but because he had lost the enjoyment of the struggle along the way. He had become so fixated on his spiraling expectations, he ceased to derive pleasure in the present. Greg was lost in a frantic search for happiness, only to forfeit any chance for contentment. I recall Greg wrestling to free himself from his golden handcuffs.

"I can't remember the last time I actually enjoyed what I do as a lawyer. Financially my work has been very rewarding, but I've been miserable for some time. I'd seriously consider giving it all up if I thought I could be happier. I've built a small fortune, yet I don't know what to do with my life to make it more fulfilling." Greg was caught on a constantly whirling vortex of rising expectations, seeing no way to escape.

He felt he could not stop and enjoy the simple things in life. Always eyeing his next goal, he was constantly looking at the next reward or accomplishment to complete his life. Happiness and gratification were always just around the corner.

Like Greg, we lose sight of the moment, yet the moment is all we have. While our body sits in the present, our mind forgets the past is over, the future not yet. In this forgetting we spend our lives imprisoned in our past or fixated on our future. We become stuck in the grief, glory, shame, guilt, and resentment of long ago. Just as sadly, we fuss and fantasize over the future, a time not yet here.

Next to reclaiming our senses, the ability to exist in the present moment is the most important skill for fully living and loving. Be in this moment; see the potency of the immediate. We must relearn the skill of being present-centered, where our full attention is concentrated in the here and now. One simple cue I've used to help people center themselves daily involves their placing a colored paper on the face of their watch, their car's rearview mirror, or their computer screen. This single visual cue acts as a frequent reminder to become present to their life.

This takes practice, though we can easily observe this in young children and many survivors. I sat just the other day watching my goddaughter playing for hours on the beach—enjoying nothing more than the texture of the sand and chill of the ocean water. By being fully present, we afford ourselves constant opportunities for new discoveries in our lives every day.

I believe the essence of happiness is pausing to savor the gift of our present moments. For me this means taking delight in the successive moments of my day, from morning walks to showering, eating a breakfast of fresh fruit and cereal, taking a few minutes to write, talking to clients, laughing with a friend, to the last moment's of consciousness, snuggling and talking with my wife. Happiness and contentment aren't in the past or future but in the morning's awakening, lunch with a friend, an evening walk, reading a bedtime story, or soaking in a hot tub.

How do we start practicing attention on an everyday level? We begin by paying more heed to the seemingly regular events happening all around us—by living our daily life with fuller focus on ordinary activities. To be a master of attention means to experience everything for the first time or, as the poet William Blake describes it, with the doors of perception cleansed. In such a state of awareness no action is trivial. There is enjoyment in the simplest of acts—washing dishes, playing with the cat, watching clouds pass by. In the small, we know we will find the great. In the ordinary, we discover the extraordinary.

Philosopher Thomas Mann reminds us, "Hold fast the time! Guard it, watch over it, every hour, every minute. Unguarded it slips away, like a lizard, smooth, slippery, faithless, a pixy wife. Hold every moment sacred. Give each clarity and meaning, each the weight of thine awareness, each its true and due fulfillment."[7]

To help you in this quest, try the following exercise to center your attention in the present. Understand that remaining present requires practice. Even with practice, you are likely to be able to stay in the moment only for brief periods. As with some of the earlier exercises, use a friend as a guide if that will help you.

BECOMING PRESENT

*Survivors often demonstrate an enhanced ability to stay present-centered, to tune in to the moment. For others, it is a skill that is learned with practice. First understand that remaining in the pres-*

*ent is a taxing discipline that can be maintained for only a few minutes at a time. Be patient and if your mind happens to wander, notice this and refocus your attention back on the exercise. Just take your time and do the best you can.*

*We can begin to anchor ourselves in the present by attending to our external world, our bodies, and our feelings. We will begin with focusing on the external world. Find a comfortable place where you can sit and not be interrupted. Eliminate any external distractions and be sure to turn off the phones, fax, and pager. Let your eyes roam around the room and focus on just one object at a time. Keep your attention on that single object; describe it in your mind. Take your time and look at just one item at a time. After a few moments, shift your gaze to another object and remain focused just on that object, appreciating its distinctive features—its color, texture, size, shape, pattern. Listen to the sounds of the room, again, just becoming aware of each sound as it comes into your consciousness. Become aware of anything you feel or smell in the room.*

*Now fully focus inwardly on your body. Close your eyes and put your full attention on what is happening physically. Tune out the external and go internal. If your mind or attention wanders, notice this and gently bring your focus back to your body. Start with your breathing. Notice your breath as it passes in and out of your body. Stay with your breathing for a few moments. Then put your attention on your right foot and toes, focus on the inside of your foot and toes, then the skin around it, the temperature, weight, and so on. Notice everything about your foot. Next, move to your left foot and toes and follow the same sequence. Slowly repeat it for every part of your body to the top of your head. Feel the pressure of the clothes on your body. Scan every part of your skin, inside and out.*

*Lastly, tune in to your feelings. Pay attention to your emotions in the moment. Do you feel calm, sad, happy, scared? Whatever you feel, try to stay focused and present with the feeling. Sometimes*

*these emotions will grow and recede, like waves; other times they*
*may become more intense. Observe and experience these feelings,*
*just as they are.*

You have just used external objects, your physical body, and
your emotions as anchors for your attention. Each works well to
keep you present and locked into the "now."

Oftentimes, staying in the present feels calming and relaxing.
We often do this without thinking. How many times have you
felt better or more alive simply by losing yourself in an activity
or experience? We lose ourselves by fully focusing on a crackling
fire, a lover's whispers, inspiring music, intense exercise, an en-
thralling book or movie, a baby's heartbeat, or the sound of waves
on a beach.

I have found physical exercise to be a wonderful way to stay
present-centered. Though intense exertion, such as running, surfing, skiing, tennis, rock climbing, and swimming, is absorbing,
even lighter exercises also anchor us in the moment. A brisk walk
provides pleasure and enjoyment as long as we remain fully focused on our experience. How we approach the activity, whether
we are "in" the moment, ultimately determines the quality of the
experience.

If you think about it, we don't remember days, we remember
moments. Your most memorable moments in life were likely
those times when you were caught up in the experience, swept
away by the sights, sounds, touch, smell, or taste of the time.
Abraham Maslow, in *Toward a Psychology of Being,* spoke of peak
experiences where we feel most alive, tuned in, balanced, clear,
and least encumbered.[8]

To experience that, we must clear the cluttered mind, open
our heart and senses, and throw ourselves into the moment. This
can occur in times of intense emotion, such as at a birth or death,

in the throes of passionate sex, while wandering in the stillness of virgin forest, or in the quiet of a contemplative trance. Allow yourself to be totally absorbed in the moment.

Mihaly Csikszentmihalyi, in his book *Flow: The Psychology of Optimal Experience,* discusses how a person in "flow" is fully invested in the moment and completely focused so there is no room for distracting thoughts or feelings. One loses track of time, self-consciousness disappears, and engagement is total.[9] This usually involves being actively involved in something enjoyable that also stretches the person intellectually or physically. Flow experiences provide flashes of intense living against the dull backdrop that is daily life.

You may have experienced this feeling when you were playing golf, skiing, mending a quilt, surfing, parachuting, dancing, singing, or gardening. It is not so much what you do, but how you approach your activity. Csikszentmihalyi suggests you experience this sensation when your goals are clear, feedback is relevant, and your skills are balanced for the task. All of these conditions facilitate full immersion in the present moment.

By being attuned sensually and in the present, people are more alive and vibrant. Many who have faced traumatic life crises become more spontaneous, less inhibited, more direct and honest, centered, open to new experiences, and ready to live to the hilt. Children, like survivors, point to a deeper experience of living.

## TAPPING THE CHILD WITHIN

As adults, many of us have lost our enthusiasm for living and find ourselves emotionally bankrupt. We have lost touch with the joy and excitement within us.

How can we recapture some of the lost fun and joy of our childhood? Where can we find some of the excitement and pleasure of our youth? What can we do to turn up the light and burn our lives brightly?

You've learned to clear your mind of muddle and negativity, open your heart to feelings, recover your lost senses, and focus your attention in the present. To enjoy our lives, to live our time fully, we must let go of the ties that bind us. Cut loose the anchor of reason and do one thing today that someone would label "foolish."

Author Joseph Heller points the way: "When I grow up I want to be a little boy." Children do all of the above without thinking about it. It is their natural state—curious, spontaneous, open, uninhibited, loving, present, and honest. These are the gifts of children if only we can accept them. They are present and available, once we make time to enter their world.

This involves stopping our busy schedules long enough to learn from our children. Take time to play with your children. Let yourself share their joy, wonder, curiosity, fear, excitement, sadness, hurt, laughter, silliness, and "childishness." If your children are grown, volunteer to be with children.

David had difficulty letting go. Bound by the thick ropes of his mental rules, he continually struggled over who he believed he "should" be, always trying to fulfill his need to be perfectly appropriate. "Since my bypass, I've made a point of taking more time with my children. At first I found myself impatient with them and was disappointed that I couldn't enjoy them the way I wanted to. I kept expecting them to act like adults, just like my parents had done with me. I would get irritated just because they were being kids, acting their age," he said, embarrassed. "I'm glad I was able to see what I was doing so I could change the way I was treating them.

"I didn't understand why the children were so quiet around me. Now I see they were afraid that I would get frustrated and correct their every behavior. I wasn't letting them be who they are, just kids." David realized how he was following in his parents' footsteps, how he was parentifying his children—transmitting the same expectations he was now trying to correct.

"Now I try to listen and watch more, meaning I bite my tongue when I feel I have to correct them. I will still discipline when it's needed, but more I'm trying to let some of their silliness rub off on me, to put myself in their place and feel what it's like to be a child, an experience I missed. David Jr. and Eva are both helping me. They get me to wrestle and tickle them. It's almost as if they recognize I need to play more," David said laughing. "They are my real therapists. Every time I let myself cut up with them I feel somehow younger, like I've recaptured a few minutes of my childhood."

David, through his new relationship with his children, was opening himself to childlike experiences and playfulness long dormant in his life. Challenging the god of reason, suspending judgment, abandoning his seriousness, he vowed to be preposterous, silly, outrageous, to play the clown with his kids and family as an experiment. "I want to let my children see a different side of me, that it's OK to have fun. I never saw that growing up."

We agreed he would do something no one would expect of him. He came back the following week with a smile on his face. "I came home from work the other night with a new puppy. The kids had been asking for one for years but I'd never agree. They were so excited, we spent the rest of the evening playing with him." David was more energized than I had ever seen him. He was turning up the light, burning his life more brightly.

Shake up your own life by doing something totally unexpected today, perhaps something you've considered or talked about for years but put off. For example, serenade your wife over dinner, bear hug your longtime yet standoffish best friend, visit a casual acquaintance in the hospital, skip work and take your little girl for a pony ride—break completely out of character. Let yourself be a kid again just for the laughs.

These are all things we must strive for, and the thought of life's impermanence aids us in our striving. By remembering that our time is limited, we recognize the importance of children, of our own lost, buried child, and the wish to honor both. Use these skills you've learned to love yourself and others more deeply than before and to live your life more brightly. Turn up the light.

PART THREE

# THE SEARCH for PURPOSE

# CHAPTER TEN

# The Meaning of Meaning

*Meaning makes a great many things*
*endurable—perhaps everything.*
                                    *—Carl Jung*

It's been said death is God's megaphone telling us to use our time wisely. In the end we look back over the sum of our lives to see what we've left behind. In the end, only love and meaning matter.

What is meaning and why does it become more important as our time grows short? For people who've faced death, the world is no longer unquestionably safe and secure. The real possibility of tragedy remains etched in their consciousness, fostering a significant transformation in their lives. Survivors recognize the preciousness of time and are compelled to meaning-making or, in other words, creating greater value in their lives.

Survivors sometimes struggle in their journey from the world of meaninglessness to a life "full of meaning." In reordering their priorities, by deciding what is most dear in life, they develop a newfound appreciation for living.

The jarring awareness of our end, the thought of our own demise, turns us to seek deeper purpose in our lives, as seen in Life Lesson 6: *Focus on the importance of purpose in life.* Because life can end at any time, it cannot be taken for granted; we must decide what truly matters and make choices. This very awareness leads us to value life more, to make sure our time counts for something.

In this quest the question arises, where has all the meaning gone? Why is it becoming more difficult to find meaning in today's world? Though people of earlier ages were beset by many problems, purposelessness didn't seem to be one of them.

In the past, meaning was supplied in many different ways. For one, citizens of past cultures were so preoccupied with meeting their most basic needs of food, water, and shelter that they had no time to luxuriate in a deep contemplation of their existence. Their focus was on the immediate, the "little" questions of daily survival and not the "big" questions of meaning and purpose.

They lived close to the earth, were caught up in tilling the soil, planting seed, raising livestock, harvesting, cooking, cleaning, and having and raising children. Strong bonds to family and community grounded them in clear roles and responsibilities. Their lives were deeply rooted in nature, meaningful work, and family.

Another early influence on meaning was the religious worldview. The religions of yesterday supplied answers so comprehensive that the questions of meaning were obscured. But much of the meaning derived from traditional religious teaching has vanished, or at least is questioned. Many people have left the church or have abandoned conventional religious teaching in search of other paths.

In addition to these influences, the nature of work itself has changed. Our work, with few exceptions, no longer supplies a strong sense of satisfaction or purpose. Many individuals in various occupations feel they experience little sense of purpose or creativity on their job, but rather consider themselves a mindless cog in some larger machine. For most, work has lost its intrinsic value and no longer seems worthwhile.

Many people have difficulty knowing what to do with the little free time they find. One small example of this phenomenon is the "Sunday afternoon neurosis," the ill ease that settles upon us after the rush of the busy week subsides and we encounter our own inner void. As the multitude of outside distractions subside, we find ourselves lost and confused.

Our roots have become diseased and weak. As technology interrupts our connection to nature, families disintegrate, religious beliefs come into question, opportunities for meaningful work diminish, and leisure time increases, we find ourselves suffocating in an existential vacuum. What are we to do with our lives to provide a deeper sense of purpose?

Many of us find our happiness or meaning from a patchwork of different activities. We golf, run, read, dine out, watch movies, attend church, work—anything to occupy our time. Yet often we're lacking any unifying purpose for our existence. The common threads tying these activities together in any satisfying way have unraveled.

As long as our enjoyment flows piecemeal from different activities, no matter how enjoyable, we are still vulnerable to the pain of purposelessness. Even the happiest family, the best friendships, the most successful career eventually runs dry. At some point children grow up and leave home, friendships fade, our spouse dies, and jobs end, leaving us susceptible to the concerns of later life.

To approach the deepest level of satisfaction, to reach as high as humanly possible, we must find a unifying purpose for our lives. Meaning provides a unifying network of experiences where all activity, our past and future goals, "make sense." This overarching vision provides background and texture to our lives. There is a feeling of congruence. Everything somehow fits together.

For years, philosophers and social scientists have told us that life has no inherent purpose, that our values are relative, and that chance rules the day. Even if we accept this conclusion, it does not mean that life can't be *given* meaning. It's one thing to accept that life in general has no meaning; it's another to accept this as an inevitable fact in our own lives.

As Victor Frankl expressed, "Meaning is something to be found rather than given." As we look around us every day we see people, some seemingly contented and others fighting against insurmountable odds, striving to find a purpose and direction for their lives. All face a common challenge. We each experience the normal human urge of wanting to feel our life mattered, that we have passed on something of ourselves of lasting value—a term psychoanalyst Erik Erickson refers to as *generativity*.[1]

In many ways it doesn't matter what we strive for—as long as our quest is compelling enough to order a lifetime's worth of psychic energy. With purpose, we feel empowered, turned on, excited about life. This added dimension carries us beyond the trivialities of every day to the next level of living. The challenge might involve providing missionary work to backward countries, educating and counseling battered women, giving support to the needy, tending an award-winning garden, raising healthy children, or finding a cure for cancer.

So there is a formula for finding a purpose for our lives. As long as our mission provides clear objectives, a means of becoming involved, and paths to action, any goal can serve to provide purpose to a person's life. But to find meaning we must first understand what it is we seek.

## THE MEANING OF MEANING

What does meaning mean? Like love, *meaning* is a word that's elusive and hard to grasp firmly. The word *meaning* refers to sense or coherence. A search for meaning implies a search for coherence. To better understand the term let's examine how we apply it in our lives.

The first leg on the journey to meaning is deciding our goals. What's most important in our lives? Death poses the question, What am I to do with my life? Reexamine your responses to the earlier awakening exercises and contemplation of your life and death. Consider your Personal Life Plan—what goals did you identify as most important for your life?

People who find their lives meaningful usually find a goal or mission they identify as challenging enough to take up all their energies, one that is significant to their lives. They have achieved a unifying vision or purpose for their existence.

What matters most is not the specific goal itself, though we may argue some are nobler than others, but the person's level of focus, energy, and enthusiasm brought to the task. One example was Mother Teresa who invested all of her energies to help the helpless. Her life was given purpose by her undying devotion to God and the unconditional love she offered to those around her.

Another example was Adolf Hitler, a man who devoted his life to the single-minded pursuit of power. In this pursuit, he brought untold suffering and death to many millions of people. Though dramatically different in their goals, each achieved comparable levels of inner purpose in their pursuit. They each created a single purpose unifying many of their goals and activities. We each can do the same by clearly identifying own passion—whether a cause, profession, or goal—and pursuing it wholeheartedly.

A second leg on the journey to meaning is resolve. What is your level of commitment to what you define as important? It is not enough to simply discover a purpose to unify your goals; you must also carry through with action to accomplish what you identify as significant. What is important is not so much whether you have actually accomplished what you have set out to do; rather it matters more that the effort is expended to reach the goal instead of being wasted or diluted. We all know those sad individuals who know exactly what they need to do yet just can't seem to muster the energy to do it.

The third and final leg on the trek toward meaning is unanimity of purpose. A person who knows his or her desires and then strives with purpose to accomplish them is a person whose thoughts, feelings, and actions are congruent and, therefore, in inner harmony. Contentment requires connecting with a totality that is beyond the apparent contradictions of daily life, a totality that reconciles these contradictions. Such persons have found their raison d'être. This is indeed what we speak of when we refer to achieving deeper meaning.

I recall a client of many years ago who came to see me guilt-stricken over the crippling of her son from a car accident. Marge, a divorced mother, had been driving and lost control of the vehicle, leaving herself and her son injured. While she recovered fully, her teenage son, Danny, was left paralyzed from the waist down and confined to a wheelchair. Marge was emotionally devastated, questioning whether she could even continue with her life.

When I asked her whether she had considered suicide, she replied, "I'll be honest. I've thought about killing myself just to relieve the pain of living with what I've done. When I talk about being miserable, Danny stops me and tells me how much he wants to live and not to feel bad. He's the only reason I've kept going and am here today."

Danny had been able to keep his life meaningful. How could we help his mother discover new meaning for her life? As we talked over the intervening weeks, Marge was able to appreciate her son's example of someone who had been able derive meaning from his limited life. At one point I asked her to imagine herself at age 90 lying on her deathbed looking back over her life. "Tell me how you would feel about your life."

She sat silently for a few moments and replied, "Well, I'd always wanted children and I had Danny, who's been a true joy in my life. Then this car accident happened and left him crippled. Yet even with his handicap, he has provided me with so much. I've provided for Danny and helped him over his life, at times when he was helpless and couldn't help himself. I feel good about having made his life fuller and, I hope in some ways, a better human being."

Marge tearfully continued, "Now I can see how my life has had meaning by what I've provided for my child. I know I've done my best for my son and as long as I am alive I will be there for him in whatever way I can." Viewing her life from her deathbed, she was able to see that her life did have meaning even with all of the suffering she had experienced.

Individuals who are in harmony, no matter their age, health, what is happening to them, or what they do, know their psychic energy is not being wasted on fear, despair, self-doubt, guilt, worry, or regret. That energy is being constructively employed to live a full life. These individuals have come to terms with who they are and are directing their lives toward something greater than themselves.

Look at your own life. Are you needlessly burning your energy in negative emotions and self-doubt or directing it toward something larger than yourself?

*Goals, resolve, and unanimity integrate our life and give it meaning.* A person who has reached this state, whose consciousness is so ordered, need not fear the unknown or even death. Every living moment makes sense, is enjoyable and fulfilling. How do we achieve such a sense of single-minded direction and purpose?

## THE PURPOSE OF PURPOSE:
## UNDERSTANDING THE IMPORTANCE
## OF MEANING

If you look closely you will find many people have a unifying purpose that justifies the things they do every day—a goal or set of goals that drive their every feeling, thought, and action. For some, it may be to better themselves or their children; for others, to help humankind; for still others, to gain fame and riches. This meaning-seeking activity provides people with a sense of purpose, a goal upon which all other goals depend.

How do we order these goals? What drives us to define the purpose for our life? Many psychologists, most notable among them Abraham Maslow, have explained this phenomenon. People develop the concept of who they are and what they need to achieve in life according to a predictable sequence of steps. Maslow refers to this stepwise progression as a hierarchy of needs.[2]

Imagine all of humankind standing beneath a large, beautiful tree. As we stand on the ground beneath this tree we come face to face with our first and most basic need of self-preservation and subsistence. At this level, the meaning of life is simple; it is safety and survival. We must eat, drink, stay warm, and satisfy our basic physiological needs in order to stay alive. It's hard to focus our attention upward when we are rocked by waves of hunger, thirst, cold, or pain. People of earlier societies largely remained within the shadow of these primary physiological needs.

Only after these most basic survival needs are met do we begin to look up at the tree's lower branches to satisfy our social needs. As we ascend to these branches we expand our meaning system to embrace the values of community—the family, neighborhood, friends, religious and ethnic groups.

I've spoken with many people who have lounged in the lower branches. Having focused their lives pursuing personal happiness, many have neglected the higher branches, never looking beyond their comfort and security. Satisfaction of our most basic needs alone does not give meaning to life. The majority of people settle in the second stage of development, lounging in the lower branches, where their survival needs are met and their focus is on the welfare of the family, community, or the nation.

The satisfaction of basic needs or at times preoccupation with worldly matters sometimes serves more as an obstacle than an aid to further growth and development. Having found satisfaction of personal desires, sensual enjoyment, material security, achievement, and personal ambition, many are left still left wanting.

I've heard the question innumerable times from people who have met their survival and social needs, "Is this all there is?" "This mate?" "This job?" "This house?" "This life?" Each individual is stirred by the notion that time is running out and that somehow life should be better or somehow different.

Take a moment to better gauge the role meaning plays in your life with the Meaning Self-Test.

The importance of meaning increases with the years. You may find yourself, like so many others, tripped up in midlife by the realization your life is half over. Perhaps you're one of those doting parents whose children have left the nest, the woman whose biological clock is ticking loudly and who has never had a baby, the wildly successful careerist stuck in a spiritually numbing job, the tired lover who discovered romance is not the answer to unhappiness. All find themselves wondering what to do with their lives while longing for something more.

Yet with this longing, few undergo the struggle and effort to reach the next level. They see the higher branches but do not climb. Unlike physical aging, spiritual and emotional maturity do not develop automatically; they exist only as a possibility. They must be intentionally and consistently pursued via commitment, effort, and struggle.

## MEANING SELF-TEST

Please respond to the items below by answering True or False.
When you have finished responding, you may check your answers with the guide that follos.

| | | |
|---|---|---|
| 1. I have clear, important goals in my life. | True | False |
| 2. I enjoy my free time. | True | False |
| 3. Whenever I am off work, I use my time in a satisfying manner. | True | False |
| 4. I look forward to my retirement; or, if I am retired, I am enjoying myself. | True | False |
| 5. My life is boring and dull. | True | False |
| 6. I often feel lost without any direction in my life. | True | False |
| 7. I frequently wonder about why I exist. | True | False |
| 8. Most days of my life seem important. | True | False |
| 9. I have never felt like I had choices in life. | True | False |
| 10. I find life exciting and stimulating. | True | False |
| 11. I feel like I have the energy and resolve to achieve the important goals in my life. | True | False |
| 12. My personal existence is meaningless. | True | False |
| 13. My work gives me a sense of value and purpose. | True | False |
| 14. If I died today, I would feel my life had been wasted. | True | False |
| 15. I have a purpose in life that makes everything I do make sense. | True | False |
| 16. Death terrifies me. | True | False |
| 17. I have little to look forward to in the future. | True | False |
| 18. I have never seriously considered suicide. | True | False |

19. I feel good about the legacy I will leave behind. True   False

20. My life is worthwhile.                      True   False

*Directions for Scoring:*

Consider these questions and your answers to develop a better understanding of the role meaning plays in your life. To score, follow these steps. Score 1 point for each *True* response to questions 1, 2, 3, 4, 8, 10, 11, 13, 15, 18, 19, and 20. Score 1 point for each *False* response to questions 5, 6, 7, 9, 12, 14, 16, and 17. Total your score.

If your score was 0–7, you may lack a clear sense of purpose or meaning in your life. This could be due to your age and stage in life, a limited attention to this aspect of your being, or distractions you allow that have blurred your vision. If you scored 8–14, you have developed some mission or value to your existence and likely understand the importance of meaning to the quality of life. If your score was 15 or higher, you have discovered the significance of meaning and have a defining direction for your life. You have clear goals, resolve to accomplish them, and your activities align to unify your purpose. Whatever your score, you may find it helpful to examine your individual responses to determine how to focus your energies and increase a sense of meaning in your life.

---

As our physiological and social needs are satisfied, we are freed to climb upward to pursue greater development of the self. Fear drives many back, for the upper limbs are thin and high. Pulled by the need for growth and self-improvement, some look inward. At this stage, the main desire in life becomes picking the riper fruits born from the actualization of our personal potential.

Only a very few climb higher to risk reaching the highest limbs and the sweetest of fruits, interdependence. The final reach involves integration with other people through interdependence rather than independence. The single, highly individualized person willingly merges his interest with those of a larger whole. This involves an expanded meaning system that transcends the individual and involves an idea, cause, work, or transcendental entity.

Not everyone progresses through these stages in ascending order. Many people in the world may never have the opportunity to get off the ground, to escape the tree's shadow. When survival demands are so insistent and you are struggling to satisfy hunger and thirst, you cannot focus much attention on anything else, nor is there sufficient energy left to move upward and support the goals of family and community. Even those of us fortunate enough to climb to the lower branches are left to decide how high we wish to go. What could move us to climb further?

Carl Jung once wrote that the great question in the later part of our life is whether human beings are "related to something infinite or not." Only a very few climb to the third or highest level of need, to forge a unity with universal values. I have seen death survivors jolted to the higher levels of consciousness, to a greater need for meaning and identification with universal values and principles.

## MEANING: AN EXISTENTIAL LIFE PRESERVER

Our mortality calls us to meaning, attempting to waken us from our spiritual slumber. Have you awakened to hear the call, the sounds in the night? One of Grimm's lesser-known fairy tales reminds us to heed the call of our end.[3]

In this story the spirit of Death accosts a giant along the highway and starts to lead him away to the Kingdom of the Dead. The giant proclaims he is not ready to die and the two titans struggle, with Death getting the worst of it. With Death beaten and bloodied alongside the road, the giant ambles off to carry on his business.

After a short while a young man happens by. Seeing the beaten victim lying in the ditch, he revives him with kind words and a sip of whisky from his flask.

"Do you know who I am?" Death asks when he is recovered. The youth shakes his head, having no idea who he has helped. "I am Death. I spare no one. Someday I will call for you as I do for all living beings. But to show how grateful I am for your help I will send my messengers to warn you before I come for your soul. This way you will have time to prepare."

The young man is delighted at his good fortune and goes merrily along his way, knowing he can carry on with his life as he wants until the messenger arrives.

Soon he comes to a town with a tavern and gambles all of his money away. Even in poverty he knows he will not starve, for Death has promised to send his messenger first.

Before long he moves on again, continuing his merry ways. As time passes a string of sorrows visit him. As he overcomes each challenge he becomes gravely ill and his friends are sure he will die. He weathers his illness confident none of these trials will lead to his demise. Death has promised, after all, and he soon recovers.

One day this carefree youth is cavorting as usual with his comrades when he hears a knock at the door. The young man opens it and finds Death waiting at the doorstep. "Follow me, your hour of departure has arrived," the hideous presence says.

"But that can't be!" cries the boy. "None of your messengers came!"

"Indeed they did," answers Death. "One after the next. First I sent poverty, then a string of sorrows, then sickness. And besides all these, did not my brother Sleep visit you every night and make you lie in your bed still and silent? All these beings were my messengers. You simply did not recognize them."

As we saw in Chapter 3, death's message comes in many forms, if only we will listen and heed its call. Too often we become distracted by the promise of things outside of ourselves. What distractions are muffling your own spiritual summons?

Many people still believe contentment comes from obtaining or achieving what we want. Contentment only grows out of our capacity to accept what is. For every desire you fill, another always follows on its heels. Whether you have a house in Aspen or more money than Bill Gates, the feeling of fullness still keeps slipping away.

Getting what we want does not promise happiness. This is a lesson as old as time yet incredibly difficult to accept. Why? Because everything we are ever taught tells us to believe in the magic of success and fortune. We have been programmed to strive to "have it all," only then realizing it is "never enough." Take time for the following exercise.

### Magic Wand

*Take a moment and reflect on what has been your quest or fantasy. What if you could wave a magic wand and have three wishes granted? Be honest. What would you ask for? Would your dream involve fame, riches, family bliss, status, or incredible power? What do you imagine would create your ultimate happiness? Be specific in your wishes and order them in priority.*

What were your wishes? Reflect on them being granted and the difference this would make in your life.

Now imagine you are a famous writer admired by millions. Notaries from around the world seek your counsel as you are considered one of the greatest minds of your time. Rich, titled, in good health, head of a happy family, lord of a vast estate, it would seem you had it all. Would all these gifts be enough to bring you contentment and happiness?

These gifts were not enough to make Count Leo Tolstoy happy.[4] In fact, the great novelist, besieged by fame in the midst of his full life, was so dissatisfied with it all he found himself falling into deep despair. How could this be?

Here was a man who had fulfilled more dreams than most of us can ever imagine, yet all of these seemingly compelling events were taking place on the outside, on the surface of his life. At age 50, deep inside, his spirit was dying.

Tolstoy wrote in *The Confession*:

I felt like something had broken within me, on which my life had always rested, that I had nothing left to hold on to, and that morally my life had stopped. My state of mind was as if some wicked and stupid joke was being played upon me by someone. One can live only so long as one is intoxicated, drunk with life; but when one grows sober one cannot fail to see that this is all a stupid trick.

Tolstoy was drowning in a sea of emptiness, grasping for an existential life preserver. He retells an ancient tale he believes sums up his plight: A traveler is running across a field pursued by a ferocious beast. Coming to an empty well the traveler starts to climb down the well to safety. Halfway toward the bottom he realizes that a hungry dragon is waiting for him below with open mouth. To save himself he grabs a small branch protruding from a crack in the well's wall.

Hanging helplessly, the traveler begins to feel his strength fade. To make matters worse a mouse appears above him and starts to gnaw through the branch he is clinging to so desperately. As the tired traveler hangs between these two oblivions, he glances up and sees a cluster of berries growing nearby. Reaching out he picks several and swallows them with gusto. How sweet they taste!

This, Tolstoy tells us, is the picture of the human condition. Hanging in the well of existence between the monsters of birth and death, we await our annihilation. While dangling, we pass time gobbling up the small pleasures that fall to our lot. Then the branch snaps and we plunge into nothingness.

We persevere, as Tolstoy portrays, and eventually see through the false promises of society's values and rewards. As we face the monsters of life and death we must ask certain questions. In his words, "What will be the outcome of my life? Why should I live? Why should I do anything? Is there in life any purpose which the inevitable death which awaits me does not undo or destroy?"

He remained stranded in a nether world between these two worlds for some years before finding his renewal. Tolstoy discovered that our mortality has been gifted to us to shake us loose from our over involvement with superficial concerns, to push us back to our spiritual roots. He writes, "I can refer to this by no other name than that of a thirst for God. This craving for God had nothing to do with the movement of my ideas—in fact, it was the direct contrary of that movement—it came from my heart."

Tolstoy's futility in the midst of a rich life ultimately was recognized for what it was—a vacuum of purpose waiting to be filled. Now was the time for him to begin a different journey, a journey of the soul. He continued his search by ignoring the honors showered on him from across the world. Following in the footsteps of his workers, he dressed as a peasant, grew his own food, lived a simple life, while providing money and spiritual guidance to all who asked.

Three decades later, after many more dark nights of the soul, he died while making a final pilgrimage to the monasteries of Tibet, where he lived out his days in service to others and in meditation. In his own words he "never regretted for a moment this time in my life when I am privileged to pursue my inner spirit."

Tolstoy's midlife conversion is not unique. Many of the people I've talked with over the past three decades have shared at least some of his experience and the impulse to grow by simplifying and eliminating the distractions cluttering their life. Usually in midlife when the sounds of death grow louder, the nourishment of the soul becomes paramount. Have you noticed an inner yearning as your soul beckons you to listen?

Of course, not all of us hear the call. To listen well to these inner urgings, you must first make time for quiet, turning down the din of external distractions. Whether by meditation, prayer, reading devotions, or simple solitude, our inner voice will guide us. But we must be willing to heed the call. For by running away we miss the opportunity to stand fast and deepen our lives. We see the message not as threatening but as a godsend, a catalytic agent generating greater spiritual growth and development.

Urgent life crises raise the question, "What is the true purpose of my life?" Each of us in our own way discovers answers in a deeper engagement in living with unified purpose, in striving for greater meaning. Let us now explore some of the more common paths to meaning.

# CHAPTER ELEVEN

# Living on Purpose

*Meaning is something to be found
rather than given. Man cannot
invent it but must discover it.*
　　　　　*—Victor Frankl*

Peple need meaning.

As time becomes more precious, meaning becomes as essential to our souls as air to our bodies. With a sense of purpose our lives become "better," possessed with greater fullness, zest, and passion.

The question of meaning takes many forms. Why do I live? What is the reason for my being here? What shall I live by? Why was I put on this earth? How do I make sense of my existence? What is the meaning of my life? We have all faced these difficult questions at some point in our lives.

Perhaps the best way to understand the importance of meaning is to observe the pain caused by its loss. Psychoanalyst Salvatore Maddi describes meaninglessness as, "a chronic inability to believe in the truth, importance, usefulness, interest, or value of any of the things one is engaged in or can imagine doing."[1] In this, we understand why trauma survivors place greater emphasis on discovering meaning in their lives.

Recall Bill who, after the death of his son, discovered a purpose for his life born out of the pain of his loss. He developed a mission, dedicating himself to caring for his daughter and children in need.

Human beings require meaning. To live without goals, values, purpose, or ideals generates considerable distress. In many cases, it is disabling. In its most severe forms, it can be terminal. Victor Frankl, the Viennese psychiatrist and concentration camp survivor, reported that those concentration camp victims without a sense of meaning were unlikely to survive.

So our challenge is clear. How do we who need meaning find meaning in a universe that has no inherent meaning? How do we begin the search for a life-sustaining sense of purpose?

As the Catholic monk Thomas Merton wrote:

> First of all, although men have a common destiny, each in-dividual also has to work out his personal salvation for him-self.... We can help one another to find the meaning of life, no doubt. But in the last analysis, the individual person is re-sponsible for living his own life and for finding himself. If he persists in shifting his responsibility to somebody else, he fails to find out the meaning of his own existence. You can-not tell me who I am, and I cannot tell you who you are.[2]

A sense of purpose is seldom handed to us. If you do not know your own identity, who will help identify you? What are we then to do? Are there no guidelines, no directions, no values? Nothing is right or wrong, good or bad? How do we decide our path to meaning, discover our reason for being?

## THE DIFFERENT PATHS TO MEANING

The simple truth is we all need to matter. Yet we're left to face the task of finding a direction for our lives. Having reached the age of majority, we search to believe in something greater than ourselves, to discover our reason for being.

We have talked about the significance of establishing clear goals, the need for resolve in pursuing these goals, and the importance of being fully engaged in the task. How do we proceed to construct our own meaning—in developing a purpose sturdy enough to support our life? Take a moment to contemplate your own life's purpose.

### LIFE'S MEANING

*Take some time to ponder your things and accomplishments and their true value in the end. Survivors often reorient themselves, turning away from things they formerly valued—status, wealth, titles, and prestige—and questioning the true meaning of their lives. How much time do you still spend trying to win out over others, rushing to save time or get ahead, working to impress, outdoing someone, or gathering and maintaining your possessions? Stay aware over the next week how much of your time and energy flows into this activity, and how much you focus on meaning-making pursuits.*

*Next, reflect on those things you are involved in that bring your life meaning and purpose. In a single sentence or two, simply state your reason for being. What sustains you through difficult times? When your life becomes unmanageable or feels out of control, what have you used as your anchor? When the time comes for you to leave this life, what would give you strength? Would it be your values, people, religion, or your sense of self-worth? Make a list of your present priorities and carefully study each one. As you did in developing your legacy and Personal Life Plan, reflect on whether you are living your present life consistent with what you say is important. Take steps to align your life to achieve greater congruence.*

People bring meaning to their lives in many ways. The path often involves work, pleasure, creativity, causes, altruism, self-actualization, self-transcendence, and spirituality and religion. Though this list is certainly not exhaustive, it captures the more common ways people have discovered a sense of purpose in their lives. Take a moment and reflect on what gives your life meaning. Perhaps it is what you give to others through volunteering, the value you place on your career and family, your devotion and hard work to a worthwhile cause or in striving to become a better person. We are each left to discover our own unique path. Search these paths, and others, until you find your way.

*Worthwhile Work: Finding Our Calling*

Work, or constructive accomplishment, has long been considered a critical component of positive mental health. Clinically profound in its simplicity is the assertion attributed to Sigmund Freud that the healthy individual loves and works productively.

For too many, work is drudgery, "the daily grind," a travail. Yet meaningless work is opportunity squandered, for through work we define ourselves, even leave a legacy that adds meaning to our lives. Blue-collar philosopher Studs Terkel tells us work is a search, "for daily meaning as well as daily bread, for recognition as well as cash, for astonishment rather than torpor, in short, for a sort of life rather than a Monday through Friday sort of dying."[3]

Maybe you're among the fortunate who love what they do for a living. They're excited about their jobs and can't wait to get to work every day, describing what they do as fulfilling, satisfying, enjoyable, and gratifying. These lucky individuals have found a way to make a living from their passion.

If you found yourself in the situation where you only had a year to live, what would you change about your work? Would you quit, would you work fewer hours, change jobs, or take up a long-admired skill or hobby? I've spoken with more than a few professionals with advanced degrees who would like to have been carpenters or bakers. Have you found yourself putting aside interests because of country, social obligations, or family responsibilities?

When I ask this question, many people I speak with say they would focus less on material acquisition and the pursuit of power and prestige. Some people speak of a love of nature they allowed to lie dormant; others would return to church, begin writing, play the cello, or sit quietly by the sea.

Many seek meaning in what they do for work, yet few are successful in their pursuit. Much of today's work lacks opportunities for creative expression, intrinsic satisfaction, or identification with a larger whole. Jobs have become tedious, repetitive, lacking the sense of greater purpose needed by many workers.

I have counseled a number of people over the years who find themselves trapped in jobs that provide financially yet give little else. Some were caught in "golden handcuffs," earning whopping incomes yet trapped in spiritually bankrupt careers.

Claire, like many clients of mine, had achieved the American dream. Having fought her way to the top of her profession, sold her computer firm, and retired at an early age, she was lost in leisure, having no idea how to find a renewed purpose in her life. Like Claire, when many of us get leisure time, we don't know what to do with it.

Work adds purpose to our living. A vocation can be a calling, a way to make a worthwhile contribution or to leave a valuable legacy. My own calling—my purpose—is to help others reach their highest potential. Others find meaning tuning pianos, designing buildings, growing and distributing food, or nursing the physically ill. Happiness is loving what you do and knowing it matters.

Consider for a moment what you would do if you inherited a large fortune. Would you continue working? Three out of four people answer yes. And nearly everyone answers yes because they experience work's nonmaterial rewards—a sense of identity, community, and purpose.

As discussed by psychologist Mihaly Csikszentmihalyi, to experience flow or satisfaction in what we do we must find challenge and meaning in our work, seeking experiences to fully engage our talents. He talks about transforming mind-numbing tasks into meaningful work by setting goals, immersing ourselves in the task, becoming present, and enjoying the immediate activity. In such ways, we turn mindless tedium into mindful engagement.[4]

As you may have noticed, trauma survivors often practice the skills of flow or engagement. Their ability to be present, appreciate what they are doing, and enjoy the moment are all essential to meaning-making.

I recently met someone who created value in his work. Raised in a poor farm family in Mississippi, Shep was determined to escape his roots. An ambitious young man, he attended college and graduated from a top law school with the idea of landing a position at a "silk-stocking" law firm. Shep was right on track, excited about his work in corporate law. Shortly after he began his new job he had a life-altering experience.

He had traveled to a party with two of his best friends, all of whom had drunk too much. On the way home Shep was dropped off first. The next morning he discovered his friends were both killed in a car accident. After attending the funerals, Shep found himself reflecting deeply on his life. He had accomplished his early goals and was quickly moving up the firm's promotional ladder. He knew he could make partner in a few years, but to what ultimate end?

Several weeks later he walked into the senior partner's office and quit. "I knew when I did it I didn't have a job and that I would likely never find a position with more potential. But as I thought about it, I knew I wasn't going to be satisfied defending corporate fat cats the rest of my life. I had to do something different, something more challenging and meaningful." Though he was offered twice his salary to stay, Shep walked out of the office and never looked back.

"It was difficult at first. I was alone, essentially broke, new to town, and with few connections. I took out a small loan and opened my office. I decided to do criminal defense work and had to build my practice from scratch."

From these meager beginnings he has practiced criminal defense law for the last 30 years, helping those who could not afford adequate legal aid, winning landmark cases, and gaining the respect of his clients and colleagues. "I love what I do. I get excited every day when I get up to go to work. Looking back, it was the best decision I ever made."

How do you feel about your own work? In addition to monetary reward, do you derive inspiration, satisfaction, and a sense of purpose from what you do? Do you find it meaningful or meaningless?

*Pursuit of Pleasure: If It Feels Good. . .*

In the extreme hedonistic solution, the purpose of life is to live fully, to search for pleasure in the deepest possible sense. Pleasure is an end unto itself, the very reason for being.

One advantage of the pleasure theme is its elasticity, as it can include each of the other meaning-making schemes in its boundaries. Activities such as love, altruism, creativity, dedication to causes, all can be viewed as important because of their ultimate pleasure-producing qualities.

Dawn, a friend I met in college, fully believed and practiced this more extreme pleasure philosophy. Life had no meaning outside of the excitement derived from the immediate moment. In making decisions about her life, she only had to consider her prime directive, what will give me the greatest pleasure? All else was irrelevant. She smoked, drank, recreated with drugs and sex, anything that would provide a sense of enjoyment in the moment. There was little thought of the future or of others unless they promised some joy or fun at the time. The purpose of Dawn's life was simple: to live in a way that was continuously stimulating and astonishing. Dawn offers one example of pleasure as purpose.

Many people who adopt this pleasure orientation early in life temper their hedonistic pursuits as they age. I know myself the things I found intensely pleasurable at 20 barely interest me as I near 50. In our later years, we create a more moderate approach to pleasure. We love our leisure and enjoy the simple pleasures of travel, exercise, a golf game, movie, play, book, or superb meal.

We can still revel in momentary pleasures, yet more as a spice than the main course in life. Pleasure adds much to our existence, yet seldom serves as our sole purpose for being.

## Creativity Compels: Touched by Fire

We would all agree creativity brings meaning to our lives. To create something new or different, to make something of beauty or depth serves as a powerful antidote to purposelessness.

Many artists create despite personal handicaps or turmoil by wrestling vigorously with the demons of meaningless and despair. Crises pushed many artists—Van Gogh, Kafka, Galileo, Keats, Nietzsche, Woolf—to the edge of madness and stoked their creative fires.

Beethoven, at the age of 32 and in despair because of his deafness, is cited in *Suicide and the Meaning of Life* as saying that art kept him from taking his life. He wrote, "Little kept me back from putting an end to my life. Art alone held me alive. Alas, it seems to be impossible for me to leave the world before I have done all that I feel inclined to do, and thus I drag on this miserable life."[5]

Creativity need not be left only to the masters. We can take a creative approach to study, gardening, bookkeeping, learning, parenting, teaching—all can add something valuable to life. For many writers, creativity overlaps with altruism in their efforts to help others or improve the world.

An artist friend of mine has lived a tempestuous life. At times ravaged by illness, divorce, and alienation from her children, she persevered with art as her center, her healer. It served as her anchor in those storms, helping to maintain her moorings when nothing else could. She loved her painting because it provided her with a safe harbor, regardless of whatever currents swirled around her.

Much of the impetus for this book derived from my need to add depth and meaning to my life, with the hope someone reading it would be helped to live life more deeply. In this way, writing has made my life richer, more satisfying, and provided me with a greater sense of purpose.

### Dedication to Causes: Joining the Whole

Another important source of meaning is dedication to causes. Have you ever invested yourself in a cause? Are there any causes you would die for? What has stirred your own interests and focus—politics, family, religion, science?

The exact cause itself is often less important than our level of involvement. Will Durant, philosopher and historian, in his book *On the Meaning of Life,* wrote that involvement must "if it is to give life meaning, lift the individual out of himself, and make him a co-operating part of a vaster scheme."[6]

In his studies of eminent men and their notions of meaning in life Durant goes on to say:

Join a whole, work for it with all your body and mind. The meaning of life lies in the chance it gives us to produce, or to contribute to something greater than ourselves. It need not be family... it can be any group that can call out all the latent nobility of the individual, and give him a cause to work for that shall not be shattered by his death.

As we examine Durant's statements, we find dedication to causes combines several aspects. First, it contains an altruistic component where meaning is found by giving to others. It also includes the aspect of self-transcendence, where we "lift the individual out of himself," a common theme to meaning-making schemas. He also describes death transcendence, or becoming a part of "something greater than ourselves," and "that shall not be shattered by death." In this last element, he is talking about our need to create a legacy to leave behind, a way to defeat our mortality.

Bill, who had lost his son, Jason, became increasingly involved in finding greater meaning in his life with his cause of helping children. He began volunteering with many of his daughter's activities, at her school, soccer league, and Indian Princess program. He participated in the Big Brothers/Big Sisters program by adopting a little brother with whom he spent a great deal of time, helping him in school and sports. Bill joined the board of the Boys Club and provided financial support for their various activities. Even after retiring from his business, his life was busy and full.

"I finally feel like I'm making a difference in my life. Sure, it was great to build and sell a business, to be successful. But this is a completely different kind of satisfaction, one I've never felt before now," Bill said smiling.

Spurred by his son's death, Bill had kept his promise, to make up for the years of neglecting his two young children. He was

lifted out of himself by his work with kids, his giving even transcending death itself.

## Altruism: Giving Ourselves Away

Doing good makes us feel good. It focuses our attention outside of
ourselves and enhances our self-esteem.

Giving of ourselves, serving others, leaving the world a better
place to live in, participating in charity—all of these things have
provided life meaning for many people. We find satisfaction by
sharing our time, talents, money, and energy with others or our favorite cause. Such activity is a worthwhile pursuit. Marion Wright
Edelman states, "Service is the rent we pay for being. It is the very
purpose of life, and not something you do in your spare time."

In my work with cancer patients I have been privileged to observe the importance of purpose. They often experience a deeper
sense of meaning and live their lives more fully and with less emotional distress than those devoid of purpose.

The type of meaning they experience, whether religious or
secular, was less important than that they experience it. Of these
types, altruism, the belief that it is good to give and be of service
to others, was one of the most common and powerful sources of
empowerment.

Karen dedicated herself to helping others with cancer. David
became more involved in his philanthropic endeavors to see how
his financial giving touched others. Both wanted to give something of themselves in service to others and, by this, fill themselves
with a sense of purpose and direction.

## Actualizing the Self: Fulfilling Our Potential

Another source of purpose in life is the belief that we should strive
to actualize ourselves, dedicating ourselves to realizing our full potential as human beings. Though popularized in contemporary

psychology, self-actualization is actually an ancient concept expressed by Aristotle in the fourth century B.C. Later the Christian tradition emphasized self-realization and offered the figure of Christ as the model to be imitated by those seeking perfection in the God-given being.

In today's secular world, "self-actualization" is entwined in the school of humanistic psychology, most notably heralded in the work of Abraham Maslow. He held that we each have within ourselves a proclivity toward growth and an inherent blueprint that lays out our unique set of characteristics and potential, only waiting to be realized.

He states in *Toward a Psychology of Being*, "the human being is constructed that he presses toward fuller and fuller being and this means pressing toward what most people would call good values, toward serenity, kindness, courage, honesty, love, unselfishness, and goodness."[7] For Maslow, the question, What do we live for? is answered, We live to fulfill our potential.

Many of the people I have presented in this book ascribe to the self-actualization orientation of meaning. They each, in their own way, struggled to gain insight and wisdom, find themselves, love others, and seek beauty and harmony in their lives. For some, this search alone provides life with fullness and substance.

### Transcending the Self: Losing Our Selves
Rather than focusing on the development of self, some find greater meaning from focusing their energies outside of the self. Victor Frankl, author of *Man's Search for Meaning,* is the leading proponent of this approach.[8] In his book, Frankl describes his tormented existence in Auschwitz, a German concentration camp, during World War II. From this experience, he concluded a sense of life meaning was crucial for his and others' survival.

Frankl's personal life experiences in Auschwitz demanded he think deeply about the relationships between pain and death, meaning and suffering. He believes and promotes that survival in extreme circumstances depends upon our ability to extract meaning out of tragedy and suffering. In the depth of despair in the concentration camp, he searched for ways to give meaning to his suffering and the pain of others.

People who have survived near-death or life-threatening accidents and illnesses often search for the reason for their experience. Why did this happen to me? How can I make this suffering or tragedy into something positive? We see this same theme in every major religious tradition—that only through pain and suffering come enlightenment and salvation.

Karen worked to take her battle with cancer and make her and others' lives better. Bill devoted his life to providing for other children the time and attention he could not give to his dead son Jason. Claire, the retired executive who was lost in leisure, later broke out of her own self-absorption and found purpose for her life in caring for her dying father.

Each survived tragedy and death to develop meaning in their own and other's lives. As Neitzsche tells us, "That which does not kill me makes me stronger." Suffering has meaning if it makes us better.

Frankl tells us what a human being needs, "is not a tensionless state but rather a striving and struggling for some goal worthy of him." He suggests meaning is essential for life and in his logotherapy, a process to help patients find meaning, he encourages people to move outside of themselves and focus on some greater purpose.

*Spirituality and Religion: Finding Our Depth*
Of all the paths to meaning, spirituality and religion offer the road most traveled. Death survivors remind us of Life Lesson 7, *Create*

*a stronger appreciation for religion and spirituality.* In facing mortality, we uncover a spiritual longing, a feeling of emptiness that cannot be filled with the ways of the world. Recognizing this hunger is the first step on our spiritual journey

I have found myself at times lost in my own search. I've studied the world religions, meditated, prayed, sat in Baptist, Unitarian, Episcopal, and Methodist churches, delved into the practice of Zen Buddhism, and been in psychotherapy. Along the way I've listened to priests, shamans, preachers, ministers, professors, and therapists, all of whom offered their own words of solace and wisdom. Through my experiences I have come to accept my need for spirituality in my life but struggled with the form it would take. Like several people I know, I felt an internal tug-of-war, pushed by my spiritual hunger yet pulled by my discomfort with organized religion. To find peace I've had to somehow reconcile this conflict.

What exactly is the difference between a religious and spiritual way? In my view, religion applies more to the outer, public aspects of worship: doctrine, ritual, and congregational practices that are often expressed institutionally and denominationally.

Spirituality, on the other hand, pertains to our deepest and innermost relationship with something sacred, for some, a Higher Power. Spiritual experiences tend to be universal, internal, affective, and private. Thus *religious* and *spiritual* overlap, though it is possible to walk a wonderful spiritual path without adhering to a religion.

The original meaning of the word *religion* is to reconnect—to put back together again, heal the wounds of separation, and make whole. Contentment comes not out of pursuing self-interest but from our capacity to connect to a larger whole—social groups, family, nature, and ultimately God. While some people

have trouble with the word *God*, all that is required is a willingness to acknowledge a power greater than ourselves.

National polls indicate 9 out of 10 Americans believe in God
and consider religion important in their lives. It is interesting that
when these figures are examined more closely we see that most
Americans want spirituality but perhaps not in a strictly conventional *religious* form. So in many cases religion may serve as a
springboard for spirituality and provide a community platform for
common worship.

Many people who've been formerly religious are searching for
an alternative or are looking for a deeper and perhaps more satisfying meaning in their present faith. Many are seeking something
beyond simple religious practice; they are seeking a deeper spirituality.

The word *spiritual* is "concerned with or affecting the soul." By
spiritual, we mean those experiences, beliefs, and phenomena that
pertain to the transcendent and existential aspects of life, such as a
Higher Power, the purpose and meaning of life, suffering, good
and evil, and death. It involves being able to open our hearts and
cultivating our capacity to experience life and all its wonders.
Most basically, it involves our experiencing awe, reverence, and
gratitude. It is in the ability to see as children do, the sacred in the
ordinary, to feel the passion and poignancy of life, to give ourselves
to something greater than ourselves.

Spirituality is not just about healing ourselves. It's about the
joys of soul-stirring music, the sight of fresh dew on an open
meadow, the laughter of children, the love we feel for a friend or
family member, or the look of wonder on a child's face. It is about
developing the ability to see the sacred in our daily lives and opening the door to a life filled with passion and depth. These are the
moments, however brief, that nourish our soul and make life
worth living.

I'm sure you've known, as I have, people who've recovered from significant obstacles such as disabling depressions and anxieties, serious illnesses, severe abuse, broken marriages, or other adversity only to be left still wanting more out of their lives. It seemed that just as they relieved their immediate problems, questions of meaning and value arose. These are concerns and needs that go well beyond the traditional model of mental health into a realm of spirituality and religion.

As these issues arose for my patients, I felt inadequate to help in their search. Wanting not to influence their beliefs, I remained silent. Often, I would keep the discussion more abstract while remaining supportive of whatever the client's beliefs happened to be. If pressed for more involvement, I talked briefly about my own beliefs then quickly sidestepped deeper discussion by referring them to their own minister, priest, or rabbi.

My professional training encouraged this attitude and approach. Sigmund Freud in his earliest teachings proclaimed religion to be nothing but a form of pathology—an obsessional neurosis growing out of a feeling of infantile helplessness. He saw religion as primitive, and spiritual searching as consolatory and regressive, not evolutionary.

In direct contrast, other respected professionals such as William James, Gordon Allport, Erich Fromm, Viktor Frankl, Abraham Maslow, and Rollo May have made spirituality a major focus of their work. Carl Jung had gone so far as to say that he could heal only those middle-aged people who embraced a spiritual or religious perspective toward life.

But professionals even sympathetic to religion are reluctant to give it wholehearted approval and support. Many mental health professionals find themselves conflicted in both their feelings and practice in this regard.

More and more I have recognized that the quest for spirituality is rooted in a growing need for more passion and depth in our lives. Psychotherapy, although generally beneficial and necessary to cure what ails us, still has a thing or two to learn from religion. I now believe some form of spirituality is essential to our happiness and overall mental health.

We all benefit from being connected to a caring community, from having a sense of importance and acceptance, a focus beyond ourselves, and a perspective on life's tragedies, especially death. And although many of us may have difficulty building a life of passion and purpose, we all share the capacity for growth and the potential to nurture and feed our souls.

Developing a deeper sense of spirituality can involve many paths, each unique and different. Contemplation, meditation, prayer, rituals, nurturing ourselves, and other spiritual practices have the power to release the "life force" contained in the deepest levels of the human psyche, levels that secular intervention cannot reach. Indeed, evidence shows that spiritual and religious methods can help when nothing else has succeeded.

A review of several studies suggests that spirituality is linked with better health, lower suicide rates, less alcohol and drug abuse, less criminal behavior, fewer divorces, and higher marital satisfaction. Thousands of other research reports support the healing qualities of spiritual belief and practice. I now often encourage my clients to first figure out what touches or moves them deeply. Developing a spiritual identity is not something far off that can only be discovered by treks to some distant land.

Those who have lived through tragedy and trauma have learned not only to live but also to radiate their spirituality, so that it emanates from within. It is practice, beyond mere belief, and expressed every day in the way we walk on this earth, the way we see our life, and the way we treat ourselves and others.

These survivors seem to have discovered what many sages and saints have advised—that too much religion impedes true spirituality. Many of us seeking a spiritual life feel compelled to adopt more formal practices—such as so many minutes of prayer or meditation daily or attending church twice weekly—and then feel guilty when we don't find the time to squeeze them into our schedule.

We need not be so obsessed about doing the "right" spiritual thing, the behavior that will "make us good or spiritual." We are already spiritual. The true measure of a daily practice is that the practice itself is gentle, loving, and joyful. As St. Teresa of Avila said, "All the way to heaven is heaven."

The heart of a full spiritual life is driven less by what we believe than by how we do it. Our actions at work, our relating to a stranger or loved one, our pick of vocation, our use of time, our ability to respond to life with wisdom and kindness—every act is an integral part of spiritual practice. "It is not the nature of the task," said Martin Buber, "but the consecration that is the vital thing."

Creating and maintaining a regular spiritual practice involves time and energy. By practice, I mean setting aside regular time for those things that honor your spiritual well-being. This could involve simple daily activities such as meditation, walking in the garden, attending services, spending a day in an art gallery, listening to Mozart or Jackson Browne, reading scripture, or volunteering at a hospice. Cleaning the garage, cooking, making love, working, driving, talking to a friend can all be spiritual activities. In my practice we work on developing a program that will help patients incorporate these activities into their daily life.

Choose what will or does make up your own spiritual practice. Consciously commit to honor that by building this time and ritual into your busy schedule—mark it down on your day planner if need be. Observe this time as sacred.

People who know they will die live very carefully. Not careful as in fearful; careful as in full of care. Every act, every word, every relationship is conducted in reverence for life. Such people seek spirituality in all that they do.

Survivors often move away from stricter, more confining rituals and belief systems to embrace those based on more universal values and tenets. They become open to all religions and feel great urgency in developing a broader spirituality.

We see this interest expressed in the media with many of the consistently best-selling books dealing with this theme—*Chicken Soup for the Soul*[9] and *The Road Less Traveled,*[10] just to name a few. Television programs such as Hugh Hewits's *Searching for God in America* and Bill Moyers's *Genesis: A Living Conversation* are other popular reminders of the importance of this topic.

This rekindling of interest has caused some to return to more traditional religious practices and congregations. An estimated 32 million baby boomers continue to remain unaffiliated today, many turning to New Age philosophies, Twelve Step programs, Greek mythology, Eastern practices, Jungian psychology, massage, yoga, and a host of other alternative methods. Some find spiritual fulfillment in literature, art, poetry, music, relationships, and nature.

How do we develop spiritual meaning and purpose in our lives? The path is wide and varied. To begin, let us consider these four possibilities.

First, consider some form of meditation and relaxation. There are literally hundreds of methods for relaxation including yoga, tai chi, transcendental meditation, strenuous physical exercise, soaking in a warm bath, deep muscle relaxation, hypnosis, massage, and structured relaxation exercises such as *The Relaxation Response* by Herbert Benson.[11] Elizabeth Lesser offers an excellent guide to mindful meditation in her book *The New American*

*Spirituality.*[12] Explore those that personally pique your interest and practice them regularly.

A second path involves prayer, one of the oldest spiritual practices and the most popular in the world. For the soul to be heard, the mind must be still. Almost all major religions consider prayer central to a spiritual life. The mental and emotional release, along with a sense of connection to a transcendent dimension, may be at the heart of prayer's effectiveness.

In Kierkegaard's *Journal* he says:

the unreflective person thinks and imagines that when he prays, the important thing, the thing he must concentrate upon, is that God should hear what he is praying for. And yet in the true eternal sense it is just the reverse: the true relation to prayer is not when God hears what is prayed for, but when the person continues to pray until he is the one who hears, who hears what God wills.[13]

A third path involves spiritual readings. Every world religion considers its writings sacred and prescribes regular reading of this material to be essential to a religious life. Browse your local bookstore or ask for recommendations from your friends, pastor, rabbi, or family to find something that speaks to you.

A fourth path to spirituality involves contact and immersion in nature. For Henry David Thoreau, who fled civilization to live in retreat on Walden Pond, nature was the temple of God and the perennial source of life. Many others have taken his lead and derive great satisfaction in their experience of the natural world.

Of the paths described, which do you follow? What direction has your search taken or will it take in the future? Whatever way you've chosen, accept and embrace it for all that it offers you.

# WITH THE END IN MIND

So how can we live our lives to the fullest? I've found that the single idea of our mortality hurls us into life's river. We use the awakening exercises and the Daily Whisper to focus us on what is most important in our lives. We clear the obstacles to loving ourselves, others, and life. We discover new meaning in our lives.

Whatever the specific approach, the antidote to isolation and meaninglessness is engagement. We must immerse ourselves in the cold stream of life. Define your goals, resolve to act intentionally, and leap into commitment and action.

Tolstoy eventually determined the solution to his own crisis with the admonition, "It is possible to live only as long as life intoxicates us." To find a home, raise children, care about other people, create projects and ideas—these are all forms of engagement.

Tragedy aids you in your search. The idea of your end helps rivet your attention on the time you have, pushes you off the ropes and into the fight of life, focusing your attention on what is most important. Facing life's frailty clears the obstacles standing between numbness and vitality. What prevents you from loving yourself? How can you deepen your relationships? How can you experience life more completely? What blocks you from greater satisfaction in your work, creative, or spiritual strivings?

In his book, *It's Not About the Bike*, Lance Armstrong talks about how he bravely battled back from the very brink of death to change his life forever:

> The truth is, if you asked me to choose between winning the Tour de France and cancer, I would choose cancer. Odd as it sounds, I would rather have the title of cancer survivor than winner of the Tour, because of what it has done for me as a human being, a man, a husband, a son, and a father.[14]

Bad things happen for good reasons. So if there's a good reason for suffering and tragedy, it's to shake you up, to inspire you to live a better life.

By embracing life's fragility, that this moment is all you ever have, you awaken to life's fullness and possibility. Awaken to what is most important. Recognize the preciousness of the jewel we call life. Love and accept your true self. Open your heart to those around you. Appreciate the treasures and gifts before you. Live fully the magic of the moment. Create meaning and spirituality every day.

Have the life you want today.

# REFERENCES

## Chapter One: Astray in a Dark Wood

1. Yalom, Irving. 1980. *Existential psychotherapy*. New York: Basic Books.
2. Heidegger, Martin. 1962. *Being and time*. New York: Harper and Row.
3. Homer. 1930. *The odyssey*. New York: Macmillan.

## Chapter Two: Exploding the Myth of Tomorrow

1. Diggory, John, and Rothman, Doreen. 1961. Values destroyed by death. *Journal of Abnormal and Social Psychology* 63 (1):205–10.
2. Castaneda, Carlos. 1972. *Journey to Ixtlan: The lessons of Don Juan*. New York: Simon and Schuster.
3. Hinton, John. 1975. The influence of previous personality on reactions to having terminal cancer. *Omega*. 6:95–111.
4. Nietzsche, Friedrich. 1959. *Life against death*. New York: Vintage Books.
5. Perls, Fritz. 1970. *Gestalt therapy verbatim*. New York: Bantam Books.

## Chapter Three: Embracing the King of Fears

1. Neuberger, Robert. Cited in J. Frank. 1962. *Nuclear death: The challenge of ethical religion*. The Ethical Platform.
2. Rosen, David. 1975. Suicide survivors. *Western Journal of Medicine*. 122:289–94.

3. Noyes, Russel. 1980. Attitude changes following near-death experiences. *Psychiatry: Journal for the Study of Interpersonal Processes.* 43:234–41.
4. Speigal, David, James Blum, and Irvin Yalom. 1980. Peer support for metastatic cancer patients: A randomized prospective outcome study. Cited in Irving Yalom. *Existential psychotherapy.* New York: Basic Books.
5. Jaques, Elliot. 1965. Death and the mid-life crisis. *International Journal of Pyschoanalysis.* 461:502–513.
6. Jung, Carl. Cited in David Levinson. 1978. *The seasons of a man's life.* New York: Alfred A. Knopf.
7. Toynbee, Arnold. 1969. *Man's concern for death.* St. Louis: McGraw-Hill.
8. Montaigne, Michel de. 1965. *The complete essays of Montaigne.* Stanford: Stanford University Press.
9. Albom, Mitch. 1998. *Tuesdays with Morrie: An old man, a young man, and the last great lesson.* New York: Doubleday.
10. Armstrong, Lance. 2000. *It's not about the bike: My journey back to life.* New York: G.P. Putnam's Sons.
11. Ring, Kenneth. 1998. *Lessons from the light: What we can learn from near-death experience.* New York: Insight Books.
12. Ring, Kenneth. 1984. *Heading toward Omega: In search of the meaning of the near-death experience.* New York: W. Morrow.
13. Atwater, P.M.H. 1988. *Coming back to life: The after-effects on the near-death experience.* New York: Dodd.
14. Ring. *Lessons from the light.*
15. Ring. *Heading toward Omega*
16. Bugental, James. Cited in Irving Yalom. 1980. *Existential psychotherapy.* New York: Basic Books.
17. Ring. *Heading toward Omega.*
18. Ring. *Heading toward Omega*

19. Ring, Kenneth. 1980. *Life at death: A scientific investigation of the near-death experience.* New York: Quill.
20. Ring. *Life at death.*

## Chapter Four: The Ultimate Wake-Up Call

1. Darwin, Charles. 1954. *The voyage of the Beagle.* New York: Dutton.
2. Seigel, Bernie. 1990. *Love, medicine and miracles: Lessons learned about healing from a surgeon's exceptional patients.* New York: Harper Perennnial.

## Chapter Five: How One Thought Can Change Your Life

1. Castaneda. *Journey to Ixtlan: The lessons of Don Juan.*
2. Albom. *Tuesdays with Morrie.*

## Chapter Six: Love Is the Cure

1. Maslow, Abraham. Cited in Rollo May. 1969. *Love and will.* New York: W. W. Norton.
2. Fromm, Eric. 1963. *The Art of loving.* New York: Bantam Books.
3. Yalom, Irving. 1980. *Existential psychotherapy.* New York: Basic Books.
4. May, Rollo. 1969. *Love and will.* New York: W. W. Norton.
5. Fromm. *The art of loving.*
6. Moustakas, Clark. 1961. *Loneliness.* New York: Prentice Hall.
7. Hobson, Robert. 1974. Loneliness. *Journal of Analytic Psychology.* 19:71–89.
8. Fromm. *The art of loving.*
9. Maslow, Abraham. 1968. *Toward a psychology of being.* New York: Van Nostrand.

## Chapter Seven: The "I" Equation

1. Branden, Nathaniel. 1994. *The six pillars of self-esteem.* New York: Bantam Books.
2. Lindbergh, Anne Morrow. 1991. *Gift from the sea.* New York: Pantheon Press.
3. James, William. 1890. *The principles of psychology.* New York: Henry Holt and Company.
4. Beck, Aaron. 1988. *Love is never enough.* New York: Harper and Row.

## Chapter Nine: Burning Life Brightly

1. James. *The Principles of Psychology.*
2. Thoreau, Henry David. 1971. *Walden.* Princeton, NJ: Princeton University Press.
3. Nietzsche, Friedrich. 1974. *The gay science.* New York: Random House.
4. Lewis, Harold and Streitfeld, Harold. 1972. *Growth games.* New York: Bantam Books.
5. Goldstein, Joseph. Cited in Rodney Smith. 1998. *Lesson from the dying.* Boston: Wisdom Publications.
6. Levine, Steven. 1997. *A year to live.* New York: Bell Tower.
7. Mann, Thomas. 1930. *Death in Venice.* New York: A. A. Knopf.
8. Maslow. *Toward a psychology of being.*
9. Csikszentmihalyi, Mihaly. 1990. *Flow: The psychology of optimal experience.* New York: Harper Collins.

## Chapter Ten: The Meaning of Meaning

1. Erikson, Erik. 1963. *Childhood and society.* New York: Norton
2. Maslow. *Toward a psychology of being.*
3. Grimm, Jacob. 1972. *The complete Grimm's fairy tales.* New York: Pantheon.

4. Tolstoy, Leo. 1929. *My confession, my religion, the gospel in brief.* New York: Scribner.

Chapter Eleven: Living on Purpose

1. Maddi, Salvatore. 1967. The existential neurosis. *Journal of Abnormal Psychology.* 72:311–25.

2. Merton, Thomas. 1978. *No man is an island.* New York: Harcourt Brace Jovanovich.

3. Terkel, Studs. 1972. *Working people talk about what they do all day and how they feel about what they do.* New York: Pantheon Books.

4. Csikszentmihalyi. *Flow: The psychology of optimal experience.*

5. Beethoven, Ludwig. Cited in M. Von Andics. 1947. *Suicide and the meaning of life.* London: William Hodge.

6. Durant, Will. 1932. *On the meaning of life.* New York: Ray Long.

7. Maslow. *Psychology of being.*

8. Frankl, Victor. 1963. *Man's search for meaning.* New York: Simon & Schuster.

9. Canfield, Jack. 1997. *Chicken soup for the soul.* Deerfield Beach, Fla.: Heath Communications.

10. Peck, Scott. 1978. *The road less traveled: A new psychology of love, traditional values and spiritual growth.* New York: Simon & Schuster.

11. Benson, Herbert. 1975. *The relaxation response.* New York: William Morrow.

12. Lesser, Elizabeth. 1999. *The new American spirituality: The seekers guide.* New York: Random House.

13. Kierkegaard, Soren. 1946. In *A Kierkegaard anthology.* Edited by R. Bretall. Princeton, N.J.: Princeton University Press.

14. Armstrong. *It's not about the bike: My journey back to life.*

# INDEX

# About the Author

Gary Buffone, Ph.D., is a practicing licensed psychologist and holds a Diplomate from the American Board of Professional Psychology. Besides his role as corporate consultant and Director of The Family Business Center at the Byron Harless group, Dr. Buffone has had extensive clinical experience working with people who have survived significant life stress and trauma. He has authored over 25 publications including the book *Transcending Trauma: Assessment, Stabilization, and Growth*. Dr. Buffone is married with two daughters and lives and works in Jacksonville, Florida.

# HAS TRAUMA POSITIVELY TRANSFORMED YOUR LIFE?

If you have had a life-threatening experience that has positively transformed your life, I would like to hear your story. Please submit your story in writing and tell me specifically about the triggering event or trauma, how your life has changed for the better, and what you learned from your experience that may inspire others who have been similarly affected. You can send your materials to Dr. Gary Buffone at the office of Byron Harless, 4651 Salisbury Road, Suite 330, Jacksonville, Florida, 32257, or forward to the author's Web site at www.docbuff.com.